The Role of Business in the Responsibility to Protect

The Role of Business in the Responsibility to Protect closes the gap between research on the Responsibility to Protect and the private sector, as previous research has focussed only on state responsibilities and state actors. This book examines in detail the developing research on the significant role that private sector actors can play in promoting peace and stability. Contributors to this volume explore the key arguments for where, why, and how private sector actors can contribute to the prevention and cessation of mass atrocity crimes, and how this can inform and extend the UN policy discussion around Responsibility to Protect. The contributors include lead voices in the Responsibility to Protect discourse as well as central voices in business and peace literature.

Professor John Forrer is Director of the Institute of Corporate Responsibility, Associate Research Professor of Strategic Management and Public Policy and Associate Faculty at the George Washington University. He has researched, taught, and written on cross-sector collaborations and public–private partnerships for fifteen years, in particular emphasizing the role the private sector can play in advancing public policy goals. Other research areas focus on business and peace, global governance, and sustainable global supply chains. He has authored a book on global governance enterprises and co-authored books on economic sanctions and cross-sector collaboration, and published more than twenty book chapters and journal articles.

Dr. Conor Seyle is the Deputy Director of Research and Development at the One Earth Future Foundation, an international research and operating foundation focussed on supporting good global governance in the interest of peace. He is a political psychologist with research interests in international governance, deliberative democracy, and the long-term impact of violence and traumatic events. He is the author or co-author of more than twenty-six academic and NGO publications.

The Role of Business in the Responsibility to Protect

John Forrer

George Washington University, Washington DC

Conor Seyle

One Earth Future Foundation

CAMBRIDGE
UNIVERSITY PRESS

University Printing House, Cambridge CB2 8BS, United Kingdom

Cambridge University Press is part of the University of Cambridge.

It furthers the University's mission by disseminating knowledge in the pursuit of education, learning, and research at the highest international levels of excellence.

www.cambridge.org
Information on this title: www.cambridge.org/9781107156128

First published 2016

A catalogue record for this publication is available from the British Library.

Library of Congress Cataloguing in Publication Data
Names: Forrer, John J., editor of compilation. |
Seyle, Conor, editor of compilation.
Title: The role of business in the responsibility to protect /
edited by John Forrer (George Washington University,
Washington, DC), Conor Seyle (One Earth Future Foundation).
Description: Cambridge, United Kingdom; New York,
New York: Cambridge University Press, 2016. |
Includes bibliographical references and index.
Identifiers: LCCN 2016025957 | ISBN 9781107156128 (hardback)
Subjects: LCSH: Responsibility to protect (International law) |
Commercial law – Moral and ethical aspects. |
Social responsibility of business. | Business ethics.
Classification: LCC KZ4082.R65 2016 | DDC 341.4/8–dc23
LC record available at https://lccn.loc.gov/2016025957

ISBN 978-1-107-15612-8 Hardback

Contents

Contributors   *page* vii

Acknowledgments   ix

Overview: The Role of Business in R2P   1
JOHN FORRER AND CONOR SEYLE

Introduction: The Private Sector, the United Nations,
and the Responsibility to Protect   9
EDWARD C. LUCK

1   Selling R2P: Time for Action   35
TINA J. PARK AND VICTOR MACDIARMID

2   Why Not Business?   51
TIMOTHY L. FORT AND MICHELLE
WESTERMANN-BEHAYLO

3   Responsibility to Protect Trumps Business as Usual:
How Corporate Leaders Build Heroism to
Face Atrocities   69
ALAIN LEMPEREUR AND REBECCA HERRINGTON

4   The Responsibility to Prevent, Inc.: The Missing
R2P–Business Link: An Anomaly in International
Affairs   98
JONAS CLAES

5   The Kenyan Private Sector's Role in Mass Atrocity
Prevention, Cessation, and Recovery   116
PATRICK OBATH AND VICTOR ODUNDO OWUOR

6   R2P and the Extractive Industries   138
JILL SHANKLEMAN

7   Information Technology, Private Actors, and the
    Responsibility to Protect   162
    KIRSTEN MARTIN

8   Corporate Responsibility to Protect Populations
    from Mass Atrocities   185
    VESSELIN POPOVSKI

9   The Private Sector and Atrocities Prevention   206
    ALEX J. BELLAMY

10 The Way Forward: Discovering the Shared Interests
    between Business and R2P   230
    JOHN FORRER AND CONOR SEYLE

    Index   241

Contributors

Alex J. Bellamy	Professor of Peace and Conflict Studies and Director of the Asia Pacific Centre for the Responsibility to Protect, The University of Queensland, Australia Non-Resident Senior Adviser, International Peace Institute, New York
Jonas Claes	Senior Program Officer, US Institute of Peace
Timothy L. Fort	Eveleigh Professor of Business Ethics, Kelley School of Business, Indiana University
Rebecca Herrington	Program Manager, Search for Common Ground
Alain Lempereur	Alan B. Slifka Professor of Coexistence and Conflict Resolution, Brandeis University
	Director of the Graduate Programme in Coexistence and Conflict, Heller School for Social Policy and Management
	Affiliated Faculty and Executive Committee Member of the Program on Negotiation, Harvard Law School
Edward C. Luck	Arnold A. Saltzman Professor of Professional Practice in International and Public Affairs and Director of the Specialization in International Conflict Resolution, School of International and Public Affairs, Columbia University

Victor MacDiarmid	Co-founder and Managing Director, Canadian Centre for the Responsibility the Protect, the University of Toronto
Kirsten Martin	Assistant Professor, Strategic Management and Public Policy, George Washington University School of Business
Patrick Obath	Vice Chairman, Kenya Private Sector Alliance (KEPSA) Foundation
Victor Odundo Owuor	Research Associate, One Earth Future Foundation
Tina J. Park	Co-founder and Executive Director, Canadian Centre for the Responsibility the Protect, the University of Toronto
Vesselin Popovski	Vice Dean of the Law School, Executive Director of the Centre for UN Studies, OP Jindal Global University
Jill Shankleman	Director, JSL Consulting Ltd.
Michelle Westermann-Behaylo	Assistant Professor of International Management, University of Amsterdam Business School

Acknowledgments

This book builds in the work of researchers who for the past fifteen years have developed the theoretical foundations for understanding how business can promote peace. It is a product that has been co-created by the scholars and practitioners who contributed their chapters. Exploring the roles business could play in addressing R2P was a collective enterprise and we wish to thank the contributors for their dedication to the project and for their spirit of collegiality.

We are indebted to our many colleagues and students who have shaped and advanced our thinking on this topic. There are several individuals we want to especially mention and thank. Timothy L. Fort, Eveleigh Professor of Business Ethics, Kelley School of Business, Indiana University, provided invaluable guidance, support, and inspiration. National Defense University Academic Dean at the Africa Center for Strategic Studies Raymond Gilpin was an early supporter of the book and contributed insights on how to approach the topic. Eamon Aloyo, currently at the Hague Institute of Global Justice, was with One Earth Future when the project was developed, and played a valuable role in promoting and developing the ideas and the project. Lee Sorensen, Director of the Business and R2P Program at One Earth Future, supported the project and played an important role in identifying project partners.

We have benefited from the assistance of the staff of the research department of One Earth Future, who provided helpful and accurate background research on R2P issues. Patti Niles gave invaluable administrative support.

We wish to thank the Carnegie Endowment for International Peace for co-hosting a symposium on R2P and business in June 2013, and the panelists, Ed Luck, Patrick Obath, and Raymond Gilpin. The event inaugurated the questions on what businesses could do to address R2P that the book attempts to answer. Also, we wish to thank the United States Institute for Peace and Jonas Claes for hosting a workshop with chapter contributors in July 2014. The event allowed contributors to present and discuss their draft chapters. The workshop was an invaluable experience for all to learn from each other and integrate their ideas throughout the book.

We are indebted to One Earth Future for their unflagging support of this project and the untold resources they have donated in support of this book. We appreciate the staff and editors of Cambridge University Press for their suggestions and improvements to the manuscript.

Lastly, John expresses his appreciation to Sharon Forrer for her patience, support, and love from beginning to end. He dedicates this book to her.

CONOR SEYLE
One Earth Future

JOHN J. FORRER
The George Washington University

Overview: The Role of Business in R2P

John Forrer and Conor Seyle

For many peace and conflict scholars, and human rights advocates, raising the issue of the role of business as a part of the international discussion about the prevention and cessation of mass atrocities – captured under the name "Responsibility to Protect" (R2P) – could mean cataloging the contemporary and historical instances when the private sector has been an instigator or a perpetuator of conflict (Cilliers and Dietrich 2000; Boele *et al.* 2001; Global Witness 2009; Stewart 2011). A frequent focus of the discourse around the private sector and conflict has been the real examples of egregious behavior by companies. Corporations are indicted for engaging in a host of practices that fosters conflict: financially bolstering repressive regimes that violate human rights; investments in commercial activities that involve forcible resettlement; by-passing international laws and norms; conducting commerce – directly and through supply chains – that impoverishes communities; complicity with undemocratic elections; and cooperation with repressive security forces. Such acts are viewed as integral to the global strategies of companies to retain access to and control of markets and resources. Popular examples include the role of the United Fruit company in advocating for US support for a coup against Guatemalan President Jacobo Árbenz (Schlesinger *et al.* 2005), and claims that Shell facilitated directly or indirectly the Nigerian military in a violent campaign against local activists in the 1990s (Boele *et al.* 2001).

Commentary and analysis that paints private sector actors as purely self-interested, including from those both critical and supportive of the private sector, further reinforce this view. Popular phrases such as "the business of business is business" or "business must act to make a profit" are invoked to justify the common assertion that businesses face an imperative to choose "profits over people." In fact, such stylized portrayals of private sector actors were never intended as faithful representations of business and the action they might take; they were developed as necessary assumptions in economic models. Assigning business a monomaniacal mission of short-term profits and maximizing investor return on investment (ROI) aligns with neo-classical economic theory: as capital

1

markets seek the highest ROI, no firm could stay competitive if it pursued anything other than profit-seeking behavior and maximization of shareholder value. But these are assertions crafted in the service of theory building, not as accurate representations of business behavior. Such views of business may be convenient abstractions, but they are misplaced as a basis for asserting the role of private sector actors in R2P situations.

The contributors to this book do not contest the claim that businesses may promote or facilitate conflict (and without doubt they have). The focus of this book is to bring recognition of the fact that businesses can play a constructive role regarding the kinds of mass atrocities that the international community has attempted to address in the development of the norms of prevention and intervention covered under the overall banner of R2P. We argue that theorizing, modeling, discourse, and policy deliberations on R2P have neglected this prospect, and as a result have impoverished our understanding of what can be done to address R2P issues. This book provides a first effort to explain the ways in which business can play a positive role in R2P situations. We do not claim to offer a comprehensive set of offerings, but insights and guidance on practical, realistic, and purposeful ways businesses can play a role in R2P.

A dedicated group of researchers from across a range of academic fields has pioneered the study of connections between business practices and peace over the past fifteen years (Nelson 2000; Fort and Schipani 2004; Fort 2007; Williams 2008; Forrer 2010; Oetzel et al. 2010; Oetzel and Getz 2012; Dai et al. 2013; Kolk and Lenfant 2015). The business and peace literature can reasonably claim to have established a prima facie case that businesses affect the peacefulness of the communities where they conduct commerce and beyond. Research continues to explore the specific actions businesses can take to promote peace and the conditions necessary for their efficacy (Oetzel et al. 2010; Forrer et al. 2012; Oetzel and Getz 2012; Dai et al. 2013; Katsos and Forrer 2014).

Although still in its "early days" as a field of study, the business and peace (B&P) literature has already inspired numerous organizations to embrace the concept and produce policy documents that offer recommendations on what business could, and in some instances should, do to promote peace. A small sampling of institutions that have published on the topic includes the UN Global Compact, the United States Institute for Peace, the Institute for Economics and Peace, the Hague Center for Global Justice, the Business for Peace Foundation, the One Earth Future Foundation, Peace Research Institute Oslo, and SwissPeace. Some individual corporations have begun to consider the connections between their own business practices and their effect on conflict and peace (Peace Through Commerce 2014; Business Fights Poverty n.d.). Although the "practice" cart has jumped well ahead of the "theory" horse, the interest in B&P studies, and how B&P can inform business strategy and policy, is expanding rapidly.

The development of the business and peace literature has happened quickly enough that it is generating more questions than answers. This volume focusses on one such example: the role of private sector actors in mass atrocity crimes – war crimes, crimes against humanity, and genocide and ethnic cleansing. The role of business in preventing or stopping mass atrocities has not been the subject of extensive discussion in either policy or research communities. B&P research has not yet explored what business can do regarding R2P situations, and the R2P community has given the role of the private sector scant attention.

In part, this reflects the fact that both the political discourse and the body of research around mass atrocity crimes is a relatively new and developing discussion. In addition, it reflects the fact that one of the major evolutions in the international response to mass atrocity crimes, the Responsibility to Protect, has been in practice – and largely in discourse – an exclusive franchise for governments and international organizations. R2P involves an amalgam of issues touching on state sovereignty, international intervention, and the definition of atrocities – all issues that have been considered to be within the exclusive province of state actors.

The result of both the focus on state concerns and the general tendency to assume that private sector actors are contributors to conflict (and not peace) means that the role of business has largely been excluded from the R2P debate. To dismiss the notion that business could contribute to preventing mass atrocities, and deter and avoid R2P situations is testimony to either a lack of real knowledge about business, or a penchant for letting ideological determinism trump practical opportunism. The role of business and R2P has been neglected for too long and deserves serious attention by scholars and practitioners.

The logic of why private sector actors should be interested in R2P extends itself quite neatly from the argument that there are well-recognized economic, legal, and corporate social responsibility (CSR) rationales for why and how private sector actors should be interested in supporting peace and the prevention of mass atrocities (Seyle and Aloyo 2015). The most familiar reasoning is economic: the kind of instability associated with mass atrocity crimes is incredibly destructive to economic activity. For example, the role of economic development and a healthy private sector is one of the strongest predictors of stability (Miguel *et al.* 2004). In the case of Kenya, which is covered at length in Chapter 5 in this book, its gross domestic product (GDP) dropped by nearly 20 percent following the post-election violence in 2007 and 2008 (Owuor and

Wisor 2014). The economic arguments for stability are clear: if a business can effectively invest in the prevention of mass atrocity crimes, it can appropriate the commercial advantages of political stability.

Second, there are legal reasons for business interest in R2P. National and international law proscribe companies from contributing to mass atrocities, as described in part by Vesselin Popovski in Chapter 8 of this volume. Several international laws bar support for mass atrocity crimes, most notably the Geneva Convention of 1949. These laws certainly apply to the directors and executives of corporations conducting business globally, barring them from contributing to mass atrocity crimes and the violations of R2P in the same way that they apply to any other individual (Scott and Rhodes 2014). More broadly, shareholder actions can provide a legal basis for structuring corporations to actively promote R2P principles if sufficient groups of shareholders can be motivated to support this.

Third, in an environment where businesses are increasingly asked to demonstrate their social commitments, shareholders and the public may encourage companies to do what they can to avoid contributing to problems and reward them when they can demonstrate their successes. The same negative influence private sector actors can have on democracy and social and economic justice that some commentators lament can be used to promote peace, and businesses can also take direct action to protect individuals and support the prevention or cessation of mass atrocity crimes. Several contributors to this volume provide specific illustrations of how these actors can support R2P, including Patrick Obath and Victor Owuor's discussion of the role of the private sector actors in supporting peace in Kenya, or Kirsten Martin's and Jill Shankleman's respective chapters discussing how telecommunications companies and extractive companies can take action to contribute to atrocity prevention. To the extent that these activities generate public goodwill, they can contribute to recognition of businesses and good corporate citizens.

We argue that business is deeply embedded in society and therefore has the potential to influence events, conditions, and attitudes that could help prevent mass atrocities. Which businesses, under what set of circumstances, at what point and time, and under what type management team and board of directors, could do what is an open question – and the topic of this book. R2P is significant because it is not a generic field of inquiry, such as the study of business and peace or business and atrocity prevention. It is a specific norm adopted by the UN General Assembly (UNGA) and defined by the UNGA and the UN Secretary-General in associated writing (UN General Assembly 2005; Ban 2009; Ban 2010).

As a result, contributors consider that both the practice of atrocity prevention without reference to the larger policy discourse and the ongoing policy and normative discussion that the term R2P specifically refers to are relevant here. Contributors to this volume have looked at the role of the private sector through both lenses, and this volume hopes to contribute to the analysis of atrocity prevention directly, and also to the conversation happening at the international level about R2P as a contribution to atrocity prevention.

Chapter Summaries

The contributors to this volume have engaged with the idea that the private sector can contribute positively and in a non-coerced manner to the prevention of mass atrocities, and also engaged with the question of what this may mean for the overall discussion of R2P. The initial chapters by Edward C. Luck (Introduction) and Victor MacDiarmid and Tina J. Park (Chapter 1) provide an initial engagement with the idea of how private sector actors may fit with the discussion around R2P. Luck provides an introduction based on his experiences in the UN, and points out the way that the UN discourse unintentionally left the private sector out of the conversation and practice around R2P, and identifies some of the places where private sector actors may be engaged. Park and MacDiarmid's chapter follows this introduction with an overview of the history of R2P in policy and practice, and highlights some of the current debates and contentious issues that may be affected by a greater appreciation of the role of the private sector. Chapters 2–5 make the discussion about the role of the private sector concrete by offering several different perspectives on how private sector groups can contribute, or have contributed, to atrocity prevention and cessation in different ways and historical contexts. Fort and Westermann-Behaylo (Chapter 2) lay out the logic and evidence for private diplomacy from the private sector as a contributor to peace and atrocity prevention, while Lempereur and Herrington (Chapter 3) underscore the human element of business. Their chapter provides several case studies drawn from World War II, the Rwandan genocide, and the 2008 Mumbai terrorist attacks where individual business leaders used their resources and role as business leaders to contribute to the protection of individuals. In Chapter 4, Claes argues that the discourse around R2P has underappreciated the impact of private sector actors, and suggests that private sector groups can be particularly impactful in "upstream" phases of violence, where they can contribute to disrupting patterns that can lead to later mass atrocities. In Chapter 5, Obath and Owuor provide a specific example of just this kind of engagement, when they detail how Kenyan companies, both individually and organized through business associations, responded to post-election violence in 2007–2008, and the threat of a repeat in the 2012/13 elections, with a series of organized activities that may have contributed to the peaceful elections in 2012–2013. Chapters 6 and 7 look at specific sectors that may be particularly impactful in preventing or stopping R2P violations. Shankleman in Chapter 6 looks at the extractive industry from the lens of the direct interest that extractive companies should have in R2P, the role they may play in addressing R2P violations, and some of the limitations and barriers to engagement that this sector may see. In Chapter 7, Martin examines the role of telecommunications companies and argues that because of the central role of telecommunications in organizing collective action, telecommunications companies may have a specific impact in preventing (or facilitating) R2P violations. Finally, the concluding chapters by Popovski and Bellamy offer some engagement with the question of what this set of arguments means as a whole for the practice of atrocity prevention or the support for the norms of R2P. Popovski reviews the arguments for private sector engagement in atrocity prevention and R2P discourse, and argues that the responsibility in the term "responsibility to protect" should apply to more than just states, and that examples like those in this volume can pave the way for an expanded discussion about what actors are invoked in preventing or addressing R2P violations. He provides a taxonomy for thinking about what roles non-state actors can play in R2P situations. Finally, Alex J. Bellamy provides an overarching review and summation in which he lays out the practical and political limitations of a state-centric approach to R2P, and uses the cases provided in this volume to make an argument for increasing appreciation for the role of private sector actors in addressing R2P. The volume concludes with a brief "agenda for action" that lays out some specific recommendations for next steps.

We do not claim that we can predict what any given business may do as it relates to R2P issues. But we also argue that there is no validity in the claim that business cannot play a positive role in promoting peace and addressing R2P issues. Contributors have established the case that businesses have and can act to prevent atrocities, and have connected specific cases to the conversation around R2P. With such precedents and insights, collectively, this book presents a strong rationale for accepting the mandate to understand the roles business might play under a broad range of conditions and circumstances. The examples and arguments advanced here offer some initial guidance for what might be possible and what is imaginable. That is a good start. We hope it is the first in a long and fruitful discussion on the topic.

References

Ban, Ki-moon. 2009. "Implementing the Responsibility to Protect: Report of the Secretary-General." A/63/677. United Nations.
———. 2010. "Early warning, assessment and the Responsibility to Protect: Report of the Secretary-General." A/64/864. United Nations.
Boele, Richard, Heike Fabig, and David Wheeler. 2001. "Shell, Nigeria and the Ogoni. A study in unsustainable development: I. The story of Shell, Nigeria and the Ogoni people – environment, economy, relationships: conflict and prospects for resolution1." *Sustainable Development* 9 (2):74–86.
Business Fights Poverty. n.d. http://businessfightspoverty.org/
Cilliers, Jakkie and Christian Dietrich, eds. 2000. *Angola's War Economy: The Role of Oil and Diamonds*. Institute for Security Studies, ISS, Pretoria.
Dai, Li, Lorraine Eden, and Paul W. Beamish. 2013. "Place, space, and geographical exposure: Foreign subsidiary survival in conflict zone." *Journal of International Business Studies* 44 (6):554–578.
Forrer, John. 2010. "Locating peace through commerce in good global governance." *Journal of Business Ethics* 89:449–460.
Forrer, John, Timothy L. Fort, and Raymond Gilpin. 2012. *How Business Can Foster Peace*. Washington, DC: United States Institute of Peace. http://permanent.access.gpo.gov/gpo30490/SR315.pdf
Fort, Timothy L. 2007. *Business Integrity and Peace: Beyond Geopolitical and Disciplinary Boundaries*. Cambridge University Press.
Fort, Timothy L. and Cindy A. Schipani. 2004. *The Role of Business in Fostering Peaceful Societies*. Cambridge University Press.
Global Witness. 2009. "Faced with a gun, what can you do? War and the militarisation of mining in Eastern Congo." www.globalwitness.org/sites/default/files/pdfs/report_en_final_0.pdf
Katsos, John E. and John Forrer. 2014. "Business practices and peace in post-conflict zones: Lessons from Cyprus." *Business Ethics: A European Review* 23 (2):154–168.
Kolk, Ans and Francois Lenfant. 2015. "Partnerships for peace and development in fragile states: Identifying missing links." *Academy of Management Perspectives*, 29:4 438–450.
Miguel, Edward, Shanker Satyanath, and Ernest Sergenti. 2004. "Economic shocks and civil conflict: An instrumental variables approach." *Journal of Political Economy* 112 (4):725–753.
Nelson, Jane. 2000. *"The business of peace: The private sector as a partner in conflict prevention and resolution."* London: International Alert. www.internationalalert.org/sites/default/files/publications/The%20Business%20of%20Peace.pdf
Oetzel, Jennifer and Kathleen Getz. 2012. "When and how might firms respond to violent conflict?" *Journal of International Business Studies* 43 (3):331–358.
Oetzel, Jennifer, Michelle Westermann-Behaylo, Charles Koerber, Timothy L. Fort, and Jorge Rivera. 2010. "Business and peace: Sketching the terrain." *Journal of Business Ethics* 89:351–373.

Owuor, Victor and Scott Wisor. 2014. "*The role of Kenya's private sector in peace building: The case of the 2013 election cycle.*" Broomfield, CO: One Earth Future Foundation. http://oneearthfuture.org/sites/oneearthfuture.org/files/documents/publications/kenyaprivatesectorreport-digital.pdf

Peace through Commerce. n.d. www.peacethroughcommerce.org/

Schlesinger, Stephen, Stephen Kinzer, and John H. Coatsworth. 2005. *Bitter Fruit: The Story of the American Coup in Guatemala, Revised and Expanded, David Rockefeller Center for Latin American Studies.* Cambridge, MA: Harvard University Press.

Scott, Kenneth and Laura Rhodes. 2014. "*Corporate social responsibility and the Responsibility to Protect: Corporate liability for international crimes.*" Broomfield, CO: One Earth Future Foundation. http://oneearthfuture.org/research/publications/corporate-social-responsibility-and-responsibility-protect-corporate-liability

Seyle, Conor D. and Eamon Aloyo. 2015. "The role of business in the Responsibility to Protect." In *The Responsibility to Protect and the Third Pillar: Legitimacy and Operationalization,* edited by Daniel Fiott and Joachim Koops. New York: Palgrave Macmillan, 171–189.

Stewart, James G. 2011. *Corporate War Crimes: Prosecuting the Pillage of Natural Resources.* New York: Open Society Institute.

UN General Assembly. 2005. "2005 World Summit Outcome." New York: United Nations.

Williams, Oliver F., ed. 2008. *Peace through Commerce: Responsible Corporate Citizenship and the Ideals of the United Nations Global Compact.* Notre Dame, IN: University of Notre Dame Press.

Introduction: The Private Sector, the United Nations, and the Responsibility to Protect

Edward C. Luck

Despite all that has been written about the Responsibility to Protect (R2P), some very large gaps persist in our understanding and scholarship. One of the more prominent and consequential omissions is a striking lack of attention by scholars and practitioners alike to the role of the private sector. There has been remarkably little appreciation of the actions that the private sector has or could take in response to, as well as in the prevention of, mass atrocities. So this book project has sought to provide fresh insights on the reasons for this oversight, on how it could be overcome, and on how the skills and capacities of the business community could be tapped to prevent and ameliorate future mass atrocities. The chapters that follow provide a promising down payment on that research and analysis. No doubt the work of these authors will spur others to build on their initial findings, opening some promising new directions for policy and practice.

During my five-year tenure as the first UN Special Adviser on the Responsibility to Protect, it was painfully evident in crisis after crisis that there was anything but a surfeit of tools to prevent, limit, or end mass atrocities, or of actors to wield them. As the Secretary-General and I repeatedly told the Member States, we intended to pursue a strategy that was "narrow but deep": narrow in terms of limiting its scope strictly to the four crimes agreed by the 2005 World Summit (genocide, war crimes, ethnic cleansing, and crimes against humanity) and their incitement, but deep in terms of employing every possible legal tool and partner to get the job done.[1] In such circumstances, expanding the R2P tent to include additional prevention and protection partners was naturally accorded a high priority.

Yet there seemed to be one blind spot: the private sector. We developed a more inclusive and dynamic model for pursuing the responsibility to protect, and, for the first time, included the private sector. I added

---

[1] See, for instance, *Implementing the Responsibility to Protect* (United Nations 2009 A/63/677, p. 8, para. 10(c)).

references to collaborating or partnering with the private sector to several of the Secretary-General's annual reports on R2P from 2009 to 2012, but the United Nations (UN) had neither a history nor an inclination nor protocols for integrating business into efforts to address such highly political matters.[2] So, given the limits of time and institutional culture, the shift in doctrine was more evident in theory than in practice.

This introductory chapter seeks to frame the discussion of the private sector's place in implementing R2P in a conceptual, cultural, and institutional context, largely from a UN perspective. It sketches the historical evolution of R2P and of relations between the UN and business communities, noting that these were parallel processes that neither intersected nor fed off of each other. The chapter begins by addressing some of the conceptual and institutional hurdles that need to be overcome if the potential contributions of the private sector to atrocity prevention are to be fully realized. It concludes that the United Nations is not the best venue through which to pursue this, given the sorry history of relations between the business community and the world body, and the practical, not normative, nature of this pursuit. It argues for the kind of fresh approach favored by the authors in this volume – one that begins with the business-like question of what can we do to prevent mass atrocities in our societies that could have devastating economic, as well as human, consequences for generations to come?

Conceptual Hurdles

The initial conception of R2P was very much the product of its times. It was shaped by changing assessments of the nature of conflict and by the challenges to traditional United Nations security doctrine posed by the turbulent events of the 1990s. The regional and sectarian instabilities of the post-Cold War world compelled the world body to devote greater attention to intra-state and transnational conflicts. The collective failure to respond to the horrendous genocide in Rwanda and the war crimes, ethnic cleansing, and crimes against humanity in the Balkans led to substantial soul-searching about doctrine, practices, and principles, as well as about capacities, will, and authority.[3] Growing concern about

[2] Ibid., p. 9, para. 11(b); p. 16, para. 32; and p. 26, para. 59; *The Role of Regional and Subregional Arrangements in Implementing the Responsibility to Protect* (United Nations 2011 A/65/877-S/2011/39, p. 4, para. 12; p. 7, para. 22; p. 8, para. 24; and pp. 8–9, para. 26); *Responsibility to Protect: Timely and Decisive Response* (United Nations 2012 A/66/874-S/2012/578, pp. 12–13, para. 46).

[3] See, especially: *Report of the Independent Inquiry into the Actions of the United Nations During the 1994 Genocide in Rwanda* (United Nations S/1999/1257 1999) and *The Fall of Srebrenica* (United Nations A/54/549 1999).

human security, alongside national security, led to fresh thinking about the nature of sovereignty and about the responsibilities it imposes. The Security Council, increasingly able to act by consensus, became more prone to adopt enforcement measures under Chapter VII of the Charter of the United Nations and to add ambitious human protection mandates to the peace operations it authorized.

When Kofi Annan, the former head of UN peacekeeping, became Secretary-General at the beginning of 1997, this changing landscape was very much on his mind. He sought to encourage fresh thinking both about the limits of sovereignty in the face of humanitarian emergencies and about the opportunities to foster public–private partnerships across a range of endeavors. There is little evidence, however, that he, or his advisers, saw a connection between the two sets of issues, which had distinct origins, constituencies, and implications. The former would require a quantum shift in Member State attitudes toward the limits and responsibilities inherent in state sovereignty. This was, and is, a highly sensitive matter with profound implications for inter-state relations, international law, and the nature of the UN system. The Secretary-General could encourage fresh thinking about such weighty matters, but he could not dictate its pace, content, or direction. In contrast, reaching across the UN–private sector divide must have looked more like low-hanging fruit. It would not entail a major conceptual leap or present an acute political risk. As the leader of the secretariat, he could take his own programmatic initiatives – discussed below – involving the business community without asking the Member States to participate in or pay for them.

Curbing atrocity crimes was a much more daunting challenge. In 1998–1999, Secretary-General Annan undertook a series of provocative and searching statements on the matter of intervention in the face of humanitarian emergencies.[4] The dilemmas posed by the use of force to protect populations in Kosovo without the authorization of a deeply divided Security Council were underscored in the Secretary-General's September 1999 address to the General Assembly. As he put it, "while the genocide in Rwanda will define for our generation the consequences of inaction in the face of mass murder, the more recent conflict in Kosovo has prompted important questions about the consequences of action in the absence of complete unity on the part of the international community."[5] The crisis, in his view, "has revealed the core challenge to

---

[4] Five of these are collected in *The Question of Intervention* (United Nations 1999). The most expansive was "Reflections on Intervention" (ibid.).

[5] "Two Concepts of Sovereignty," Statement by the Secretary-General to the General Assembly (September 20, 1999).

the Security Council and to the United Nations as a whole in the next century: to forge unity behind the principle that massive and systematic violations of human rights – wherever they may take place – should not be allowed to stand." For all its eloquence, his address was not well received by sovereignty-conscious delegations, especially from the developing world. As a whole, the Assembly demonstrated little interest in his efforts to foster a dialog on humanitarian intervention, the obligations of the Security Council, or the limits of sovereignty.

Rather than launching his own initiative to address this dilemma, the Secretary-General gave quiet but enthusiastic support to the Canadian launch of an independent International Commission on Intervention and State Sovereignty (ICISS), co-chaired by Gareth Evans and Mohamed Sahnoun, former Foreign Ministers of Australia and Algeria, respectively. By any measure, the report produced by the Commission in December 2001 was a landmark achievement.[6] It introduced the concept of the Responsibility to Protect and, in doing so, shifted the locus of international debate from an alleged right to intervene to the inherent obligation that governments have to protect their people from mass harm. Not surprisingly, given the state-centric questions it was asked to address, and its emphasis on rules for the use of force, the report, for all its strengths, virtually ignored the private sector as a potentially significant player in the prevention of mass atrocities and the protection of populations.[7]

In seventy-five pages of comprehensive and thoughtful analysis, the seminal ICISS report mentions "the business community" only once, as one of a long list of actors that should work together on prevention.[8] It also comments that "these days peace is generally regarded as much better for business than war."[9] An extensive chapter on post-intervention rebuilding never refers to the private sector, nor is its potential role in prevention through early warning, assessment, messaging, education, and communication, in protection, or in influencing national or international decision-making, ever acknowledged. In contrast, nongovernmental organizations (NGOs) are frequently touted in the report

---

[6] *The Responsibility to Protect* (ICISS 2001).

[7] The report includes a detailed discussion of prevention on pp. 19–27, which it asserts "is the single most important dimension" of R2P (p. XI), but then fails to mention the subject in its conclusions and recommendations. This omission is striking in that the Secretary-General had made prevention one of his top priorities and had just published his own report on the subject: *Prevention of Armed Conflict* (United Nations A/55/985-S/2001/574 2001). Also see *Preventing Deadly Conflict* (Commission on Preventing Deadly Conflict 1998).

[8] Ibid., pp. 25–26, para. 3.36.

[9] Ibid., p. 72, para. 8.15.

as being critical and essential players in the implementation of R2P. This imbalance in the treatment of these two groups of stakeholders received little attention at the time, because it was common practice for scholars and practitioners to leave the potential contributions of the private sector out of discussions of security and humanitarian matters.[10] One of the conceptual casualties of this tendency, however, has been the exclusion of any serious exploration of the ways in which business could assist NGO efforts at prevention and protection, and vice versa.[11]

Though the initial reactions to the ICISS report among governments were mixed or muted, Secretary-General Annan, the co-chairs of the Commission, and other prominent "norm entrepreneurs" recognized the importance of R2P and its emphasis on state responsibility as an alternative to having to choose between doing nothing or undertaking unilateral humanitarian intervention. R2P featured prominently in the late 2004 report of the Secretary-General's High-level Panel on Threats, Challenges and Change, but the Member States continued to be sharply divided about the new concept in the debates leading up to the September 2005 World Summit.[12] Much to the surprise of most observers, the consensus Outcome Document of the Summit included three paragraphs (138–140) on R2P.[13] That text, however, as adopted by the heads of state and government in 2005, differed in several important respects from the initial version of R2P proposed by the International Commission four years earlier.[14] It limited the application of R2P to the four crimes of genocide, war crimes, ethnic cleansing, and crimes against humanity, as well as their incitement. It emphasized prevention, non-coercive action under Chapters VI and VIII of the Charter, and assisting states "under stress" alongside "timely and decisive" response through the Security Council and under the Charter "should peaceful means be inadequate and national authorities are manifestly failing to protect their populations" from the four specified crimes.

---

[10] Over the years, there have been important exceptions to this general rule, such as the participation of chemical producers in the development of the chemical weapons convention, the nuclear power industry in the design and implementation of international safeguards and safety standards, and the diamond industry in the Kimberley Process to ban the sale of "conflict diamonds."

[11] The Outcome Document from the 2005 World Summit makes no direct reference to either NGOs or the private sector in its three paragraphs on R2P.

[12] *A More Secure World: Our Shared Responsibility* (United Nations 2004).

[13] The Outcome Document was adopted by the General Assembly, again by consensus, in resolution 60/1 of October 24, 2005.

[14] To this author, the specificity of the 2005 version made it much more amenable to practical implementation than the original ICISS conception. For a comparison of the two versions, see "From Promise to Practice: Implementing the Responsibility to Protect" (Luck 2012).

In the Outcome Document, the first inter-governmental statement on R2P, the Member States made no mention of the private sector, NGOs, or even civil society. Does this mean that they intended to limit the implementation of R2P solely to governments and inter-governmental organizations? As the first Special Adviser on R2P, this was one of the most pressing questions that I needed to address in terms of understanding what the heads of state and government had intended and – most immediately – what they expected. In a somewhat liberal reading of those three paragraphs, I came to the following conclusions:

–One. I read the references in paras. 138 and 139 to "international community" as encompassing civil society, and I did so in crafting the Secretary-General's R2P strategy and in explaining it to the Member States. It was necessary to clarify this interpretation of the intent of the world leaders in 2005 because "international community," not unlike "civil society," does not have a single, strict, and generally accepted definition.

It is certainly true, as Alex J. Bellamy argues persuasively in his chapter, that the Outcome Document does not assert that states, international organizations, and civil society bear the same level or nature of responsibility.[15] By 2005, however, references to civil society and to partnerships or collaborations with civil society had become so commonplace in UN documents as to seem almost mandatory. In operational, as opposed to normative, endeavors, it was and continues to be standard operating procedure for the United Nations to seek partnerships and collaborations with others. To this author, the omission in this case suggested that collaboration with civil society was implied, especially in tasks such as "encourage and help States to exercise this responsibility" for prevention, and employing "humanitarian and other peaceful means" to protect populations. As Bellamy acknowledges, no one would have expected states or international organizations to fulfill these tasks without some cooperation from civil society. Tellingly, when the text in para. 139 turns to enforcement under Chapter VII of the UN Charter, its references to "the international community" disappear.

–Two. Though there are divergent schools of thought on such things, this author believes that the private sector should be considered to be an integral part of civil society for these purposes.[16] In most countries, the private sector produces the bulk of the goods, services, and employment that serve the purposes of both development and human security. Likewise, often working in partnership with governments and non-profit institutions, business provides a significant portion of the investment and technological innovation economies need to thrive and

---

[15] As discussed below, the notion of differentiated responsibilities was also critical to resolving international debates about a possible Code of Conduct for the private sector and human rights.

[16] Though the concept of civil society is often seen as a western invention, there have been variations of the notion in a range of ethical and cultural traditions. On this point, see *Alternative Conceptions of Civil Society* (Chambers and Kymlicka 2001). For a broad conception of civil society that encompasses the private sector, see *Global Civil Society?* (Keane 2003, 8, 14, Chapter 2).

to compete in an era of globalization. The financial, technical, and human contributions of corporations, their leaders, and their workers have helped to build programmatic and intellectual bridges between the private sector and other civil society actors. In many fields, old barriers have begun to fade as corporations, investors, and consumers have become more socially and ecologically sensitive.

On the one hand, even in an era of public–private partnerships, the critical distinction should be retained between government and civil society, as it is essential that civil society actors retain their independent and voluntary nature. That independence could prove critical when some in government seek to divide their societies along sectarian lines and to incite violence between groups. On the other hand, highlighting distinctions within civil society between the profit or non-profit motivations of individuals and groups could be divisive and even fatally dysfunctional in such a situation. There is no reason to assume that those working in the private sector would be any less concerned than those in non-profit organizations about the futures of their societies or the dangers inherent in moving down the path toward atrocity crimes. These broader social concerns typically cut across all of these imputed societal distinctions, particularly when partnerships across sectoral lines are so widely encouraged and when people, ideas, and programs move so easily across the lines that distinguish the non-profit, commercial, and government sectors.

–Three. I also concluded that if the purpose of R2P – to reduce the likelihood and severity of mass atrocity crimes – was to be achieved, then the pledge in para. 138 to protect "populations" by preventing the four crimes and their incitement would have to be extended to non-state actors as well.[17] Again, there is no reference to armed groups in the text of paras. 138–140, but the intent of those paragraphs, it seemed to me, was to extend R2P principles to all actors who would consider committing or inciting any of the four specified crimes. There had already been a number of situations in which armed groups had committed horrific crimes of mass murder, maiming, and/or sexual and gender-based violence. Indeed, some groups – even then – had made atrocity crimes their calling card as they sought to intimidate civilian populations. When governments were unable to control their territory and armed groups had been able to commit such crimes with impunity in territory they effectively controlled, there was a pressing need for international military assistance and/or consent-based intervention to help defeat the armed groups and prevent further mass atrocities. It is worth recalling, in this context, that the Kimberley Process, which involved governments, civil society, and the private sector, was developed to help prevent the sale of "conflict diamonds," whose profits had been helping to fund armed groups that had, among other things, been committing atrocity crimes.

Some aspects of R2P, particularly provisions relating to the use of armed force, have been controversial among the Member States, but I encountered little or no resistance in putting forward these interpretations of the intent of the Outcome Document concerning civil society,

---

[17] This point was incorporated in the Secretary-General's implementation strategy and in a number of his statements and reports. See, for instance, *Implementing the Responsibility to Protect* (United Nations 2009, pp. 18–19, paras. 40 and 42).

the private sector, and armed groups. Moreover, as strategies for implementing R2P have put greater emphasis on prevention and on individual responsibility (discussed below), the opportunities for contributions from the private sector have expanded apace.[18] Therefore, at this point, there should be no serious conceptual, normative, or political barriers to including the private sector fully in strategies and plans for realizing R2P in action as well as in words.

Institutional and Cultural Hurdles

For many years, in human rights circles, business has been treated more often as part of the problem than as part of the solution. Doubts about partnering with commercial enterprises have long been most pronounced in the NGO and UN communities – precisely where the technical and material assets and the managerial and communications know-how of the private sector have been most needed. To many commentators and activists, the profit motive forms a dividing line that is just too wide to be crossed, even in helping societies to heal after the trauma of mass violence. In turn, business leaders, most markedly in the United States, have tended to be rather skeptical of the politics, inertia, and inefficiencies of the United Nations. Unless attitudes on both sides change substantially, efforts to curb mass atrocity crimes are unlikely to reach their full potential. If this book succeeds only in triggering a conversation, and perhaps some fresh thinking, among business leaders, the R2P/atrocity prevention community, and officials in governments and international institutions, that would be a significant step forward.

The historical roots of this mutual ambivalence are deep rooted and well known.[19] Yet they bear repeating briefly here, because the negative stereotypes on both sides continue to infect the prevailing culture at the United Nations despite the progress that has been made over the past two decades in reaching out to the private sector in a more engaging and productive manner. As noted below, the last three Secretaries-General have attempted to bridge this gap both rhetorically and programmatically, but when social and cultural biases become institutionalized over

---

[18] The first exposition of the notion of an Individual Responsibility to Protect (IR2P) as a bottom-up complement to the state-centric principles of R2P can be found in "The Individual Responsibility to Protect" (Luck and Luck 2015). IR2P encompasses both individuals and civil society groups, including the private sector.

[19] Several chapters in this volume, including those by Jonas Claes, Jill Shankleman, and Vesselin Popovski, offer useful insights on the reasons for this gap in literature, policy, and practice.

decades, even generations, they take time and persistent effort to eliminate. What is most needed – and this book provides a starting point – is evidence that the private sector has made significant contributions to mass atrocity prevention in the past and is positioned to do much more in an increasingly information and technology-oriented future. First, however, the topic has to appear on the world's collective radar screen.

For much of its first quarter century, the UN's political agenda revolved around efforts to tame the military excesses of the Cold War and to keep local conflicts from escalating into dangerous East–West confrontations. At the world body, there was neither room for nor interest in the place of the private sector in international affairs. In the early 1970s, however, this began to change with revelations about the attempts of ITT to interfere in the domestic affairs of Chile in order to undermine the left-leaning regime of President Salvador Allende. These sensational and well-documented reports provoked widespread concern among UN delegates from developing countries, many of whom were suspicious of possible "imperialist" interference as they faced post-colonial governance and economic challenges. They worried that unaccountable multinational corporations, based in the North, could infringe with impunity on their newly won political and economic sovereignty.

Developed countries, in turn, were concerned about efforts by some of these regimes to nationalize the facilities and assets of foreign investors, and about the steps by the Organization of the Petroleum Exporting Countries (OPEC) to manipulate international energy supplies and prices. As a result, through much of the 1970s and 1980s, debates at the United Nations about the place of the private sector in international and domestic affairs were as polarized, ideological, and unproductive as they were lively. As Karl Sauvant recounts in authoritative detail in a recent article, much of the debate was about whether and how to control, tame, and regulate transnational corporations through a Code of Conduct.[20]

The ultimately unsuccessful effort to negotiate a Code of Conduct followed attempts, led by the Group of 77 developing countries, to craft a New International Economic Order (NIEO) that could facilitate a process of what some experts called "economic decolonization."[21] The Sixth Special Session of the General Assembly in 1974 did adopt a Declaration and a Programme of Action on the Establishment of an NIEO without a vote, though a number of developed countries expressed profound

---

[20] See "The Negotiations of the United Nations Code of Conduct on Transnational Corporations" (Sauvant 2015).

[21] The calls for a sweeping, even radical, restructuring of global economic relations were not restricted to the developing world. See, for instance, "For a New World Economic Order" (de Montbrial 1975).

reservations.[22] Noting that there had been "irreversible changes in the relationship of forces in the world," the Declaration sought to "correct inequalities and redress existing injustices" and to address "the remaining vestiges of alien and colonial domination, foreign occupation, racial discrimination, apartheid and neo-colonialism in all its forms."[23] Among the principles on which the NIEO would be based were "full permanent sovereignty of every State over its natural resources and all economic activities," "the right to nationalization or transfer of ownership to its nationals," and the "regulation and supervision of the activities of transnational corporations by taking measures in the interest of the national economies of the countries where such transnational corporations operate on the basis of the full sovereignty of those countries."[24] Section V of the Programme of Action was devoted to "Regulation and Control over the Activities of Transnational Corporations."

The developing countries were not alone in calling for greater oversight of multinationals, as the US Senate Select Committee on Intelligence Activities – the so-called Church Committee – focussed attention on the clandestine collaboration between the CIA, ITT, and other multinationals in undermining the Allende regime.[25] As social movements to address a range of labor, consumer, and environmental concerns grew in the US, Western Europe, and other developed countries, activists turned their attention to similar or more damaging multinational practices in the developing world as well. As a result, as Craig Murphy has pointed out, in the late 1970s "specific UN agencies responded to the calls of non-governmental organizations (NGOs) for more aggressive forms of regulation of some practices of multinational firms that were poorly controlled, especially in the developing world."[26] Concerns grew, as well, about corruption and collusion between governments and the private sector actors they were supposed to oversee.

Members of the UN secretariat, moreover, tended to have a statist orientation, as one would expect in an inter-governmental organization.

---

[22] A/RES/S-6/3201 of May 1, 1974 and A/RES/S-6/3202 of May 1, 1974, respectively. The General Assembly later that year adopted a Charter of Economic Rights and Duties of States (A/RES/29/3281) by vote, with six negative votes from developed countries, including the United States, United Kingdom, and West Germany, and ten abstentions. A more balanced approach was taken by an experts group commissioned by ECOSOC that included some private sector participants – see *The Impact of Multinational Corporations on Development and on International Relations* (United Nations 1974).

[23] Para. 2, preambular para. 3, and para. 1, respectively.

[24] Paras. 4e and 4g, respectively.

[25] See *Covert Action in Chile, 1963–1973* (US Senate 1975, Sec. IIC).

[26] See "Private Sector" in *The Oxford Handbook on the United Nations* (Murphy 2007, 264). For instance, he refers to the "adversarial, regulatory approach of the relatively successful infant formula campaigns" led by advocacy NGOs (ibid., 269).

Relatively few had much experience working in the private sector, as most came from government service, academia, or civil society organizations. Their partners in human rights NGOs had been particularly vigilant in tracking human rights and labor violations by transnational enterprises. Meanwhile, a number of scholars and think tanks – to some extent reprising the spirit, if not the content, of the "merchants of death" themes of an earlier era – started to draw attention to greed, as well as grievance, as a cause of conflict, especially in resource rich but less developed countries of the Global South.[27]

More fundamentally, the structure of the United Nations, as the world's premier inter-governmental forum, left little room for the voices of business and private enterprise. Despite repeated calls for economic and social cooperation among the Member States, the Charter mentions "commercial matters" only twice, once in Article 74 on non-self-governing territories and once in Article 76 on the International Trusteeship System. The Charter relegates the private sector, at best, to third-class status. On the one hand, Article 71 authorizes NGOs approved by the Member States to apply for consultative status with the United Nations Economic and Social Council (ECOSOC), and more than 4,000 of them have done so successfully.[28] On the other hand, even private sector firms with truly global reach and "special competence" cannot qualify because they lack the required democratic and representational character of UN-recognized NGOs and their funding is not from the contributions of their affiliates.[29] Only two international business associations, the International Chamber of Commerce (1946) and the International Organisation of Employers (1947), are on the list of 142 NGOs that have been granted General Consultative Status with ECOSOC.[30] A much larger number of labor groups and unions, however, have achieved that status.

The interests and perspectives of the private sector, therefore, generally have had to be advanced in the world body by western governments. This has tended to reinforce public and NGO suspicions about

---

[27] See "On the Economic Causes of Civil War" (Collier and Hoeffler 1998, 563–573); "Greed and Grievance in Civil War" (Collie and Hoeffler 2004, 563–595); and *Greed and Grievance: Economic Agendas in Civil Wars* (Berdal and Malone 2000).

[28] The United Nations, *List of Non-Governmental Organizations in Consultative Status with the Economic and Social Council as of 1 September 2014*, Economic and Social Council, E/2014/INF/5 (December 3, 2014).

[29] For these criteria, see principles 10, 12, 13, and 20 of ECOSOC Resolution 1996/31 of July 25, 1996 (United Nations Economic and Social Council 1996).

[30] The list of those NGOs with Special Consultative Status, which is tied and limited to specific areas of expertise, is much longer at 2,926. Another 977 are on the ECOSOC Roster.

the alleged collusion between governments and the business community.[31] Moreover, as a general rule, despite selected protectionism, those governments have largely favored reductions in barriers to free trade and investment as contributions to the general welfare. A number of advocacy NGOs have not been so sure. They doubt, based on unhappy experience, that the unfettered profit motive would maximize the interests of workers, consumers, or the environment, especially in places where governance and economic development are weak. They have tended to favor regulatory approaches and to see their work as reflecting the broader social, political, and economic interests of the general public, both nationally and internationally. Enjoying a more direct voice in the United Nations than their business counterparts, they have generally championed its unique role as an incubator and disseminator of international norms in many areas, including the regulation of the private sector. These divergent expectations have fed caricatures and stereotypes on both sides, making it that much harder to narrow the gap between the private sector and the UN community.

During the 1970s and 1980s, North–South differences over the role of transnational enterprises were compounded by the continuing East–West ideological divisions over socialism, capitalism, and the relationship between the state and the means of production, as well as the Soviet–American competition for influence in the developing world. The place of the private sector became a political and ideological, as much as an economic, question. The economically advanced countries may have possessed the world's most prosperous economies, but they were perpetually outnumbered in UN forums on a range of political, economic, and social issues. This led to broadly cast damage-limitation strategies, especially by the United States, where moderate as well as conservative pundits began to question the value of international norms and institutions.[32] In the multilateral debate over the role of the private sector and multinationals, there seemed to be much to lose and little to gain. During these difficult years, there was simply little incentive for western countries to expend much political capital to try to bridge the North–South and East–West differences on these matters.

---

[31] For a critique of the efforts to encourage cooperation between the UN and the private sector, and for a call for a binding international instrument to hold transnational corporations accountable, see MISEREOR, the Global Policy Forum, and *Corporate Influence on the Business and Human Rights Agenda of the United Nations* (Brot für die Welt 2014).

[32] On American ambivalence toward international institutions, see *US Hegemony and International Organizations* (Foot et al. 2003), *Multilateralism and US Foreign Policy* (Patrick and Forman 2001), and *Mixed Messages: American Politics and International Organization, 1919–1999* (Luck 1999).

It took the end of the Cold War, therefore, as well as more nuanced views of foreign direct investment in many developing countries, to allow a somewhat more productive international discourse on these matters over the course of the 1990s. According to Karl Sauvant, the rapid rise in the number of multinational corporations based in developing countries may have contributed to the more encouraging trend in the discourse.[33] Economic and political reform within countries that were transitioning from socialism offered fresh perspectives on the transnational, as well as domestic, role of the private sector. Globalization, with its pervasive mix of risks and benefits, had become a fact of international life that could no longer be denied, especially as eastern markets themselves began to open. Economic interdependence was here to stay, and most countries that embraced it, on balance, prospered, despite uneven effects on different domestic groups and constituencies. Even in the General Assembly and ECOSOC, exchanges on these questions became less shrill, more constructive, and more searching.

When Boutros Boutros-Ghali of Egypt became UN Secretary-General in 1992, one of his first acts – much to Washington's delight – was to eliminate the Centre on Transnational Corporations unilaterally and with little explanation. His 1992 *Agenda for Peace* report, mandated by the Security Council, noted that "national boundaries are blurred by advanced communications and global commerce."[34] Respect for sovereignty remained "crucial to any common international progress," but "the time of absolute and exclusive sovereignty … has passed; its theory was never matched by reality." Leaders should "find a balance between the needs of good internal governance and the requirements of an ever more interdependent world. Commerce, communications and environmental matters transcend administrative borders."[35] Moreover, "peace in the largest sense cannot be accomplished by the United Nations system or by Governments alone. Non-governmental organizations, academic institutions, parliamentarians, business and professional communities, the media and the public at large must all be involved."[36] In other words, the private sector could play a legitimate – if hardly central–role in advancing the core business of the world body – the maintenance of international peace and security.

As noted above, when he became Secretary-General in January 1997, Kofi Annan sought to make progress both on atrocity prevention and

---

[33] Sauvant 2015, 72–74.
[34] See *Agenda for Peace*, para. 11 (Boutros-Ghali 1992).
[35] Ibid., para. 17.
[36] Ibid., para. 84. In 1995, Kofi Annan's remarks to the World Economic Forum in Davos reportedly took a relatively open and positive tone toward transnational business.

on building ties to the business community, though these efforts would have to proceed in different ways and at different speeds. In January 1999, he told the World Economic Forum in Davos of his "hopes for a creative partnership between the United Nations and the private sector'" and for "a global compact of shared values and principles, which will give a human face to the global market." Specifically, the compact would "embrace, support and enact a set of core values in the areas of human rights, labour standards, and environmental practices … in which universal values have already been defined by international agreements."[37] The Global Compact, though not without its critics, has grown impressively through the years, perhaps in part because it grew out of an appeal to a business, not inter-governmental, forum and because it was presented "as a complement rather than substitute for regulatory regimes."[38]

This dichotomy in approaches to the two sets of issues was reflected in Secretary-General Annan's *We the Peoples* report, prepared for the 2000 World Summit. On the one hand, it placed collaboration with the private sector on the fast track, indeed in the vanguard of efforts to deal with both the upside and downside of globalization:

Better governance means greater participation, coupled with accountability. Therefore, the international public domain – including the United Nations – must be opened up further to the participation of the many actors whose contributions are essential to managing the path of globalization. Depending on the issues at hand, this may include civil society organizations, the private sector, parliamentarians, local authorities, scientific associations, educational institutions and many others.

Global companies occupy a critical place in this new constellation. They, more than anyone, have created the single economic space in which we live; their decisions have implications for the economic prospects of people and even nations around the world. Their rights to operate globally have been greatly expanded by international agreements and national policies, but those rights must be accompanied by greater responsibilities – by the concept and practice of global corporate citizenship.[39]

Yet even these relatively bold words reflected the persistent ambivalence within the world body toward the private sector. Unlike NGO or other civil society partners, business would have to earn its way into the global community by assuming greater responsibilities and by practicing an ill-defined "global corporate citizenship."

[37] "Secretary-General Proposes Global Compact on Human Rights, Labour, Environment, in Address to World Economic Forum in Davos" (United Nations 1999).

[38] "Overview" (United Nations Global Compact n.d.).

[39] *We the Peoples: The Role of the United Nations in the Twenty-First Century* (United Nations 2000, p. 8, paras. 46–47).

On the other hand, the matter of humanitarian intervention was largely side-tracked, as the *We the Peoples* report appeared to take a step backward from the Secretary-General's path-breaking addresses of 1998 and 1999. No longer was he pushing the Member States to consider the limits of sovereignty in the face of mass atrocities. Though it acknowledged the tragedies in Rwanda and Srebrenica, the report did little more than to highlight "the dilemma of intervention" and to underscore – with considerable understatement– that "humanitarian intervention is a sensitive issue, fraught with political difficulty and not susceptible to easy answers."[40]

The broader question of the relationship between the private sector and human rights also remained unsettled and, in UN and NGO circles, contentious. In 2005, Secretary-General Annan appointed an American academic, John Ruggie, to the post of Special Representative for Business and Human Rights, as mandated by the Commission on Human Rights. His principal task was to find an alternative to a draft set of Norms on the Responsibilities of Transnational Corporations and Other Business Enterprises with Regard to Human Rights, which was based on the questionable premise that firms should have the full range of duties as do states. After several years of research and consultations, he presented a new "protect, respect, and remedy" framework that was accepted in 2011 by the reconstituted Human Rights Council. The Council, however, continued to call for the "proper regulation, including through national legislation, of transnational corporations and other business enterprises" and to warn against "the negative impact of globalization on vulnerable economies."[41]

Charting a New Path

In some ways, the acceptance of the Framework was a landmark event. Its relevance to the parallel but distinct effort to integrate the private sector into strategies for curbing mass atrocity crimes, however, should not be over-emphasized.[42] It was developed and designed for a different

---

[40] Ibid., p. 34, paras. 215–219.

[41] Human Rights Council, A/HRC/RES/17/4, July 6, 2011, preambular paras. 5 and 6.

[42] As the 2014 R2P report of the Secretary-General acknowledges, compliance with the Guiding Principles on Business and Human Rights might reduce the risk that private sector actors would contribute directly or indirectly to the commission of atrocity crimes. However, the Principles do not speak to the many positive ways that businesses and business leaders could – and have – actively worked to prevent atrocities and/or to protect populations. Many of these are mentioned later in this and other chapters in this volume, as well as in earlier reports by the Secretary-General. *Fulfilling Our Collective Responsibility* (United Nations 2014, p. 7, para. 26).

purpose. For at least five reasons, the Framework would not be a promising place to start the latter task:

1 It does not address the key players or core challenges to curbing mass atrocity crimes. Encouraging private firms to respect human rights and labor standards is certainly a worthy enterprise, and one that could be indirectly helpful to achieving R2P goals. Mass atrocities are committed by governments, their security forces, and/or armed groups. As several chapters in this volume acknowledge, there have been a number of cases in which corporations have aided and/or abetted the commission of such crimes.[43] With the possible exception of war crimes, which can be an individual act without mass casualties, the four crimes identified under R2P by the 2005 World Summit (genocide, war crimes, ethnic cleansing, and crimes against humanity) require mass violence on a scale that could not be contemplated by individual firms or even groups of business leaders without the active participation of government forces or of non-state armed groups in places where governments have failed to maintain a monopoly on the instruments of large-scale violence.[44] If corporations in countries under stress can be persuaded both to do no harm and to practice exemplary human rights standards, that could be a helpful factor in fostering a political, economic, and social climate that is less fertile for the kind of extremist ideologies or highly sectarian political agendas that are often associated with the commission of mass atrocities. But this would be a circuitous route to curbing mass atrocity crimes, just as traditional approaches to conflict resolution have missed the mark in this regard, despite the fact that mass atrocities tend to be statistically associated with ongoing armed conflict.[45] What is needed

[43] See, for instance, the chapters by Vesselin Popovski and Alex J. Bellamy.

[44] Through the years, there have been any number of reports of commercial enterprises employing or hiring others to employ violence or intimidation to further their perceived business interests, but the author has not seen accounts that would be of the scale or nature to qualify as true mass atrocities.

[45] In Rwanda, Bosnia-Herzegovina, Sri Lanka, and possibly South Sudan and Syria, the international focus on conflict resolution arguably diverted attention from sufficient consideration of the risks of mass atrocities. The author's experience at the United Nations as Special Adviser, in fact, suggested that more often than not the emphasis in strategy and policy on related matters, such as conflict resolution and humanitarian affairs, made it more difficult to pursue an effective mass atrocity prevention strategy in a number of crisis situations. This was less true of human rights, given that mass atrocities are the most extreme form of human rights violations, but even there the optimal strategies tended to be somewhat distinct. On the distinction between atrocity prevention and conflict prevention, see *Early Warning, Assessment and the Responsibility to Protect* (United Nations 2010, p. 4, para. 10(b)) and *Responsibility to Protect: State Responsibility and Prevention* (United Nations 2013, p. 3, paras. 12–13). For this author's reflections, see "Getting There, Being There: The Dual Roles of the Special Adviser"

is more focussed, more direct, more energetic, more imaginative, and more consistent efforts by both governments and corporations to prevent atrocity crimes and protect populations, not treating this as a subset of related endeavors.

2   Finding a place for the private sector in the implementation of R2P is an operational challenge, not a normative issue. The normative battles to gain near universal acceptance of R2P principles among the 193 UN Member States have been fought and largely won. The remaining contentious issues relate to how Pillar Three (on timely and decisive response) of the Secretary-General's implementation strategy will be carried out when coercive measures, particularly military force, are to be employed. As the chief architect of that strategy, this author led the conversation with the Member States from 2008 to 2012, including the preparation of annual reports from the Secretary-General and informal interactive dialogs in the General Assembly. Through that process, three things became abundantly clear. One, over time there was less and less objection to R2P in normative terms, with virtually universal acceptance of its normative and legal foundation by the end of that five-year period. Two, there was little or no controversy about our decision to include the private sector in the Secretary-General's reports as one of the stakeholders that could play a positive role in prevention and even response.[46] In essence, the private sector would be helping states to fulfill their R2P obligations, as would other civil society actors. Three, Member States and the UN secretariat have both made it abundantly clear that they are eager to move from normative debate to practical implementation. The question now is how to get the job done.

3   Therefore, the matter of how the private sector could contribute to ongoing efforts to curb atrocity crimes should not be the subject of inter-governmental debates or negotiations. No resolutions, declarations, or codes of conduct are needed in this area. Nor would it be helpful to have such questions addressed by the General Assembly, ECOSOC, the Human Rights Council, or other inter-governmental forums that

---

(Luck forthcoming) and "The Responsibility to Protect at Ten: The Challenges Ahead" (Luck 2015) Policy Analysis Brief, May 2015, The Stanley Foundation.

[46]   Indeed, the Secretary-General's reports refer to ways that the private sector could contribute to each of the three pillars of his implementation strategy: 1) to the protection responsibilities of the state (United Nations 2011, p. 4, para. 12); 2) to assisting the state and building capacity (United Nations 2009, p. 9, para. 11(b) and p. 16, para. 3; United Nations 2011, p. 7, para. 22, p. 8, para. 24, and pp. 8–9, para. 26; and United Nations 2014, p. 7, para. 26); and 3) to timely and decisive response (United Nations 2009, p. 26, para. 59; United Nations 2012, pp. 12–13, para. 46).

are inherently and intensely political. Issues raised in these bodies often become entangled in extraneous political struggles, as has been the case with the private sector and human rights, as briefly chronicled above. Moreover, such bodies, by their very nature, have a statist orientation. As noted above, their appreciation of the private sector has been limited, conditional, and of recent vintage. There would be much to lose and little to gain by adding R2P matters to the ongoing, but still unsettled, debates in the Human Rights Council about business and human rights.[47] Conflating two sets of contentious issues would benefit neither, as each could end up gaining the detractors of the other.

4 The United Nations would also be the wrong venue to address the relationship of the private sector to R2P, as this is a matter that needs to be worked out as much at a local and national level as at a global one. At the world body, there would undoubtedly be a strong inclination to stress the role of transnational corporations over that of domestic-based enterprises. As the chapter by Patrick Obath and Victor Owuor on Kenya suggests, however, local and national firms might actually be more critical to influencing the way troubled situations evolve, to identifying ways to prevent possible atrocities, and to mobilizing commercial enterprises on the ground to take effective political and preventive action.[48] R2P's normative and conceptual development has, quite properly, been a global affair. Yet, in this author's experience, its application had to be adapted to the distinct characteristics of each situation, as no two were fully alike. According to Secretary-General Ban, his implementation "strategy stresses the value of prevention and, when it fails, of early and flexible response tailored to the specific circumstances of each case."[49] Ironically, the effective and consistent application of global norms on preventing mass atrocities

---

[47] Many of the old divisions within the UN Human Rights Council resurfaced in 2014 over competing resolutions on business and human rights, one sponsored by Ecuador and South Africa and the other one by Norway. Though their respective provisions were inconsistent regarding the critical question of whether to pursue a legally binding instrument to regulate transnational corporations, both passed by narrow margins anyway. The episode demonstrated that the political situation in the Human Rights Council remains unsettled and that the consensus that had been won earlier is still fragile. In response, on June 26, 2014 the International Organisation of Employers released a statement that it "deeply regrets that the adoption of the Ecuador initiative has broken the unanimous consensus on business and human rights achieved three years ago with the endorsement of the UN Guiding Principles on Business and Human Rights" (IOE 2014). Also see Sauvant 2015, 70.

[48] For a fuller account of the interaction between local and national firms and the international mediators, see *Back from the Brink: The 2008 Mediation Process and Reforms in Kenya* (The Office of the African Union Panel of Eminent African Personalities 2014).

[49] *Implementing the Responsibility to Protect* (United Nations 2009, p. 2).

entails enlisting local, national, and regional stakeholders – including the private sector – in the development of plans, practices, and policies that are shaped to meet the political, economic, and cultural dynamics of the society under stress.

5 What is needed is a positive, forward-looking agenda about how the assets, capacities, and skills of the private sector could contribute to efforts to curb atrocity crimes, not one built on the premise that commercial enterprises need to mend their ways in this regard. The core principle is simple, but powerful: curbing mass atrocities is good for business. They generally thrive in stable, predictable environments, where markets are expanding, not contracting, where governments are accountable and transparent, not corrupt or irrational, and where laws are enforced fairly, openly, and consistently, not used to stifle dissent or to crush minorities. They generally seek to sell their products and services across sectarian lines and social divisions. Those are the places, as well, where foreign investors and assistance agencies alike prefer to place their capital, and tourists prefer to visit. Since substantial capital and infrastructure investments are made for the long term, they tend to go to societies that exhibit promise and demonstrate resilience, not those that are riven by sectarian divisions and tensions.

The bottom line is that the private sector, if left to its own devices, without untoward political influence, will tend to favor public policies and social standards that discourage the incitement and commission of mass atrocities. There are exceptions of course, principally where a government and the bulk of its people have already turned against a minority group or groups, as in Germany under National Socialism. But the general rule is that, for the private sector, long-term self-interest equates with enlightened self-interest. Most commercial enterprises, most of the time, should be natural allies of those in government, international organizations, or civil society that are working to curb atrocity crimes. That is why the divide that has long existed between the private sector and UN and human rights circles appears so dysfunctional from an atrocity prevention perspective, and why the path of posing more rules, standards, or codes for business in this regard sounds so untimely and counterproductive.

The four case studies presented in the chapter by Alain Lempereur and Rebecca Herrington, as well as additional examples mentioned in other chapters, are valuable reminders that there is a history of business figures intervening, often in quiet ways, to save lives even as mass atrocities are unfolding around them. We need to know more about what motivates business leaders and others to take personal and financial risks to help the vulnerable at such critical times, as well as why others choose to be bystanders or even perpetrators. We need greater understanding, as well, about what moves group and political leaders – domestically and internationally – to get involved in trying to make a difference. The stories presented in this volume suggest, at the same time, that more could be done by the private sector to prevent such mass crimes in the future with a more concerted effort, a more focussed sense of purpose, and a more refined and articulated partnership among key governmental, inter-governmental, and civil society actors.

The chapters by Alex J. Bellamy and Vesselin Popovski provide more comprehensive and rigorous typologies of ways the private sector can assist with prevention and protection, but it might be useful here to give a sense of how wide these range. For instance, business could help through the following measures:

1) Employment and business practices. In societies that are divided along sectarian lines and that may be at risk of atrocity crimes, companies can provide a positive example by stressing diversity in their hiring and promotion practices, by encouraging tolerance and multiculturalism in their internal and external practices, and by developing infrastructure, marketing, and advertising in a manner that cuts across sectarian lines and builds the widest possible corporate identity and customer base. It may help, as well, to seek investors from a range of cultural backgrounds and beliefs. In most of the world, these steps would simply be considered to be integral to growing a business and expanding its markets, rather than as examples of altruism or social activism. As the Secretary-General's 2014 R2P report notes, a successful private sector can help to build a country's resilience in the face of domestic divisions.[50] In a larger sense, since researchers have long asserted a statistical linkage between a country's poverty and its proclivity for atrocity crimes, it may well be that a thriving and profiting private sector may indirectly inhibit mass atrocities by giving populations a perceived stake in their larger societies, not just their cultural or sectarian groups.[51] Building on lessons from the Sullivan Principles on investment in South Africa, international investors and multinational corporations could develop standards for investing in countries and societies that could be at risk of or have experienced mass atrocity crimes.

2) Training, messaging, and outreach. To succeed, businesses need to be good at reaching out to the communities in which they work and

---

[50] *Fulfilling Our Collective Responsibility* (United Nations 2014, p. 7, para. 26).
[51] See "Second-Generation Comparative Research on Genocide" (Strauss 2007).

to which they sell their products and services. They need to excel at communicating with existing and potential markets and at utilizing whatever media is available and cost effective. They need, also, to train their staff not only about technology, procedures, and products but also about the standards, expectations, and culture the firm seeks both to internalize and to project. All of this provides multiple opportunities for companies, large and small, to participate actively in the lives of their workers, their families, and the larger communities in which they live. As they prosper, firms can choose whether to sponsor public service announcements and where and how to contribute – financially, materially, and personally – to local projects and community activities. They may choose to partner with local civil society groups that seek to build bridges, encourage tolerance, or mediate differences between disparate groups. In the approximately forty-five countries where the governments have appointed atrocity prevention/R2P focal points, businesses or business groups could select their own private focal points to work with their official counterparts on atrocity prevention activities, ranging from community-building projects to supporting legislation on civil rights to countering hate speech aimed at minority groups.[52] None of this need be limited to the activities or policies of firms themselves, as both workers and employers have unions, associations, and/or professional groups and networks that can make a larger collective difference.

3) Political influence. Though business leaders do not always seek political access for the best purposes, at a time of crisis and sectarian divisions within a country, their instincts – for the reasons discussed above – may tend to lean toward unity, healing, and stability. My experience at the United Nations was that in most situations governments and political elites are, at least initially, uncertain about how to proceed when sectarian tensions rise and/or when some political leaders start on a course toward violence against certain groups within the country. There usually is a period in which the political waters for such destructive steps are being tested and more moderate voices can still get a public and political hearing. It does matter whether timely messaging and political engagement are forthcoming at those points, whether from the business and labor communities, religious, cultural, and educational leaders, parliamentarians, media figures, or international partners. Given the enormous and lasting economic and

---

[52] For more information about the ongoing effort to develop the governmental atrocity prevention/R2P network, see the website of the Global Centre for R2P, which backstops the inter-governmental initiative.

social costs of mass atrocity crimes, the reasoned and united voice of prominent and respected business leaders – acting individually or, better, collectively as described in the chapter by Patrick Obath and Victor Owuor on Kenya – can make a significant difference in domestic political calculations in such cases. Depending on the size and reach of the firm or industry, such voices can also provide added legitimacy to those in foreign capitals and international organizations who are pressing for early international engagement.

4) Early warning. This is clearly an area of considerable promise in an age of exponential growth in the capacity of mobile communications technology, of information technology, and of advanced analytical techniques. As several of the authors in this volume point out, the possibilities for marrying these new technologies to the expanding international human protection mandates are much greater than they were even a few years ago, especially as much of this capacity is becoming increasingly affordable.[53] The private sector could be very helpful in providing technical expertise and advice regarding the employment of new technology in detecting the incitement of mass violence and in facilitating early warning of rapidly unfolding events that could be precursors to mass atrocities. There has been considerable communication among businesses, civil society partners, governments, and international agencies about such matters, but not enough exchange among local, national, regional, and global actors about how they could collaborate on such matters.

5) Assessment. In this author's experience, the most difficult and pressing challenges come in the realm of assessment, not early warning. International decision-makers, for instance, are unlikely to have as full, as detailed, as timely, and as reliable information as they would like about the critical players in a given situation, about their motivations, perceptions, and intentions, about the evolution of relationships among different groups, and about interactions with other groups and countries within the region and immediate neighborhood. One needs a dynamic, not static, understanding of such things, particularly if an international engagement is to do no harm and is to be sustainable over time. The risk management techniques employed by corporations in similar difficult environments might provide useful insights for government and international organization officials as well, for example in conjunction with the Framework of Analysis prepared by the UN's Joint Office on Genocide Prevention and R2P.[54]

[53] See, especially, the chapters by Kirsten Martin and Jonas Claes.
[54] Jill Shankleman makes a similar point in her chapter. Also see *Framework of Analysis for Atrocity Crimes: A Tool for Prevention* (United Nations Joint Office on Genocide Prevention and the Responsibility to Protect 2014).

6) Physical protection. At the World Summit, heads of state and government accepted the primary responsibility to protect populations, and nothing should be done to undermine that solemn commitment. Nevertheless, when national authorities manifestly fail to do so, all elements of the international community – including the private sector – should do what they can to provide whatever modicum of protection that they can manage. As noted in several chapters, there is a long, if spotty, history of corporations and their leaders finding sometimes creative ways to protect the most vulnerable. This has generally involved employing them, assisting their transit away from immediate danger, bribing officials or armed groups to look the other way, or providing housing or physical space to hide them until the worst danger has passed. The numbers affected have been relatively modest, but the example of courage under extreme pressure has often been quite compelling. It would be worthwhile to engage the business community in a conversation about two current and horrific challenges: the record number of forcibly displaced globally, but especially in the Middle East, and the growing role of non-state armed groups with highly sectarian agendas in fomenting so much of the violence aimed at displacing populations.[55] With tens of millions of internally displaced and refugees forced to live in camps for what could be generations, the question of physical protection, especially for children and women, demands the most innovative and generous answers that business, other civil society partners, governments, and regional and global institutions can muster.

None of this suggests that the private sector is, or should be, one of the primary actors in preventing mass atrocities or in providing protection when they do occur. But efforts at prevention and protection need all the partners and collaborators they can get, and the potential intellectual, technical, material, and financial contributions of the private sector have hardly been tapped.

There are, moreover, good, practical reasons for private sector actors to want to help. Yet for all that has been said and written about R2P, we still lack avenues, strategies, and procedures for encouraging and organizing cross-sectoral collaborations among businesses, other civil society groups, governments, and regional and global institutions. The first step,

---

[55] According to the United Nations High Commissioner for Refugees (UNHCR), at the end of 2014 there were 59.5 million forcibly displaced people in the world, the highest number since the establishment of the United Nations seventy years ago and more than 8 million over the number of the previous year, which at that time was also a record (UNHCR 2015).

of course, is to acknowledge that the private sector can be and should be seen as a natural partner in mass atrocity prevention efforts, domestically and internationally. This seems obvious when one looks at such challenges through the bottom-up lens of the Individual Responsibility to Protect (IR2P), rather than solely through the state-centric template of the initial conception of R2P presented in 2001. IR2P underscores that every member of society, not just top office holders, has a personal responsibility to try to prevent mass atrocity crimes.[56] Under IR2P, the business community – like every other sector of national and international society – needs to do its part. This book, by shining light on past heroics and by offering some fresh ideas for future initiatives, can help illuminate the way forward.

References

Berdal, Mats and David M. Malone, eds. 2000. *Greed and Grievance: Economic Agendas in Civil Wars*. Boulder, CO: Lynne Rienner Publishers.

Boutros-Ghali, Boutros. 1992. *An Agenda for Peace*. Report of the Secretary General Pursuant to the Statement Adopted by the Summit Meeting of the Security Council on 31 January 1992, A/47/277-S/24111 (June 17, 1992).

Brot für die Welt. 2014. *Corporate Influence on the Business and Human Rights Agenda of the United Nations*. Working Paper.

Chambers, Simone and Will Kymlicka, eds. 2001. *Alternative Conceptions of Civil Society*. Princeton University Press.

Collier, Paul and Anke Hoeffler. 1998. "On the economic causes of civil war." *Oxford Economic Papers* 50:563–573.

2004. "Greed and grievance in civil war." *Oxford Economic Papers* 56:563–595.

Commission on Preventing Deadly Conflict. 1998. *Preventing Deadly Conflict*. New York: Carnegie Corporation of New York.

de Montbrial, Thierry. 1975. "For a new world economic order." *Foreign Affairs* 54 (1):61–78.

Foot, Rosemary, Neil MacFarlane, and Michael Mastanduno, eds. 2003. *US Hegemony and International Organizations*. Oxford University Press.

International Commission on Intervention and State Sovereignty (ICISS). 2001. *The Responsibility to Protect*. Ottawa: International Development Research Center.

International Organization of Employers. 2014. "Consensus on business and human rights is broken with the adoption of the Ecuador initiative." www.ioe-emp.org/index.php?id=1238

Keane, John. 2003. *Global Civil Society?* Cambridge University Press.

Kimberley Process. 2000. www.kimberleyprocess.com

Luck, Edward C. 1999. *Mixed Messages: American Politics and International Organization, 1919–1999*. Washington, DC: Brookings Institution Press.

---

[56] See "The Individual Responsibility to Protect" (Luck and Luck 2015).

Luck, Edward C. 2012. "From promise to practice: Implementing the Responsibility to Protect." In *The Responsibility to Protect: The Promise of Stopping Mass Atrocities in Our Time*, edited by Jared Genser and Irwin Cotlar. Oxford University Press.

Luck, Edward C. and Dana Zaret Luck. 2015. "The individual Responsibility to Protect." In *Reconstructing Atrocity Prevention*, edited by Sheri Rosenberg, Tiberiu Galis, and Alex Zucker. Cambridge University Press.

Murphy, Craig N. 2007. "Private sector." In *The Oxford Handbook on the United Nations*, edited by Thomas G. Weiss and Sam Daws. Oxford University Press.

The Office of the African Union Panel of Eminent African Personalities. 2014. *Back from the Brink: The 2008 Mediation Process and Reforms in Kenya*. Addis Ababa, Ethiopia: The African Union Commission.

Patrick, Stuart and Shepard Forman, eds. 2001. *Multilateralism and US Foreign Policy*. Boulder, CO: Lynne Rienner Publishers.

Sauvant, Karl P. 2015. "The negotiations of the United Nations Code of Conduct on Transnational Corporations." *Journal of World Investment and Trade* 16:16–17.

Strauss, Scott. 2007. "Second-generation comparative research on genocide." *World Politics* 59 (3):476–501.

United Nations. 1974. *The Impact of Multinational Corporations on Development and on International Relations*. Report of the Group of Eminent Persons to Study the Impact of Multinational Corporations on Development and on International Relations, E/5500/Rev. 1, ST/ESA/6.

1998. "Reflections on intervention." Annual Ditchley Foundation Lecture. United Nations Press Release SG/SM/6613 (June 26).

1999. "Secretary-General proposes global compact on human rights, labour, environment, in address to World Economic Forum in Davos." Press Release SG/SM/6881 (February 1).

1999. "Two concepts of sovereignty." Statement by the Secretary-General to the General Assembly, September 20.

1999. *The Question of Intervention: Statements by the Secretary-General of the United Nations Kofi Annan*. New York: United Nations Department of Public Information.

1999. *Report of the Independent Inquiry into the Actions of the United Nations During the 1994 Genocide in Rwanda*. Annex to Letter Dated 15 December 1999 from the Secretary-General Addressed to the President of the Security Council, S/1999/1257 (December 16).

United Nations Economic and Social Council. 1996. Official Records, 1996, Supplement No. 1. ECOSOC Resolution 1996/31 of July 25, 1996. New York: United Nations.

2014. *List of Non-Governmental Organizations in Consultative Status with the Economic and Social Council as of 1 September 2014*. E/2014/INF/5 (December 3).

United Nations General Assembly. 2005. "2005 World Summit Outcome." Document A/Res/60/1, October 24. www.un.org/womenwatch/ods/A-RES-60-1-E.pdf

1974. Declaration on the Establishment of a New International Economic Order, A/RES/S-6/3201 (May 1).

1974. Programme of Action on the Establishment of a New International Economic Order, A/RES/S-6/3202 (May 1).

1999. *The Fall of Srebrenica*. Report of the Secretary-General Pursuant to General Assembly Resolution 53/35 A/54/549 (November 15).

2000. *We the Peoples: The Role of the United Nations in the Twenty-First Century*. Report of the Secretary-General A/54/2000 (March 27).

2009. *Implementing the Responsibility to Protect: Report of the Secretary-General*, A/63/677 (January 12). www.unrol.org/files/SG_reportA_63_677_en.pdf

2010. *Early Warning, Assessment and the Responsibility to Protect*. Report of the Secretary-General A/64/864 (July 14).

2011. *Human Rights and Transnational Corporations and Other Business Enterprises*. Human Rights Council A/HRC/RES/17/4 (July 6).

2011. *The Role of Regional and Sub-regional Arrangements in Implementing the Responsibility to Protect*. Report of the Secretary-General A/65/877-S/2011/393 (June 27).

2012. *Responsibility to Protect: Timely and Decisive Response*. Report of the Secretary-General A/66/874-S/2012/578 (July 25).

2013. *Responsibility to Protect: State Responsibility and Prevention*. A/67/929-S/2013/399 (July 9).

2014. *Fulfilling Our Collective Responsibility: State Responsibility and Prevention*. Report of the Secretary-General A/68/947-S/2014/449 (July 11).

United Nations Global Compact. 2015. "Overview." Accessed April 24. www.unglobalcompact.org/what-is-gc

United Nations High Commissioner for Refugees. 2015. *Global Trends Report: World at War*. Geneva: UNHCR.

United Nations High-level Panel on Threats, Challenges and Change. 2004. *A More Secure World: Our Shared Responsibility*. New York: The United Nations.

United Nations Joint Office on Genocide Prevention and the Responsibility to Protect. 2014. *Framework of Analysis for Atrocity Crimes: A Tool for Prevention*. New York: The United Nations.

United Nations Security Council. 2001. *Prevention of Armed Conflict*. Report of the Secretary-General A/55/985-S/2001/574 (July 7).

United States Senate. 1975. *Covert Action in Chile, 1963–1973*. Staff Report of the Select Committee to Study Governmental Operations with Respect to Intelligence Activities. Washington, DC: Government Printing Office.

1   Selling R2P: Time for Action

Tina J. Park and Victor MacDiarmid

Introduction

The Responsibility to Protect, also referred to as RtoP or R2P, is an emerging norm in international relations coined in 2001, which states that when sovereign states are unable or unwilling to fulfill their responsibility to protect their own populations from genocide and other mass atrocities, the international community has the responsibility to do so. The R2P principle, as endorsed by the 150 heads of state and government at the 2005 World Summit, has a "narrow but deep" approach – it is confined to situations of four specific crimes (genocide, war crimes, crimes against humanity, and ethnic cleansing) but calls upon multiple actors to exercise collective responsibility in protecting people in peril (United Nations 2005). At its core, R2P marks a fundamental shift in our Westphalian understanding of state sovereignty into sovereignty as a responsibility.

In addition to the political commitment by the heads of state and government in 2005, various actors, including the United Nations system, academics, and civil societies around the world, have helped to solidify the R2P principle in the past decade. The UN Secretary-General Ban Ki-moon, in particular, has been one of the key champions in promoting R2P and can be seen as one of the norm entrepreneurs for R2P.[1] In his speech on "Responsible Sovereignty: International Cooperation for a Changed World" in Berlin in 2008, Ban made his personal commitment to turn R2P from a concept to a policy (Ban 2008). The Secretary-General's annual reports on R2P have served as important guiding posts in clarifying the conceptual bases of R2P, while also continuing the dialogue across all regions.[2] There has been growing support for Ban's special advisers

---

[1] For a detailed discussion on the term "norm entrepreneur," please see Martha Finnemore and Kathryn Sikkink, "International norm dynamics and political change," *International Organization*, 52 (4), Autumn 1998.

[2] Since 2009, Ban's annual reports have developed a three-pillar approach for implementing R2P (A/63/677/2009), analyzed early warning and assessment capacity (A/64/864/2010), explored the role of regional and sub-regional organizations (A/65/877/-S/2011/

on the Prevention of Genocide and R2P, who have worked closely with national and regional governments and civil society organizations to promote political implementation. Since the 2005 World Summit, the UN Security Council has adopted thirty resolutions and six presidential statements that refer to the responsibility to protect, while also repeatedly emphasizing the need to support national authorities in implementing R2P in resolutions authorizing UN peace operations. The UN Human Rights Council has adopted thirteen resolutions that have reference to R2P, including three on the prevention of genocide and nine on country-specific situations. At the time of writing, six annual UN General Assembly's informal interactive dialogs on R2P have taken place, with a steady increase in consensus and support for R2P from the Member States every year (United Nations 2015). The 2014 annual UNGA dialog followed the release of the UN Secretary-General's sixth report on R2P entitled *Fulfilling Our Collective Responsibility: International Assistance and the Responsibility to Protect*, which focussed on the responsibility of the international community in upholding protection responsibilities. Sixty-seven states spoke at this dialogue emphasizing that R2P reinforces state sovereignty and underscoring crucial roles of national, regional, and sub-regional organizations for the second pillar of R2P (United Nations 2014).

Concurrently, there have been important milestones in the political implementation of R2P across all regions. In 2013, the Inter-Parliamentary Union Assembly, which brought together more than 600 parliamentarians from around the world, unanimously adopted a resolution entitled "Enforcing the Responsibility to Protect: the Role of Parliamentarians," in Quito, Ecuador, in consultation with Dr. Edward C. Luck, then UN Secretary-General's Special Adviser on R2P, and the Canadian Centre for the Responsibility to Protect (IPU 2013). The African Commission on Human and Peoples' Rights has adopted a resolution on strengthening the responsibility to protect in Africa, and the European Parliament has recommended the European Union for the full implementation of R2P (United Nations 2015). As of July 2016, fifty-five governments and the European Union appointed a National Focal Point on R2P to help facilitate information sharing and strengthen protection capacity on mass atrocity prevention and response (Global Centre for R2P 2016).

---

393), investigated timely and decisive response (A/66/874-S/2012/578), and identified state responsibilities for prevention (A/67/929/S/2013/399). The 2014 report (A/68/947-S/2014/449) focussed on the second pillar of R2P on international assistance, and the most recent report in 2015 (A/69/981–S/2015/500), entitled "A Vital and Enduring Commitment: Implementing the Responsibility to Protect," focusses on seizing the momentum for political implementation.

As the Honorable Lloyd Axworthy, former Canadian Minister of Foreign Affairs, once observed, "The debate over R2P today is not some abstract, academic exercise of hypothetical simulations. This is real, because the issue of intervention – of how, when and who goes in to influence the affairs of another state – is probably the most critical and difficult conundrum in this new century of ours" (Axworthy 2005). Over the span of merely a decade since the 2005 World Summit Outcome (WSO), discussions on R2P have shifted from the acceptance of R2P as a viable concept in international relations to the issue of political implementation at national, regional, and international levels. There have been some clear R2P successes in Kenya, Kyrgyzstan, and Côte d'Ivoire, where careful national and international efforts helped to avert crises from escalating (United Nations 2015). Yet, serious concerns remain in situations like North Korea, where Justice Michael Kirby's Commission of Inquiry found that "systematic, widespread and gross violations of human rights" constituting crimes against humanity are being committed (Kirby 2014). There are serious ongoing challenges in Iraq and Syria, with the on-going terror attacks by the Islamic State in Iraq and the Levant (ISIL), as well as conflicts in Yemen and on the Gaza Strip (United Nations 2015).

These continuing challenges in the political implementation of R2P provide compelling reasons for the relevance of R2P in our world today. Although R2P was traditionally considered from the UN-centric perspective, there has been growing interest in working with a more diverse set of actors with different capacities for timely and decisive action. This brief chapter is aimed at providing a historical and conceptual overview of the R2P principle in the field of international relations. It also seeks to highlight the relevance and importance of the role of the private sector in implementing R2P. Ultimately, it will argue that in light of the growing momentum of the R2P principle, it is important to move beyond the UN-centric approach on R2P and carefully examine the ways in which other actors, such as the private sector, could usefully engage in the implementation of R2P.

Origins of R2P

To fully appreciate the remarkable speed at which R2P has traveled in the realm of international relations, it is useful to first consider the historical context that gave birth to the R2P principle. With the end of the Cold War and the outbreak of new conflicts in the 1990s, "humanitarian intervention" became the new buzzword for the international community.[3] The

---

[3] The most prominent cases include Liberia (1990–1992), Northern Iraq (1991), Bosnia and Herzegovina (1992–1995), Somalia (1992–1993), Rwanda (1994), Haiti (1994),

clash of competing imperatives about human rights and intervention, coupled with the removal of some superpower constraints, led to more confusion and chaos than ever before (Evans 2008, 25). While they were few in number, the 1990s saw a number of cases in which military action by foreign powers were explicitly supported by humanitarian rationale (Welsh 2004). Nevertheless, humanitarian intervention was controversial both when it took place (Somalia, Bosnia, and Kosovo) and when it failed to take place (Rwanda). The delayed and half-hearted actions of the international community in Rwanda, and the deaths of 800,000 civilians over the course of 100 days in 1994, prompted a serious questioning of our Westphalian notion of state sovereignty (ICISS 2001). In cases when intervention did take place, such as the 1999 NATO bombing of Serbia without UN Security Council authorization, compelling questions arose about the use of military force and selective application of humanitarian intervention (Welsh 2009, 2).

The conscience-shocking crises in the 1990s proved that neither humanitarian intervention nor traditional UN peacekeeping provided sufficient mechanisms for protecting people in peril. At the same time, these crises also prompted the UN to reassess its own intervention framework. Of special importance is the notion of "protection of civilians" (POC), introduced by UN Secretary-General Kofi Annan in 1998 as a humanitarian imperative (Banda 2007, 7–8). By 1999, the UN Security Council had issued a *Presidential Statement on the Protection of Civilians in Armed Conflicts* and subsequently approved two resolutions on POC. The *UN Security Council Resolution 1265* (1999) and *Security Council Resolution 1296* (2000) made an important turning point in how the UN system approached the issue of POC. These resolutions recognized that targeting civilians or denying humanitarian access may constitute a threat to international peace and security, thereby enabling the possibility of coercive action under Chapter VII of the UN Charter.

In the fall of 1999, amidst continued controversies and debates about the Kosovo intervention, then UN Secretary-General Kofi Annan urged the UN Member States to "find a common ground in upholding the principles of the Charter and acting in defence of our common humanity" (Annan 2005). Responding to Annan's call to build a new consensus for state sovereignty, the Canadian government sponsored the

Albania (1997), Kosovo (1998–1999), and Iraq (2003). From Welsh, Jennifer. 2004. "Authorizing humanitarian intervention." In *The United Nations and Global Security*, edited by Richard M. Price and Mark W. Zacher. Basingstoke: Palgrave Macmillan, 177–192.

establishment of an international commission called the International Commission on Intervention and State Sovereignty (Tomlin *et al.* 2008, 214–215). The Commission was tasked to investigate "a whole range of questions – legal, moral, operational and political" and to produce a report that could help reconceptualize our notion of sovereignty as responsibility. The core tenet arising from the ICISS report is the principle that sovereignty implies responsibility and the primary responsibility for the protection of its people lies with the state itself (ICISS 2001). In accordance with this paradigm, the ICISS sought to achieve three main things: change the conceptual language from humanitarian intervention to responsibility to protect, pin the responsibility on state authorities at the national and at the international level, and ensure that international interventions are carried out in a proper manner. The ICISS report also provided a set of six criteria before military intervention can take place for humanitarian purposes: right authority, just cause, right intention, last resort, proportional means, and reasonable prospects for success. Marking a departure from political paralysis prevalent with humanitarian interventions, the ICISS report refocused attention on protection of people at risk, using the United Nations as the main channel (ICISS 2001).

According to the ICISS report, R2P embodied three main aspects – the responsibility to *react* to protect populations from grievous harm, to *prevent* such situations, and to *rebuild* in their aftermath. Signaling a key turning point from the Westphalian notion of state sovereignty, R2P announced that it was no longer a matter of the external state's right to intervene but the responsibility of *all states* to protect their own people and help others in such endeavor (Evans 2008a). Accordingly, the ICISS report sought to change the language from a "right of intervention" which focussed on the coercive prerogatives of interveners to a "responsibility to protect" which focuses on the state's duty to protect its own people (Welsh 2009). At the normative level, R2P embodied both sovereignty as responsibility and the collective international responsibility to protect victims within a sovereign state if necessary, with right authority and through military intervention if necessary. The Commission also stressed the importance of responsibility to prevent, through means such as building state capacity, remedying grievances, and ensuring the rule of law. Whatever the measures chosen to fulfill our responsibilities – political, legal, economic, and others – the less coercive measure was to be prioritized. On the controversial issue of military intervention, the ICISS proposed a number of criteria on legality and legitimacy, which would provide a set of benchmarks before any military intervention would be undertaken (Evans 2008, 43).

The R2P report produced by the ICISS was then adopted in the 2004 report from the UN Secretary-General's High-level Panel on Threats, Challenges and Change entitled *A More Secure World*, which was convened to "recommend clear and practical measures for ensuring effective collective action, based upon a rigorous analysis of future threats to peace and security." The Panel's report, *A More Secure World: Our Shared Responsibility*, was far wider in scope than the ICISS report, encompassing poverty, disease, and environmental degradation as well as the notion of human security. On R2P, the Panel noted that it "endorses the emerging norm that there is a collective international responsibility to protect, exercisable by the Security Council authorizing military intervention as a last resort, in the event of genocide and other large-scale killing, ethnic cleansing, or serious violations of humanitarian law which sovereign governments have proved powerless or unwilling to prevent" (Evans 2008, 44–45).

While revolutionary in the encompassing of international responsibility for protection, the core beliefs of R2P have historical roots in "sovereignty as a responsibility" first expressed by Roberta Cohen of the Refugee Policy Group in 1991: "Sovereignty carries with it a responsibility on the part of governments to protect their citizens" (Cohen 1991). Francis Deng, who served as the UN Secretary-General's Special Representative on Internally Displaced Persons, further developed "sovereignty as a responsibility" through open dialogues on IDP-related issues (Deng *et al.* 1996). Erin Mooney, Senior Adviser at the UN on IDP issues, drew an important parallel between R2P and the *Guiding Principles* on IDPs: "National authorities have the primary duty and responsibility to provide protection and humanitarian assistance to internally displaced persons within their jurisdiction" (Mooney 2011).

Unfortunately, the publication of the ICISS report on R2P took place in the same year as the 9/11 terrorist attack in the United States, when the "War on Terror" seized the front page of international politics. The British prime minister Tony Blair's use of R2P as a justification for the American invasion of Iraq to topple Saddam Hussein generated legitimate suspicions in the developing world about the motive behind R2P (Thakur and Weiss 2009, 36). Despite vigorous arguments from R2P's architects that the Iraq invasion did not constitute an R2P situation, this misuse nevertheless affected how the concept was perceived by the public and governments, especially those in the Global South. In that vein Thomas Weiss outlined the implications of the War on Terror on R2P's discourse. First, the decision made by Washington and London to go to war against Iraq in March 2003 without Security Council approval has distorted the legitimacy of UN-approved military action. Second, the rhetoric used by Tony Blair and George W. Bush to justify the invasion of Iraq on "humanitarian" grounds elicited hostile reactions from the Global South, who came to equate the R2P as another tool of an "imperial" North. Lastly, global preoccupation with the counter-terrorist invasions have shifted attention from the R2P. Weiss concluded: "Military overstretch and the prioritization of strategic concerns to the virtual exclusion of humanitarian ones is the sad reality of a post-9/11 world" (Weiss 2006, 749–750).

With the global attention on the War on Terror, it was not until the 2005 UN World Summit that R2P regained attention in the international arena. After much debate and consultation, the heads of state and government from 150 countries unanimously endorsed the R2P principle expressed through paras. 138 and 139, pledging that when a sovereign state fails to protect its own people from genocide, war crimes, ethnic cleansing, and crimes against humanity, the responsibility will fall upon the international community to take whatever action is appropriate, including the use of force (United Nations 2005). The full text of two R2P paragraphs in the WSO are worth examining in detail for both the clarity and brevity it offers on R2P's normative development:

138. Each individual State has the responsibility to protect its populations from genocide, war crimes, ethnic cleansing and crimes against humanity. This responsibility entails the prevention of such crimes, including their incitement, through appropriate and necessary means. We accept that responsibility and will act in accordance with it. The international community should, as appropriate, encourage and help States to exercise this responsibility and support the United Nations in establishing an early warning capability.

139. The international community, through the United Nations, also has the responsibility to use appropriate diplomatic, humanitarian and other peaceful means, in accordance with Chapters VI and VIII of the Charter, to help protect populations from genocide, war crimes, ethnic cleansing and crimes against humanity. In this context, we are prepared to take collective action, in a timely and decisive manner, through the Security Council, in accordance with the Charter, including Chapter VII, on a case-by-case basis and in cooperation with relevant regional organizations as appropriate, should peaceful means be inadequate and national authorities manifestly fail to protect their populations from genocide, war crimes, ethnic cleansing and crimes against humanity. We stress the need for the General Assembly to continue consideration of the responsibility to protect populations from genocide, war crimes, ethnic cleansing and crimes against humanity and its implications, bearing in mind the principles of the Charter and international law. We also intend to commit ourselves, as necessary and appropriate, to helping States build capacity to protect their populations from genocide, war crimes, ethnic cleansing and crimes against humanity and to assisting those which are under stress before crises and conflicts break out.

Paras. 138 and 139 were extremely significant for breaking through a political *impasse*, specifically on the basic questions of when, how, and under whose authority international intervention should occur. The inclusion of R2P paragraphs marked a major turning point for the normative trajectory of R2P, because it was the first time the principle was endorsed universally after some intense cross-regional dialogues, debates, and lobbying efforts. These two paragraphs explicitly make links to recognized international crimes under international law, marking a step forward from the 2001 ICISS report (Badescu 2011, 107). The 2005 WSO document also urged the General Assembly to continue consideration of R2P, which prompted the beginning of the UN Secretary-General's annual report on R2P and the UN General Assembly's annual informal debates on R2P.

Following the 2005 World Summit, the Security Council adopted a thematic resolution (Resolution 1674) of the protection of civilians in armed conflict in April 2006, reaffirming the R2P principle, and passed in August 2006 Resolution 1706, which specifically reiterated the key R2P provisions (para. 138 and 139) of the World Summit Outcome. To this date, the UN Office of Special Adviser on the Responsibility to Protect has maintained that it is important to promote a "strict and narrow definition" of the 2005 consensus on R2P and resist the temptation to broaden the scope beyond the four agreed principles. Furthermore, a variety of policy tools under Chapters VI, VII, and VII of the UN Charter should be used to prevent, deter, and react to the violations of four R2P crimes. Dr. Edward C. Luck, the former Special Adviser on the Responsibility to Protect, also highlighted that while no sequence was proposed in terms of which crime has more serious grave consequences than others, it was understood that many of the risk factors behind these four crimes were usually interconnected, and prevention and protection efforts should "encompass the whole range of R2P crimes and violations" (Luck 2008). The R2P paragraphs in the 2005 WSO further clarified the kinds of tools, actors, and procedures involved in implementing R2P.

Based on the recommendation of the 2005 World Summit Outcome, the UN Secretary-General Ban Ki-moon has developed a mutually reinforcing three-pillar approach on R2P. These pillars are non-sequential and to be adopted as needed on a case-by-case basis, simultaneously if necessary, in full partnership with regional, sub-regional, and international organizations. As formulated in the Secretary-General's 2009 Report (A/63/677) on *Implementing the Responsibility to Protect*, the three pillars of R2P entail: 1) The State carries the primary responsibility for protecting populations from genocide, war crimes, crimes against humanity, and ethnic cleansing, and their incitement; 2) the international community has a responsibility to encourage and assist States in fulfilling this responsibility; and 3) the international community has a responsibility to use appropriate diplomatic, humanitarian, and other means to protect populations from these crimes. If the State is manifestly failing to protect its populations, the international community must be prepared to take collective action to protect populations, in accordance with the Charter of the United Nations. The latest Secretary-General's report on R2P further noted that in implementing these pillars, the real question is not so much whether the R2P "applies" in a given situation, since states have a responsibility to protect their populations at all times, but rather how best to use specific measures identified under each pillar to prevent and respond to R2P crimes in a timely and decisive manner (United Nations 2014).

Greater input from the Global South into the theoretical conceptualization and practical implementation has been crucial for R2P's relevance in today's world. In that light, Brazil's "Responsibility while Protecting" (RwP) in the aftermath of the Libyan intervention marked an important contribution from a major actor in the Global South that can greatly strengthen the credibility of the R2P principle. RwP proposed a set of criteria for military intervention, a monitoring-and-review mechanism to assess the implementation of Security Council mandates, and a renewed emphasis on capacity building to avert crises before they happen. RwP therefore stressed three major principles: accountability, assessment, and prevention (United Nations 2014).

Most recently, the Rights up Front initiative, launched in December 2013 by UN Secretary-General Ban Ki-moon, has added another dimension to the debate on R2P. The Rights up Front initiative was inspired by the Petrie Report of 2012, which assessed the UN's response to the final months of the 2009 war in Sri Lanka. This independent review panel report, chaired by Charles Petrie, was extremely critical of the United Nations in its protection capacity and called its actions a "systematic failure" in Sri Lanka. It also called for a comprehensive review of the UN system regarding the implementation of its humanitarian and protection mandates. Hence, the Rights up Front strategy is mainly aimed at enhancing coordination capacity within the UN system and attempts to strengthen the actions of the General Assembly, the Security Council, and the UN Human Rights Council for greater coherence and efficiency (Boon 2014). There are six action plans outlined in the Rights up Front initiative:

ACTION 1: Integrating human rights into the lifeblood of the UN so all staff understand their own and the Organization's human rights obligations.
ACTION 2: Providing Member States with candid information with respect to peoples at risk of, or subject to, serious violations of human rights or humanitarian law.

ACTION 3: Ensuring coherent strategies of action on the ground and leveraging the UN system's capacities to respond in a concerted manner.

ACTION 4: Clarifying and streamlining procedures at headquarters to enhance communication with the field and facilitate early, coordinated action.

ACTION 5: Strengthening the UN's human rights capacity, particularly through better coordination of its human rights entities.

ACTION 6: Developing a common UN system for information management on serious violations of human rights and humanitarian law.

While there is no explicit reference to the R2P principle, the Secretary-General's Rights up Front initiative has been seen as an important development in the future implementation of R2P, especially as the Member States and the UN organs look toward mainstreaming R2P at national, regional, and international levels. In particular, Action 4 has strong correlations to Pillar One and Pillar Two of R2P, and also underscores the centrality of human rights in the works of the UN system. As we look ahead to the new UN Secretary-General sustaining and further enhancing the momentum built during Ben's service will be critical in mainstream R2P in the US system.

R2P Today and the Role of the Private Sector

As evident in the previous discussion on the normative trajectory of R2P in the last decade, R2P has generally been considered in the state-centric perspective, with the UN as the main channel for both discussion and action. While the central role of the UN in maintaining global peace and security cannot be dismissed, the complex nature of today's conflicts calls for a paradigm shift in how we prevent and respond to R2P crimes. Ranging from the General Assembly to the Human Rights Council to the Security Council and the Peacebuilding Commission, as well as various UN programs and specialized agencies, different organs of the UN system have been instrumental in responding to humanitarian crises and building capacity against mass atrocity crimes (United Nations 2014). Hence, the focus of our attention should not be on replacing the capacities and roles already played by the international organizations such as the UN or regional bodies, or a state's primary responsibilities, but about how best to fill the gap found in our existing mechanisms for protection capacity.

Undoubtedly, profit-making is the first priority for the private sector. At the same time, it is useful to remember that a stable political environment is generally conducive to business interests, and building a positive reputation in the community is in line with many firms' business objectives. In fact, there are many examples of corporations behaving altruistically since the dawn of the nineteenth century, ranging anywhere from selfless giving to self-interested giving (Crowther 2008, 59). While human rights may appear to be a public good, most often in the hands of the state, the private sector may have leverage with the political leadership within the state and partake in activities that may eventually promote peace.

When John Ruggie was appointed as the UN Special Representative of the Secretary-General on human rights and transnational corporations in 2005, applying human rights law to the private sector was a highly contested issue. The business community and the human rights community disagreed on whether corporations have, or should have, direct responsibilities under the international human rights law (Knox 2012). Since then, important milestones have been reached in terms of key frameworks within the UN system for engaging the business community on human rights issues. Furthermore, the *UN Guiding Principles on Business and Human Rights*, endorsed by the Human Rights Council in 2011, and the *Corporate Responsibility to Protect Human Rights*, released by the Office of the UN High Commissioner for Human Rights in 2012, provide useful frameworks for understanding the role of business in promoting human rights. The commentary to the *UN Guiding Principles* states that "there are strong policy reasons for home States to set out clearly the expectations that businesses respect human rights abroad, especially where that State itself is involved in or supports those businesses" (*UN Guiding Principles on Business and Human Rights*, 7).

The twenty-four guiding principles and the "Protect, Respect and Remedy" framework is also based on a three-pillar approach:

• the State duty to protect human rights;
• the corporate responsibility to respect human rights;
• the need for greater access to remedy for victims of business-related abuse.

The *Guiding Principles* also make it clear that in many cases, the responsibility of enterprises to respect human rights is not optional, and many of their activities are already governed by domestic law or existing tenets of international law. In light of these frameworks, it is valuable to consider the role of the private sector in promoting Pillar Two of the R2P, concerning the assistance to states for capacity building (early warning capability and assisting before crisis breaks out).

Timely intervention is critical for communities affected by conflict. When a situation is declared "R2P applicable," a timely and decisive intervention will largely depend on the institutional culture of relevant organizations. While institutions such as the United Nations or the African Union may have the best intentions for responding to a crisis situation, finding consensus and taking action will require mobilization of capital and other resources. The latest UN Secretary-General's Report on R2P explicitly asserts that private sector actors can "contribute to building resilience by strengthening local economies and employing a workforce inclusive of all social groups" (United Nations 2014). This can be done sometimes through public–private partnerships to enhance the impact of national measures aimed at R2P prevention. As the experience in Kenya's post-election crisis demonstrated (OEF 2014), the private sector can also indirectly contribute to the commission or suppression of atrocity crimes through its operations and business practices, as well as mobilizing itself for a culture of peace. While norms and practices differ by industries and countries, the private sector can also actively develop risk management tools to explicitly incorporate atrocity crime risks in its business strategies (United Nations 2014). Most importantly, it is crucial for the private sector to recognize that preventing R2P crimes is in its business interest as well, and for the UN agencies to actively engage with relevant private sector representatives under the broader protection umbrella.

Conclusions

The UN Secretary-General Ban Ki-moon once said that R2P today is "a principle, not yet a policy; an aspiration, not yet a reality." Yet, since its inception in 2001, the support for R2P has grown across all regions and at all levels of governments, quickly becoming an emerging norm in international relations. This chapter has considered some key turning points in the normative and conceptual evolution of the R2P from 2001 until today. From the unanimous endorsement by world leaders at the 2005 World Summit to the annual informal General Assembly debates at the United Nations, R2P has traveled a long journey in the realm of international relations over a remarkably short span of time. To date, there have been heated debates across the globe on the scope and depth of R2P, despite the UN Secretary-General's advocacy for a "narrow but deep" approach and limiting the applicability to four specific international crimes. Some attempted to apply R2P to natural disasters, some mistakenly equated R2P with regime change or military intervention, and some inevitably became frustrated about the usefulness of R2P as we witnessed grave humanitarian crises in Sudan, Central African Republic, Syria, and Iraq. Some worried about infringement of state sovereignty, while others worried about overstretching of limited resources. Today, the international community's engagement on R2P still presents challenges on political implementation, timely and decisive deployment of resources, and consistent application as an emerging norm in international relations.

Moving forward, three interrelated aspects of intelligence gathering, coordination mechanism for prevention, and collaborative partnership for action will determine the future of R2P as an established norm in international relations. Successfully tackling these challenges will require input from various actors, including the private sector. The risk factors outlined in the Analysis Framework of the UN Office of the Prevention of Genocide provide a useful starting point for identifying the risks of four R2P crimes. Many of the risk factors, such as triggering factors of genocide or the presence of illegal arms, are already being tracked by a number of UN organs and civil society groups. What is lacking at this stage is a mechanism to measure the degree of risk found in each individual case and to consolidate various sources of information collected by different agencies. In line with such information-gathering mechanisms, a comprehensive strategy for preventing R2P crimes would be extremely useful. An effective prevention strategy must reflect the unique circumstances of each crisis and cultural sensitivities surrounding that case, and encourage collaboration at all levels of the society to turn early warning into early action. Moving away from the reactionary approach seen so far with R2P-related cases, a new pro-active prevention strategy will require financial and institutional resources on a long-term basis, as well as political leadership at the national, regional, and international levels. Lastly, there is a dire need to encourage collaboration between national, regional, and international actors. Regional bodies such as the African Union are uniquely suited to adopt targeted diplomatic measures or deploy military, police, or civilian personnel in case of impending crisis. For R2P to become an applicable norm in international relations, it must move outside the debating chambers of academia and the UN system and become more institutionalized at local levels, involving all key actors of society.

Despite all the challenges, there is much to be hopeful about as we consider the state of R2P in our world. As the latest UN General Assembly on R2P has amply demonstrated, an overwhelming number of UN Member States – even the former critics of R2P – are no longer debating the merits of R2P but discussing how best to "own" and implement R2P in their domestic environment. Our knowledge base on R2P is stronger than ever before thanks to the flourishing scholarship on various aspects of R2P. The UN Secretary-General's annual reports, as well as his three-pillar approach for implementation, have provided a clearer roadmap for decisive and timely intervention. His Special Advisers on R2P have reached out to various nation-states, civil society representatives, and scholars around the world, which has helped to build a global consensus on R2P. The civil society groups around the world, as well as sub-regional and regional organizations, are working closely with their national governments to promote political implementation of R2P. The private sector, with its immediate access to capital and political leverage, undoubtedly has an important role in the future of R2P to prove that selling R2P in a timely and decisive manner is in everyone's interest.

References

Annan, Kofi. 1998. *Speech at the 35th Annual Ditchley Foundation Lecture.* Retrieved from www.ditchley.co.uk/page/173/lecture-xxxv.htm
  2005. *In Larger Freedom: Decision Time at the UN.* May. Retrieved from www. unis.unvienna.org/pdf/freedom_annan.pdf
Axworthy, Lloyd. 2005. *The Responsibility to Protect: Prescription for a global public domain.* Joan B. Kroc Distinguished Lecture Series. San Diego, CA: Joan B. Kroc Institute for Peace & Justice, February 10. Retrieved from http:// peace.sandiego.edu/events/DLS/AxworthyPDFBook.pdf
Badescu, Christina. 2011. *Humanitarian Intervention and the Responsibility to Protect: Security and Human Rights.* New York: Routledge.
Ban, Ki-Moon. 2008. *Responsible sovereignty: International cooperation for a changed world.* Berlin: UN News, July 15. Retrieved from www.un.org/press/en/2008/ sgsm11701.doc.htm
Banda, Maria. 2007. *Responsibility to Protect: Moving the agenda forward.* Ottawa: UN Association In Canada. Retrieved from www.responsibilityto-protect.org/files/ UNA%20Canada%20Report%20on%20R2P.pdf
Bellamy, Alex. 2006. *Whither the Responsibility to Protect? Humanitarian Intervention and the 2005 World Summit, Ethics & International Affairs.* Retrieved from www.cerium.ca/IMG/pdf/BELLAMY-_ALEX Whither_ the_ Responsibility_to_ Protect-2.pdf
Bellamy, Alex and Sarah Davies. 2009. "Introduction." *Global Responsibility to Protect Journal* 1. Retrieved from www.brill.com/global-responsibility-Protect
Boon, Kristen. 2014. "Assessing the UN's New Rights up Front initiative," *Opinio Juris.* February 27. Retrieved from http://opiniojuris.org/2014/02/27/ assessing-uns-new-rights-front-action-plan/
Cohen, Roberta. 1991. *Human Rights Protection for Internally Displaced Persons.* Washington, DC: Refugee Policy Group.
Crowther, David, ed. 2008. "Stakeholder perspectives on social responsibility." In *The Ashgate Research Companion to Corporate Social Responsibility.* Burlington, VT: Ashgate Publishing Ltd.
Deng, Francis M. and Donald Rothchild *et al.* 1996. *Sovereignty as Responsibility: Conflict Management in Africa.* Washington DC: Brookings Institution Press.
Evans, Gareth. 2003. "Humanity did not justify this war." *Financial Times,* May 15.

2008. "The Responsibility to Protect: An idea whose time has come...and gone?" *International Relations* 22 (3):283–298.

2008. *The Responsibility to Protect: Ending Mass Atrocity Crimes Once and For All.* Washington, DC: Brookings Institution Press.

Finnemore, Martha and Kathryn Sikkink. 1998. "International norm dynamics and political change." *International Organization* 52 (4):887–917.

Global Centre for Responsibility to Protect. 2016. "R2P focal points." Retrieved from www.globalr2p.org/our_work/r2p_focal_points

Hardt, Heidi. 2014. *Time to React: The Efficiency of International Organizations in Crisis Response.* Oxford University Press.

International Commission on Intervention and State Sovereignty (ICISS). 2001. *The Responsibility to Protect: Report of the International Commission on Intervention and State Sovereignty.* Ottawa: International Development Research Centre. Retrieved from http://iciss.ca/pdf/Commission-Report.pdf

Inter-Parliamentary Union. 2013. *Resolution Adopted by the 128th IPU Assembly: Enforcing the Responsibility to Protect: The Role of Parliament in Safeguarding Civilians' Lives.* www.ipu.org/conf-e/128/res-1.htm

Kenkel, Kai Michael. 2012. "Brazil and R2P: Does taking responsibility mean using force?" *Global Journal for R2P* 4(1). Retrieved from http://booksand-journals.brillonline.com/content/journals/1875984x/4/1

Kirby, Michael. 2014. *Report of the Commission of Inquiry on Human Rights in the Democratic People's Republic of Korea.* New York: United Nations. Retrieved from www.ohchr.org/EN/HRBodies/HRC/CoIDPRK/Pages/ReportoftheCommissionofInquiryDPRK.aspx

Knox, John H. 2012. "The Ruggie Rules: Applying human rights law to corporations." In *The UN Guiding Principles on Business and Human Rights,* edited by Radu Mares. Boston, MA: Martinus Nijhoff Publishers.

Luck, Edward. 2008. *The United Nations and Responsibility to Protect.* New York: Stanley Foundation. www.stanleyfoundation.org/publications/pab/LuckPAB808.pdf

Mooney, Erin. 2011. "The Guiding Principles and the Responsibility To Protect." In *Ten Years of the Guiding Principles, Foreign Migrations Review.* Retrieved from www.fmreview.org/en/FMRpdfs/GP10/11–13.pdf

One Earth Foundation. 2014. "The role of private sector in Kenya's peacebuilding: The case of 2013 election cycle." http://oneearthfuture.org/sites/oneearthfuture.org/files/documents/publications/kenyaprivatesectorpolicybrief_1.pdf

Thakur, Ramesh. 2003. "Chrétien was right: It's time to redefine a just war." *Globe and Mail,* July 22.

(2009). "Ban Ki-moon a champion of U.N.'s role to protect." *The Daily Yomiuri,* March 10. Retrieved from www.yomiuri.co.jp/dy/world/20090310DY13001.htm

Thakur, Ramesh and Thomas G. Weiss. 2009. "R2P: From idea to norm – and action?" *Global Responsibility to Protect Journal.* Retrieved from www.brill.com/global-responsibility-protect

Tomlin, Brian, Norman Hillmer, and Fen Hampson. 2008. *Canada's International Policies: Agendas, Alternatives and Politics.* Toronto: Oxford University Press.

United Nations. 2005. *2005 World Summit Outcome Document* (General Assembly Resolution 60/1). Retrieved from www.responsibilitytoprotect.org/index/php/united_nations /398?theme=alt1

———. 2014. *Secretary-General's Annual Report on R2P: Fulfilling our Collective Responsibility: International Assistance and the Responsibility to Protect.* New York: United Nations. http://responsibilitytoprotect.org/N1446379.pdf

———. 2015. *Secretary-General's Annual Report on R2P: "A Vital and Enduring Commitment: Implementing Responsibility to Protect."* New York: United Nations. www.un.org/en/ga/search/view_doc.asp?symbol=S/2015/500

UN Guiding Principles on Business and Human Rights. www.ohchr.org/Documents/Publications/GuidingPrinciplesBusinessHR_EN.pdf

Utting, Peter. 2011. "Promoting CSR through the United Nations: Developmental and governance implications." In *The Responsible Corporation in a Global Economy*, edited by Colin Crouch and Camilla Maclean. Oxford University Press.

Weiss, Thomas. 2006. "R2P after 9/11 and the World Summit." *Wisconsin International Law Journal* 24. Retrieved from http://hosted.law.wisc.edu/wordpress/wilj/files/2012/02/weiss.pdf

Welsh, Jennifer. 2004. "Authorizing humanitarian intervention." In *The United Nations and Global Security*, edited by Richard M. Price and Mark W. Zacher. Basingstoke: Palgrave Macmillan.

Welsh, Jennifer. 2009. *Policy Brief: Implementing the R2P.* Oxford: Oxford Institute for Ethics, Law and Armed Conflict. Retrieved from www.elac.ox.ac.uk/downloads/r2p_policybrief_180209.pdf

2 Why Not Business?

Timothy L. Fort and Michelle Westermann-Behaylo

"I work hard. I try to do my best every day. I try to be responsible in what I do too. Now, you are telling me that I'm supposed to create world peace through my work?"

A General Motors executive once said that to one of the authors of this chapter. Though sympathetic to the idea that business might contribute to a better world – even by reducing the amount of violence in the world – the idea proved a bit overwhelming when he thought of adding the task to his job description.

Indeed, it can seem that assigning a role to business for peacebuilding – or for acting to address atrocities – is far removed from the work of businesspeople in at least two important ways. While it is tempting to think of "business" in institutional terms, the reality is that to ask business to build peace or to reduce the likelihood of a mass atrocity is asking some human being, balancing work and family life and juggling demands of bosses and colleagues, to add something seemingly enormous and complicated to a normal work day. The term "business" can cloud the reality that such demands are one among any number of requests people receive and face pressures to accomplish.

Even from a more institutional basis, the notion that businesses are to take on a role of creating the governance structures that inhibit war and atrocities seems somewhat far afield from commercial institutions' central task of creating wealth. Yet, while bearing these perspectives in mind, in this chapter we wish to argue that businesses can play a role in creating a more peaceful world, one that contributes to peace generally and, by doing so, also lessens the likelihood of mass atrocities.

How would business do this? In the first section, we review a traditional, almost neo-mercantilist kind of approach in which business is viewed as an agent of or facilitator of state action and, independently, has philanthropic opportunities. In the second section, we introduce a perspective in which corporations, as independent institutional actors on the global stage, conduct their own diplomacy and foreign policy that could be aimed at creating a structural world with less violence. We continue this argument in the third section, where we examine arguments that demonstrate that the world may be more peaceful than in the past, and how gentle commerce and business diplomacy can be key, incremental contributions to that process.

In making this argument, we risk conflating war and atrocities. They are not, of course, the same things. War crimes by definition happen in the context of major armed violence, and genocide is almost always preceded by political instability or civil war (Goldsmith *et al.* 2013). War itself may not produce genocide and war crimes (though in the existential, emotional struggle of killing, it is not surprising that genocide and/or war crimes may take place). But it is hard to imagine times and places where war crimes (by tautology) and genocide are not part of or immediately connected with warfare. Putting ourselves in the shoes of that General Motors executive, the roadmap of how his work would prevent genocide has yet to be drawn. However, an emerging literature over the past fifteen years has demonstrated how business can contribute to peace and to reducing the chances of war. The authors of this chapter have been deeply immersed in the business and peace literature for those fifteen years and so our contribution draws from that roadmap. We hope that in sketching it here, we contribute to a new map that might further show businesspeople how they can mitigate the horrors of atrocities as well.

A Traditional Approach to Reduction of Violence and Atrocities

Many authors in the realist school of political thought begin and end analysis of organized violence with states as the unit of analysis. In just the past few years, two scholars, Ian Morris and Charles Kupchan, have made the case that while civil society and economic trade may flourish with peace, the parameters of conflicts and borders with which disputing parties navigate are created by nation-states (Kupchan 2012; Morris 2014). To be sure, we agree that nation-states' influence on issues of war and peace are enormous. At the same time, by concentrating on state action, one risks the possibility of not only marginalizing what civil society and business might be able to contribute but considering those contributions only as agents of states themselves. This is a neo-mercantilist vision that has enough truth to it to bear consideration, but at the same time misses the possibilities (in our case) of how business can contribute to peace and to the reduction of the likelihood of atrocities.

For example, GDP per capita is a strong predictor of civil war and instability (Collier and Bank 2003; Dixon 2009; Blattman and Miguel 2010) and so, when businesses pay their workers fairly, they can contribute to an increase in GDP per capita. Governmental social service programs, paid for by taxes, can significantly reduce the likelihood of civil war (Taydas and Peksen 2012) and so when businesses pay their taxes fairly, they are providing funding to governments that they can use to pay for these social services. When ethnic groups are marginalized in a society, and excluded from economic (and political) activity, civil war is much more likely (Cederman *et al.* 2011). Businesses that consciously construct their hiring practices to make sure that benefits are spread out among local groups can reduce inequality and support peace.

Transparency in government activity and financing is an important part of establishing government accountability and legitimacy (Florini 2002), which may reduce civil war. Private sector actors, particularly multinational corporations, can contribute by being transparent about their activities and how funding is directed to host governments. There is some evidence that as more information flows from international organizations to citizens of less transparent countries, the governments of those countries become more transparent (Grigorescu 2003). Because civil war tends to be longer when armed groups are able to make money from the violence, typically by capturing local resources – including, potentially, tax resources (Fearon 2004; Kaldor 2007) – businesses' refusal to allow resources to be diverted to rebel groups or violent groups can potentially reduce violence.

In each of these examples, the role business plays is to strengthen government. One necessary assumption, of course, is that the governments businesses strengthen are those unlikely to foment war crimes and genocide. Yet, even if we make this assumption, the role business plays is to bolster the political sector so that it can have the resources and legitimacy to do its traditional work. Moreover, to the extent that businesses contribute philanthropically to civil society institutions working toward the goals of justice and peace, those businesses continue to strengthen a social structure that is thereby empowered to do its work effectively.

Corporate Foreign Policy

With each of these points, businesses undertake actions that strengthen other social institutions in their world and create more stable structures that inhibit violence and atrocities. We do not dismiss this approach, but businesses are powerful actors in their own right. What does it mean that Apple is a US company when labor and materials for its products come from all over the world? The same holds true for numerous companies and industries. Moreover, while business associations may strengthen government efforts in peacemaking, the work of businesses in Northern Ireland spoke directly to the population in arguing that incessant violence between Catholics and Protestants was bad for business, bad for the country, and bad for the people. We want to take a step back and ask what businesses, as independent actors, might do to foster structures of peace that would inhibit violence. Because this argument is rooted in an incremental approach to peacebuilding and is one that emphasizes day-to-day actions of business, we can sometimes miss it. Moreover, to explain it, we need to contextualize the approach.

A Sociological Context

In his landmark research, sociologist Randal Collins, perhaps the world's leading expert on violence, reports that the evidence shows that human beings rarely are violent and when they are, they are pretty incompetent at fighting. People – even violent youth gangs – might bluster a good deal, but they do not fight all that much or that well (Collins 2008). More typically, when individuals do fight, there is a lot of yelling and a few punches thrown or other weapons used, but a long, engaged fight is rare. Indeed, where one is more likely to find an evenly matched, drawn-out altercation is when there are prescribed rules of engagement with enforcers of those rules, such as in a boxing match (Collins 2008). A primary purpose of such rules is so that the violence does not get out of control.

Yet, things change dramatically, in local brawls and in organized battle itself, when one side gains a clear advantage. When a rout ensues, a darker side of human nature is exposed. It is a disturbing aspect that terrorizes and tortures the defeated and the helpless (Collins 2008). When defenseless, the vulnerable become easy prey for the victors, flushed with success and power. In this regard, mass atrocities that scourge the planet are not especially different from issues of war and peace; they are an unfortunately common next step in war itself. Atrocities might not be best seen as an independent phenomenon to be addressed generally – and by business specifically – but rather as a connected phenomenon.

This assertion is not mere conjecture. In societies where there are histories of ethnic, religious, or other divisions, resentments may simmer just below a superficially civilized surface. So was the case in Rwanda or Yugoslavia and other multi-ethnic societies. A match lit at the wrong time can turn relations ugly and victors take out resentment on the vulnerable.

To take a more specific example, John Forrer and John Katsos have documented a similar phenomenon in Cyprus, with strong divisions between Christians and Muslims. Resentments, they explain, lie below the surface, but are especially noticeable to an outsider. Small things, such as allowing churches to fall into disrepair in Muslim territories, stoke such resentments, awaiting the match lit at the wrong time (Forrer and Katsos 2014).

What does it look like when such a match is lit? Amy Chua detailed numerous examples of exactly this issue in her book *World on Fire* (2002). Chua argued that crony capitalism often favors a wealthy ethnic minority – Chinese in Southeast Asia; Israelis in the Middle East; Americans in a global context. When pure democracy – a system without systems of checks and balances and protection of minority rights – takes over, the majority gleefully punish the now vulnerable ethnic minority (Chua 2002). It is this one-sidedness, this imbalance of power, combined with socially stoked resentments, that provides the tinder for atrocities.

This context offers a unique vantage point for business. Once the point is reached where there are refugee camps and terror, the avenues businesses might pursue to constructively mitigate suffering may be limited. But one could identify at least two concrete ways in which businesses might cool the tempers of violence and atrocities before they fully set in. For example, consider Forrer and Katsos's work on Cyprus and the deterioration of churches in Muslim-held territories, a phenomenon that fuels resentment. Businesses could act to restore some of these religious edifices themselves, thereby mitigating a source of anger.[1] In this respect, businesses could play a role in protecting vulnerable people by acting in advance of the violence, conflict, routs, and atrocities.

Or return to our earlier comments about Northern Ireland. Not only did business associations join forces to condemn violence between Protestants and Catholics, but also some companies intentionally hired Catholics as half their workforce, with the other half being Protestants, in order for the two sides to have the experience of working together (Fort 2008). This is an example of how business – completely separate from state action per se – can undertake efforts to dampen resentments and build common ground among conflict parties.

Could business do the opposite? That is, could business spark the flames not just of violence but of an ethnic anger that could boil over? McDonald's faced such anger when it changed the way it cooked its French Fries from using vegetable oil to using beef tallow, thereby causing vegetarians and Hindus to violate philosophical and religious precepts. Angry protestors smashed McDonald's restaurants in India as a result (Fort 2008). Or consider the toilet seat manufacturer that faced

---

[1] I am grateful to Professor Forrer for this insight.

angry protests for depicting sacred Buddhist figures on its commodes. The company claimed no disrespect was intended because it also sold toilet seats with the Virgin Mary on them (Fort 2008). These actions can get under people's skin. They may not result in either war or atrocities, but such insults can fuel the kinds of resentments that do boil over.

Yet, there are also the instances cited by Forrer and Katsos (2014) or noted in Nicaragua, Guatemala, South Africa, Northern Ireland, and Palestine where businesses served as the agents of understanding rather than stoking resentments (Fort 2015).

More broadly speaking, it is worth seeing how business can be oriented toward peace and away from war as a way to prevent atrocities from happening in the first place prior to assessing what business might do in the aftermath of conflict when the darker side of human nature has set in. Indeed, this business contribution to peace fits better into business strategy itself and so likely finds its most efficacious impact.

Business, Peace, and R2P

An anthropologically based argument similarly documents that our contemporary observations and experiences are deeply rooted in human history. As Douglas Fry and others have shown, human beings were relatively peaceful in deep history (Fry 2012). When we lived in nomadic hunter-gatherer groups, the incidences of warfare were low. To be sure, there was still violence from time to time, but it was limited and certainly not on the scale of organized warfare. Over time, the argument goes, as humans progressed to equestrian hunter-gatherer groups, and then especially when they turned to agriculture, organized warfare became much more prevalent. With agriculture, there was specific territory to defend and economic surpluses that provided the resources for large-scale fighting. The industrial revolution further enhanced this combination of economically productive property and resources for organized fighting, including the efficiency with which these phenomena were combined by modern nation-states. World War II resulted in the deaths of 20 million people.

In this narrative, it is hard to see any positive role business might play in reversing these fatal trends. After all, business drives agriculture and industry. It is exactly the essence of profits – creating the surpluses governments can use to build fighting forces – that allows for warfare on a large scale. Often, governments have used business vehicles and interests to further political aims, such as via colonialism. The profit-driven excesses of business violate human rights, enslave and exploit, and teach a cultural attitude of self-interest that seems far away from the spirit of community and peace one would need to make the world a safer place. Indeed, if business fosters an ethos that diminishes the importance of human beings, viewing them as manipulable labor inputs or vague externalities with no human face or spirit, business shares with others the dehumanizing practices that make atrocities easier. In this respect, "business as usual" may contribute to large-scale evils.

Thus, it comes as a surprise to see newer arguments claiming that the world is in fact far more peaceful now than it has ever been. Steven Pinker (2011) has made the more comprehensive argument on this point, and while Pinker provides original evidence for why we are more peaceful, he also relies on extensive evidence that has been building that shows that exactly *because* of the rise of nation-states, and what Pinker calls *gentle commerce*, we live in a safer world. Even more surprising is that when one digs below the surface of the debate between those who think we are more violent and those who think the opposite, one finds some common themes. Among them is that a certain kind of business could provide a significant contribution to peace.

As with other studies of businesses working in conflict-sensitive zones, there is a temptation, after examining a given conflict, to ask what businesses might do. As a matter of logical inference, this places the question of businesses' role in that realm of peacemaking and peacekeeping. In other words, the question becomes what businesses can do to respond to violence and stop it from occurring.

Businesses have played a role in such conflicts ranging from El Salvador to Northern Ireland, Columbia, Sri Lanka, Cyprus, and elsewhere (Fort 2015). Businesses sometimes act as independent, third-party honest brokers. Sometimes they coalesce as a voice to demand change and thereby provide the political support that creates room for warring parties to resolve differences. On occasion, business leaders find themselves at negotiating tables to help resolve conflict. At still other times, businesses provide financial and other material resources to maintain peacekeeping personnel and/or to provide the wherewithal for assisting victims. As we will suggest, businesses may engage in these activities for moral reasons, for instrumental reasons, or as a result of a combination of both.

To be clear, we celebrate the times and places when businesses make these contributions. However, we suggest that there is also a role, perhaps more powerful and constructive, that businesses can take on in peacebuilding in addition to those times and places when they may be able to undertake peacemaking and peacekeeping.

We also want to be clear about two other aspects of our approach. First, we are business and peace scholars and so we make our argument primarily as a point of this relationship as an independently valuable area of research and practical phenomena. Second, however, because we earlier stipulated that atrocities may be an extension of the consequence of war and of rout, our treatment has direct implications for the ways in which businesses can fight atrocities themselves.

We wish to briefly describe the argument of whether or not we are more peaceful, acknowledging that this debate is dealt with more extensively elsewhere. Then we wish to explore further this notion of gentle commerce, the promise it holds, and the contributions it may make. These two sections provide a foundation for approaching business's involvement with issues directly pertaining to war and to mass atrocities. They offer a framework for business engagement with such social and political issues of life and death that incorporate businesses's role rather than proposing a particular case and asking businesses to address such a case without a contextual understanding of the role businesses might play in the first place. Finally, with this as background, we then wish to draw upon the insights from business strategy to argue for a more rigorously instituted sense of business diplomacy. Such diplomacy may call for business engagement to reduce conflict and respond to mass atrocities, but a greater role for business may well be in incremental building cultural practices that make both war and atrocities less likely to occur in the first place.

More or Less Peaceful

Whether rooted in contemporary political study or through anthropological resources, the notion that the world is an increasingly violent place seems to have the status of conventional wisdom. Contemporary studies of conflict demonstrate the increasing amount of warfare, especially within states between organized groups. Think, for example, of Yugoslavia in the 1990s, Iraq in the 2000s, or Ukraine in the 2010s. In each case, there is a question as to whether nation-state borders are drawn correctly.

Or, to build on the references contained in the introduction, consider the anthropological arguments. Many such arguments claim that (a) human beings are inherently violent (especially young males) so that (b) there has always been and always will be warfare and violence, and (c) such warfare and violence have increased over time with the domination of agriculture and industrialization.

These arguments are both well supported and commonly observed. They are also reinforced by a twenty-four-hour news cycle that captures news from around the world. Given the old media adage that "if it bleeds, it leads," the headlines tend to focus on confrontation and violence. Peace and serenity are not news except in a special segment added to lighten a given day. The same critique can be made of our entertainment. As one commentator once wrote, if one watches a sports event, one may attentively observe the game while sitting, but if a fight breaks out, everyone stands up. From cowboy westerns to science fiction to myriad other film genres, violence claims a market. Fighting gets our attention. Saturated by this exposure to violence, it is not surprising that we tend to think there is a great deal of violence, even if studies show that we rarely experience it ourselves.

A good representative to the counter of this conventional wisdom is anthropologist Lawrence Keeley (Keeley 1996). Keeley relies on evidence that shows incidents of violence from the recent past (for instance, the twentieth century's world wars) to deep history (for example, mass burial sites that suggest that atrocities have a long history) to make calculations on the number of deaths compared with populations living at the time of the violence. Based on this evidence, he argues that the so-called peaceful hunter-gatherers inflicted twenty times more death via violence than did the deaths from war in the twentieth century. While the economic and organizational structure of hunter-gatherers did not support large-scale warfare (there were, after all, only an average of thirty persons living in a hunter-gatherer band, so "large-scale" anything is impossible), smaller raids were every bit as lethal and ended up killing more people, on a percentage basis, than Hitler's tanks or Allied bombs.

This is the argument Pinker and others (Human Security Centre 2005; Goldstein 2011; Gat 2012) build on. Bringing an enormous amount of data to bear on the issue, Pinker argues that we are indeed less violent. That is true, he argues, in comparison with our distant past (though a vigorous argument can be joined in terms of the interpretation of much of the hunter-gatherer data), and is certainly the case if one's timeline is greater than, say, the past fifty years, but shorter than the past six thousand. Pinker argues that the rise of nation-states and wealth also led to a civilizing process. A thousand years ago, he argues, human beings relieved themselves in the streets, had sex in public, and blew their noses on their shirtsleeves. In a graphic illustration drawn from "sport," he notes that a popular sport was to tie a person's hands behind their back and a cat to a post; the game was for the person to kill the cat by hammering it with one's head, with the cat, of course, clawing the attacker's head until both participants were bloody messes and the cat was dead. We may complain about the violence in football, hockey, and mixed martial arts, but they are a far cry from this "entertainment."

This civilizing process occurred incrementally. Strong governments (that could enforce behavioral laws and provide dispute resolution), literacy (especially with the development of printing), and the arts all facilitated this civilizing process. All of these factors spurred increasing protection of human rights and reductions in violence. Pinker cites strong, correlative evidence to suggest that violence also reduced – on a per capita basis – during this time. He argues that the conventional wisdom that things are more violent now rests on a misperception driven by news sources and entertainment that focus on such things, but in reality, more people drown in bathtubs each year than are killed in terrorist attacks, for example.

To be sure, there is a difference of opinion here. Pinker and his allies' claims that we are more peaceful are not likely to convince Fry and his supporters, nor may they win over those who argue that our world seems to be slipping into a darker time. What is interesting, though, is how much all parties turn to common solutions for improving things, however their debate comes out. All parties seem to endorse the idea of transnational organizations helping to resolve disputes. All seem keen on the importance of protecting human rights, especially as they pertain to gender-related issues. All seem supportive of a greater spirit of communal responsibility from all parties in order to make the world more peaceful. This consensus – especially amidst their disagreement – provides a fruitful platform for considering the final, crucial factor that Pinker identifies in this incremental movement toward peace: gentle commerce.

Gentle Commerce

Pinker does not define the term gentle commerce. He leaves commerce in the generally accepted sense of trade and economic development. Following a long line of research, he argues that economic development reduces poverty and the violence long associated with it. It also can be a dynamic that improves relations among nation-states and the organizations and individuals within them who see efficient advantages to trading with each other rather than fighting each other. This trade and economic development argument is well known and needs little further elaboration.

In considering Pinker and his allies' enthusiasm toward the aforementioned civilizing values, however, one has to think that not just any commerce gives rise to peace. Exploitation and offensive, cultural domination do not seem to foster any sense of peace. Colonialism may provide a kind of economic development, but one that brings with it a host of other problems. Trade at the point of a gun would seem to run afoul of the entire thrust of the argument toward incremental, civilizing improvements as well. Of course, those who view commerce as inherently problematic will find little to disagree with in all of this.

Pinker argues that commerce is gentler than swords and guns, but it is not any kind of commerce that facilitates peace. It is a certain kind of commerce, what we have identified elsewhere as an ethically driven commerce that is gentle in incorporating these other incrementally civilizing features within the benefits that commerce provides. It is this vantage point that provides the basis for authors coming from the ethics field to argue that business contributes to peace through an economic development that follows rule of law practices (especially the avoidance of corruption), is sensitive to the values of local communities, and organizes itself in a way that is respectful of its constituents.

Indeed, citing contemporary studies, Fort and Schipani have argued that business actions along these lines correlate directly with other correlations of peace that provide a practical agenda for businesses to adopt in fostering peaceful practices (Fort and Schipani 2003). At some times and places, businesses might become directly involved in efforts to resolve conflicts. At other times, businesses may find that it is instrumentally smart to engage in political diplomacy. At still other times, businesses may have no conscious awareness of the impact of their actions on issues of peace and violence but have an impact – positively or negatively – because of their practices.

Moreover, there are reasons to believe that businesses are crucial to peace. Businesses have enormous influence in the world. Many businesses are larger than nation-states themselves. Smaller businesses do the most to provide people with jobs and all the good that goes with being employed.

Many of the technologies that are often credited for health improvements (think, quite pedestrianly, of toilets) or improving people's ability to "connect" (perhaps the twenty-first-century buzzword and exemplified by cell phones and the Internet) have been brought to us by business. Would the world be better off relying on outhouses?

In ways often more difficult for government, religious organizations, and other NGOs to do, businesses can bring together people from different backgrounds, cultures, religions, and races to work on a common project. Businesspeople were the ones who confronted King John with the demands to sign the Magna Carta and to usher in modern democratic government.

It thus seems rather strange to think that peace in the world would be anything but enhanced if businesses were contributing positively and, as indicated in brief above, and as has been argued extensively elsewhere, the arguments for how businesses can make these contributions have already been identified. Finally, these contributions capture the essence of a gentle commerce that would seem to find consensus support from parties searching to find ways to make the world more peaceful.

Business Diplomacy

How might business itself conceive to do this? It is telling, even within this book and its effort, that while there may be acknowledgment of a business role to foster peace, few businesspeople are involved. One might propose that businesses should promote peace, but how does this translate into a business strategy? In this section, we identify four reasons for why businesses might address themselves to the issue of peace and then offer a strategy, rooted in diplomacy that provides a roadmap to do this.

As a general matter, some businesspeople have argued that business needs to attend to business issues in a way more serious than in the past. Per Saxegaard, an investment banker in Oslo, has suggested that the Internet changes everything in business. Prior to the Internet, a corporation could hide its practices from all but the most dedicated district attorney or investigative reporter. Now, anyone with a smartphone can capture a corporate indiscretion and broadcast it worldwide in a matter of seconds. Companies have always had to be concerned with their reputation, but the Internet equips constituents with a greater capacity to influence that reputation.

Further, Saxegaard argues, a significant dimension of the new economy is the shared economy. This is true of services such as taxi hailing firm Uber, but more fundamentally, companies rely much more on feedback and partnerships in designing and selling products and services. The essence of any enduring relationship is trust and it is exactly this trust – what Saxegaard calls "businessworthiness" – that calls on the gentle commerce practices we have already mentioned. Saxegaard converts these into essential business strategies. Indeed, Saxegaard is not only an investment banker but the founder and chairman of the Business for Peace Foundation. Thus, the ethically grounded strategies identified that contribute to peace may also have significant salience for successful business practice (Saxegaard 2014).

Some entrepreneurs, of course, may consciously seek to integrate peace and business. Such social entrepreneurs specifically identify their brand with peace, and so peaceful practices, identified throughout this volume, chapter, and elsewhere, would be brought to bear in doing business. It is certainly possible that, once established as successful practices, they may be more broadly adopted by others imitating success.

A third business integration of peaceful practices was already hinted at. Some companies may be ethical and integrate gentle commerce approaches with no conscious awareness of – or perhaps even interest in – their impact on peace. Yet, if these practices are part of a way of behaving that contributes, even incrementally, to peace, then those businesses are having a positive impact. After all, Pinker's incremental practices may not have been consciously oriented toward peace but positively contribute to it nonetheless.

This leaves a final business approach to peace that is more instrumental and can be characterized as business diplomacy or corporate foreign policy.

Given the way that businesses today cross borders for the production and sale of goods and services, they take on an independent institutional identity. Component parts for a product may come from various parts of the world and be assembled in another part of the world away from corporate headquarters. Then with a market for the product around the world, the sales and marketing function also has an international dimension. Asking whether a company is American, Chinese, German or something else is difficult to answer. The identity of the company can stand apart from its origin or its headquarters.

This can make a difference when a company finds itself in crisis. When Google faced shutdown orders by Egyptian President Hosni Mubarak, it had to decide whether to comply (as other telecommunications companies did) or to defy Mubarak. Relying on values of free flow of information, Google joined with Twitter to develop work-around solutions that aligned with its values.

In making decisions, companies rely on some sense of strategic values that define what they are and do in the marketplace. Companies' global reach means that they cannot simply rely upon their affiliation with a given nation-state. Instead, companies must set forth their own claims to legitimacy in the market, at least among the constituents who invest in, work for, and purchase from them.

Companies have clear models from which to draw in crafting what might be called corporate foreign policy. For example, Heinz shows how senior executives negotiate and create alliances with the government, media, NGOs, and analysts. In today's market, this is what successful companies do. They are not participants isolated from political and social concerns, but are directly in the midst of such issues. Moreover, except for the 5 percent of companies that are in the so-called military-industrial complex, most companies tend not to do well when bombs are falling, especially on their own buildings and delivery trucks. Thus, diplomacy is a sense of navigating pressure points, but peace tends to be an advantageous set of affairs for business to be in. A peace-focussed foreign policy thus has instrumental benefits for a company's bottom line as well as socially.

These kinds of concerns have already been embraced, to some extent, within corporate risk management and corporate (political) social responsibility departments. Both of these functional areas recognize the importance of the social issues with which companies engage. As companies become more aware of the advantages peace and stability provide for their company, as they realize that they themselves are actors on the political stage, and as social media brings to bear pressures on businesses' reputations, we believe that the time is ripe for companies to see the positive contribution they can make to peace through gentle commerce.

If businesses remained in silos producing goods and services to sell, then they would not have to concern themselves with social and political issues. They could just "do their thing" in their financial markets and let social and political markets take care of issues within their own markets. Yet, as already suggested, markets are not hermetically sealed from each other; the economic market is impacted by the political and social markets just as the latter two are impacted by the economic market.

Indeed, many critics of business argue that the modern popularity of corporate social responsibility is purely an exercise in window dressing. They argue that there is little to CSR programs other than public relations. In fact, some critics within the business community of CSR make the same criticism. These criticisms have much to be said in support of them, but they miss the more important point that businesses do have to be aware of public opinion. That itself is something to build on. One may hope – we certainly do – that this awareness deepens, but this awareness is a positive step.

This is a reason why companies need to concern themselves with issues of conflict and mass atrocities. Governments, NGOs, consumers, and other stakeholders think these are important issues. If that is true, businesses need to concern themselves with them in order to maintain their reputation, brand, and legitimacy. From the perspective of diplomacy or corporate foreign policy, it is simply mismanagement to not find ways to participate in responses to conflict and mass atrocities if constituents that impact the company believe it is important to do so. Even a "profits-only" economist such as Milton Friedman argued that corporate philanthropy and other public involvement could be justified if it directly impacted the company's performance.

Companies may well find that in responding to these issues, they see a difference in their workforce as well. Shoe company Timberland, for example, provides its employees with forty hours a year of paid time to do volunteer work. The company does this in part out of social commitment, but it also sees differences in workers' attitude and motivation as a result. David Hess has presented studies that show the impact of such involvement. Whether because of empathy, role reversals, or meaning making, companies might well find other instrumental benefits to engaging in these kinds of social and political issues (Hess 2007).

One could, of course, simply claim that a given company doing whatever work it is doing should join in a response to a mass atrocity. Some may do just that. However, the likelihood of companies doing this will be more likely, we suggest, if they are previously oriented toward an approach to business (gentle commerce) that already opens them up to considering such issues, and if they conceive of their strategic focus as a kind of corporate foreign policy that makes issues of legitimacy and reputation cornerstones of their work in the twenty-first century. *Those* kinds of companies will be the ones most likely to partner with others.

Moreover, the companies that do undertake their work based on ethical principles of gentle commerce, and that do conceive of their work as a kind of corporate foreign policy, may also contribute to the kind of incrementally improving political and social world in which peace grows and violence dwindles.

Conclusion

From this analysis, one can see that businesses fight atrocities by cutting off warfare and conflict to begin with. Businesses have strong economic interests in doing so and therefore it makes strategic sense for them to engage at this level. This is where businesses can do the most to prevent atrocities from occurring.

To be sure, businesses may still have opportunities to engage directly in providing relief for atrocities. Yet, like peacemaking and peacekeeping, these are more difficult, rarer areas where business is likely to have less expertise. Businesses may still provide resources to help efforts to mitigate suffering. They may be able to use their influence on governmental parties involved in the situations as well. Yet these situations are likely to be more occasional than the peace-building approach we propose that could be implemented by any and all business and could contribute to the mitigation of these situations through prevention.

Gentle commerce has an important role to play in enhancing peace in the twenty-first century. It stands as a common denominator among very different accounts of how peace occurs, and because of that unifying capability, it should be something strongly developed and supported. There are already supports for the ways in which business can contribute to peace, precisely through an ethically informed kind of business that makes incremental contributions to a more peaceful society. The good news is that such an approach also can find its way into strategic management practices in enhancing business's own success in the twenty-first century. What will make this contribution even more powerful and valuable is for people inside and outside of business to take a step back and to recognize the possibilities business has to contribute to peace rather than to immediately label business as a problem or view it as apart from the processes that promote peace. Business itself will enhance its own contribution as it sees how its reputation and financial success are intertwined with political and social markets.

Of course, the traditional model remains open to business. Business actions that provide tax revenues and take actions that support (presumably "good" governments), and which philanthropically support civil society, remain vital contributions to governance structures that head off war to begin with and the atrocities that could follow. We simply wish to add to this traditional viewpoint a complementary one that suggests that businesses, as independent actors in their own right, have the motivation, practices, history, and background to contribute directly to such peaceable endeavors. The good news is that business fostering peace really is not a stretch. Business has contributed to peace throughout history already. It will continue to do so. It simply needs to be a bit more consciously gentle to have its maximum impact.

References

Blattman, Christopher and Edward Miguel. 2010. "Civil war." *Journal of Economic Literature* 48 (1):3–57.

Cederman, Lars-Erik, Nils B. Weidmann, and Kristian S. Gleditsch. 2011. "Horizontal inequalities and ethnonationalist civil war: A global comparison." *American Political Science Review* 105 (3):478–495.

Chua, Amy. 2002. *World on Fire*. New York: Anchor Books.

Collier, Paul, V. L. Elliott, Havard Hegre, Anke Hoeffler, Marta Reynal-Querol, and Nicholas Sambanis. 2003. *Breaking the Conflict Trap: Civil War and Development Policy*. World Bank Publications.

Collier, Paul, and Anke Hoeffler. 2004. "Greed and grievance in civil war." *Oxford Economic Papers* 56 (4):563–595.

Collins, Randall. 2008. *Violence: A Micro-Sociological Theory.* Princeton University Press.

Dixon, Jeffrey. 2009. "What causes civil wars? Integrating quantitative research findings." *International Studies Review* 11 (4):707–735.

Fearon, James. 2004. "Why do some civil wars last so much longer than others?" *Journal of Peace Research* 41 (3):275–301.

Florini, Ann. 2002. "Increasing transparency in government." *International Journal on World Peace* 19 (3):3–37.

Forrer, John and John E. Katsos. 2014. "Business practices and peace in post-conflict zones: Lessons from Cyprus." *Business Ethics: A European Review* 23 (2):154–168.

Fort, Timothy L. 2007. *Business, Integrity, and Peace.* Cambridge University Press.
2008. *Prophets, Profits and Peace.* New Haven, CT: Yale University Press.
2015. *Diplomat in the Corner Office: Corporate Foreign Policy.* Palo Alto, CA: Stanford University Press.

Fort, Timothy L. and Cindy A. Schipani. 2003. *The Role of Business in Fostering Peaceful Societies.* Cambridge University Press.

Fry, Douglas P. 2005. *Beyond War: The Human Potential for Peace.* New York: Oxford University Press.

Gat, Azar. 2012. "Is war declining – and why?" *Journal of Peace Research* 50 (2):149–157.

Goldsmith, Benjamin E., Charles R. Butcher, Dimitri Semenovich, and Arcot Sowmya. 2013. "Forecasting the onset of genocide and politicide: Annual out-of-sample forecasts on a global dataset, 1988–2003." *Journal of Peace Research* 50 (4):437–452.

Goldstein, Joshua S. 2011. *Winning the War on War: The Decline of Armed Conflict Worldwide.* New York: Dutton.

Grigorescu, Alexandru. 2003."International organizations and government transparency: Linking the international and domestic realms." *International Studies Quarterly* 47 (4):643–667.

Hess, David. 2007. "A business ethics perspective on Sarbanes-Oxley and the organizational sentencing guidelines." *Michigan Law Review* 105 (8):1781–1816.

Human Security Centre, Liu Institute for Global Issues. 2005. *Human Security Report 2005: War and Peace in the 21st Century.* Oxford University Press. Retrieved from https://books.google.com/books?hl=en&lr=&id=rSIrNeFW IfcC&oi=fnd&pg=PA1&dq=human+security+report&ots=ZbkpygYhPd&s ig=Kz9CLWWxzagwnHR7JtYAK7BO3q4

Kaldor, Mary. 2007. *New & Old Wars.* Palo Alto, CA: Stanford University Press.

Keeley, Lawrence H. 1996. *War Before Civilization: The Myth of the Peaceful Savage.* New York: Oxford University Press.

Kupchan, Charles. 2012. *How Enemies Become Friends: Sources of Stable Peace.* Princeton University Press.

Lord, Michael D. 2000. "Corporate political strategy and legislative decision making: The impact of corporate legislative influence activities." *Business & Society* 39 (1):76–93.

Morris, Ian. 2014. *War! What Is It Good For?* New York: Farrar, Strauss, and Giroux.

Owuor, Victor Odundo and Scott Wisor. 2014. *The Role of Kenya's Private Sector in Peacebuilding: The Case of the 2013 Election Cycle.* Broomfield, CO: One Earth Future Foundation.

Pinker, Steven. 2011. *The Better Angels of Our Nature: Why Violence Has Declined.* New York: Viking.

Regan, Patrick M. and Daniel Norton. 2005. "Greed, grievance, and mobilization in civil wars." *The Journal of Conflict Resolution* 49 (3):319–336.

Saxegaard, Per. 2014. "Are you businessworthy?" In *Vision of the Firm*, edited by Timothy L. Fort. St. Paul, MN: West Academic Publishing.

Taydas, Zeynep and Dursun Peksen. 2012. "Can states buy peace? Social welfare spending and civil conflicts." *Journal of Peace Research* 49 (2):273–287.

3 Responsibility to Protect Trumps Business as Usual: How Corporate Leaders Build Heroism to Face Atrocities

Alain Lempereur and Rebecca Herrington

In the midst of atrocities, how can business rise to the challenge of heroism against all odds? Whether the focus is on corporate leaders at the top or the bottom of organizations, whether their call is duty or necessity, how can the responsibility to protect become their fundamental mission in drastic circumstances, trumping business as usual and making the impossible possible – saving lives? How can corporations learn from their behaviors in order to build the right teams, teams that will adjust based on lessons learned, put the right processes in place to prevent future incidents, and perform reliably to the best of their ability in emergency situations?

Cases of heroism in the private sector uncover the role of business owners or leaders who have paved the way. The first story that comes to mind is that of Nazi business leader Oskar Schindler and his wife Emilie, who through the Emalia enamel factory helped save more than a thousand Jews during the Holocaust. Similarly, in Holland, Frits Philips made R2P business as usual at Koninklijke Philips N.V. His father and his uncle founded the well-known electronic giant company, Philips. Frits Philips was the only member of the family and executive board to stay in the Netherlands during World War II. He used his position to responsibly circumvent the extermination of several hundred Jews and maintain business operations. In both accounts, the value of human life and dignity became the key purpose of business, as it can or must when we remember our core common values as human beings.

Responsible business leaders can serve a critical role "at the top" to mitigate genocide and mass atrocities, especially when they get the support of others in their organization and beyond. Internally, leaders "from below" in the chain of command need to intervene as "business righteous" in daily intercourses to help prevent the worst from happening. Leaders "from outside," namely from the press or the security sector, also play an important supportive role to protect people in danger.

Two other bright spots illustrate the remarkable power of entire organizations when they strive for R2P. Organizations have a multiplier effect and demonstrate that responsible business is capable of making a difference in management of a crisis until timely support from outside makes a decisive move. Both stories originate from the hotel sector and reinforce the examples seen in the aforementioned heroic acts. The first bright spot is what happened in the Hotel des Mille Collines in Kigali during the 1994 Rwandan genocide. Paul Rusesabagina, a well-educated businessman who quickly rose in rank working at Sabena hotels in Kigali, used his influence, access to high-quality goods, and position as general manager during the crisis to help save lives amidst chaos. Hollywood may have romanticized Paul Rusesabagina's leading role in the movie *Hotel Rwanda*, but the reality remains that more than 1,200 lives were saved thanks to the support of hotel staff, the Sabena company, and others in Kigali and abroad who came together to protect and finally rescue the hotel "guests."

While terrorism does not qualify as genocide, its impact can be mitigated by any organization that commits to avoid mass atrocities. Business under terror is put to the test of what it can achieve in mobilizing as a non-violent rapid-reaction force. A striking example of this stems from staff dedication at the Taj Mahal Palace Hotel during the Mumbai terrorist attacks of November 26, 2008. The Taj Mahal Palace has long been a sought-after hotel and convention center due to its reputation for preeminent customer service. But on that day in 2008, from the top to the bottom of the business pyramid, the true heroism of the hotel's 600 personnel helped them rescue more than 1,000 hotel and restaurant guests. This event shone the spotlight not only on brave individuals but on a business model tested by fire that put values and people first. The Taj Mahal Palace Hotel heroes extended the meaning of R2P, making it look like business as usual, creating buffer zones that gave enough time for state authorities to intervene and evacuate hundreds at risk.

This chapter will summarize each of these four real-life cases and draw lessons for business leaders, managers, and staff, making the point that leadership is everyone's responsibility when the right to life of so many stakeholders is threatened, whether it concerns a thousand people or one. In a world where business is global and where threats to human lives can test anyone, anywhere on the planet, we assert the role business can play in fighting against mass atrocities. It starts with business leaders, it strengthens with staff involvement, and ends with state authorities intervening along the accepted definition of state or international community intervention for R2P. We will emphasize the role of business leaders but also that of personnel, while recognizing that business cannot act alone, and must rely on external intervention. We will also stress how essential it is to build the right teams and the processes that integrate R2P efforts in business.

Part 1: When Business as Usual Shifts to R2P

Conducting responsible business does not mean forgetting the financial bottom line. Successful corporate leaders want profitable business. This proves true for the four cases we examine. However, exceptional circumstances might require taking into account something more timely than money – life. This is when our success cases become exemplary, because they all originate in situations where business was taking place "as usual" in a profit-making context, but suddenly horrors happened, which dictated a major shift in mindset that dictated a broader focus.

The Schindlers and the Emalia Factory

Oskar Schindler's story of saving almost 1,200 Jews during the Holocaust has been told in many different lights. While Schindler may not have been the humbly reformed hero that Hollywood's Steven Spielberg in *Schindler's List* and biographer Thomas Keneally would make him out to be, there is no doubt about the humanitarian impact of Schindler's actions during World War II.

Oskar Schindler was an ethnic Catholic German born in Moravia in 1908. He attended various trade schools and worked several odd jobs, starting at his father's farm machinery business. Though he served in the Czechoslovak army, he joined the *Abwehr*, the Nazi Office of Military Intelligence, in 1936 (Crowe 2004; US Holocaust Memorial Museum 2014), and became an official member of the Nazi Party in 1939. Schindler saw the German invasion of Poland and the "Germanization" of businesses as an opportunity, buying Rekord Ltd., a previously Jewish-owned enamelware factory in Krakow, which he converted to his Emalia factory (US Holocaust Memorial Museum 2014). He began by inviting the previous owner of the factory, Abraham Bankier, who was now bankrupt, to assist him in his conversion (Holocaust Research Project 2008), and he utilized the nearby workforce in the Jewish ghetto as a cheap labor force. So far, Schindler cannot be painted as a hero at all. He is a Nazi profiteer who acted on business opportunities in a manner and in a context that most of us would find illegitimate. He resembles many other German business leaders of the period who supported Nazi ideology simply because it made them rich.

In mid-1942, when the Krakow ghetto was dissolved, Schindler appealed for his Jewish workers to stay at Emalia overnight (US Holocaust Memorial Museum 2014), starting his more protective engagement toward his workers. A year later, when the Plaszow concentration camp opened, Schindler fought and bribed Nazi officials to have his factory excluded from the move inside the camp. At his own expense, he built a sub-camp to house his workers and an additional 450 from other nearby factories (Thompson 2002, 20). As the situation for Jews increasingly deteriorated, and at the behest of his wife Emilie, Schindler maneuvered to have his business transitioned solely into an armaments factory and moved to Czechoslovakia where his Jewish workforce would be in less danger (Burkeman and Aris 2004; Yad Vashem 2014c).

The move to Czechoslovakia is where the famous Schindler's List came into play – a list of so-called "essential personnel" he would need to operate the factory for the war effort. The paradox is that this "business" decision led to the rescue of hundreds of Jews, including children and the elderly. Schindler was incarcerated twice on charges of irregularities and of favoring Jews, and his wife Emilie carried out many copies of the list and cared for the factory's Jewish workforce (*The New York Times* 2001; Thompson 2002; Yad Vashem 2014c). The SS qualified the new factory in Czechoslovakia as a sub-camp of Gross-Rosen concentration camp. Farther from the intentional violence and extermination plans at the concentration camp, Schindler was able to provide better food rations and some basic healthcare to his workers. Schindler and his wife continued to utilize black market dealings, bribes, and business appeals, including arranging for the release and rescue of Jews from Auschwitz and other concentration camps (Crowe 2004, 383–401). When workers arrived too weak and feeble due to horrific transportation methods, Schindler's wife established a makeshift hospital to care for them (Thompson 2002, 24; Yad Vashem 2014c). The Schindlers fought through Germany's surrender to protect the most vulnerable. In turn, after the war, the Schindlers were protected by the "Schindlers' Jews" and Schindler himself even received some support from Jewish societies until he died in 1974.

Oskar Schindler began his career as a business leader who profiteered from opportunities such as the availability of an inexpensive labor force. As he witnessed severely worsening circumstances, he expressed his full humanity toward his workers. Taking ever more risks, he used all his accumulated wealth to buy "his enlisted Jews" who were supposedly indispensable to the war effort. His ability to positively impact the threatened lives of Jews was in large part due to his business acumen. His profits, bribes, and connections appeared necessary to carry out operations that in his Czechoslovak plant became a mere cover-up for a humanitarian cause. Schindler learned all these skills at the start of his opportunistic and less than honest business career (Crowe 2004; US Holocaust Memorial Museum 2014; Yad Vashem 2014b). Some of the stories told by survivors from his factories detail the small things that created a sanctuary of dignity amongst chaos and atrocities. From dropping barely smoked cigarettes to respectful morning greetings to his workers (Page 1992), the humanity Oskar Schindler showed to his workers, when so much dehumanization was happening all around, left a lasting mark on those who worked for him.

Schindler offered assistance available to him because of his status, connections, and resources. He identified who needed assistance. Whether Schindler identified the Jewish population as a workforce based on coordination and feasible involvement (i.e. the closest ghetto when he started the factory was primarily Jewish), or as a target of mass atrocity, is hard to tell. However, he used the information and knowledge of the conflict responsibly and he pursued his factory's transition to Brunnlitz, a safer location for his workers and the longevity of his efforts and business. Schindler's process was more ad hoc than strategic, stemming from his personal transformation, his wife's influence, and the realization of the extent of violence and dehumanization taking place. He reacted to shifting circumstances, leadership needs, and escalation of violence as they occurred, and strove to perform the best he could with the position and power he had gained earlier in life.

In his life after the war, Schindler failed in his subsequent business ventures (Roberts 1996, 86, 88; Thompson 2002, 25; Crowe 2004, 455), but the countless lives he saved marked history. They constitute a first bright spot, a launch platform for thinking about the private sector's role in R2P in unlikely circumstances.

Frits Philips and the Philips Electronics Company

Frederick Philips, or "Frits," was the son of Anton Philips and nephew of Gerard Philips, founders of a light bulb factory in Eindhoven that would later become the behemoth electronics company, Philips (Smith 2006). The Philips family had ties to Karl Marx, and held humanitarian and social concerns, despite their capitalist pursuits. Frits officially joined the family's company in 1930. When the Germans invaded and occupied the Netherlands in May 1940, he was singularly left in charge of maintaining operations, while the rest of the board and high-level employees evacuated to the United States (Crouch 2005; Smith 2006). "Frits saw the task as keeping the company together whilst making the least possible contribution to the German war effort" (Smith 2006, 2).

In 1943, Frits took advantage of a humanitarian opportunity to establish a plant inside the concentration camp at Vught. This decision allowed him to hire more Jewish workers and, as such, offer them better working conditions than the camp, thanks to his personal control over the factory operation (Yad Vashem 2014a). He built such a good rapport with his workers that when he was arrested during a sweep in retaliation for the allies' liberation efforts, his workers went on strike until he was released (Smith 2006). He was recognized righteous by Yad Vashem (the World Holocaust Remembrance Center) in 1996.

Frits not only led the Philips company through the dangers of Nazi occupation while protecting Jews, but he also followed through with the same sense of responsibility during reconstruction. Alongside fellow industrialists and union leaders, he established the Foundation of Labor in the Netherlands, an organization that helped hold the country's workforce together through the rebuilding phase (Smith 2006), showing an acute sense of engagement toward all the stakeholders. He became the head of Philips in 1961 and greatly expanded the company's market, product line, profits, and collaboration with similar manufacturers. Philips Electronics is still on the list of the most reputable companies in the world (Adams 2014).

Frits' work continued even after retirement, when he launched the Caux Round Table (CRT), which was comprised of Japanese, European, and American business executives and aimed at building trust and transparency within the industry. The CRT *Principles for Business* manual "incorporated the concept of human dignity and the Japanese approach of *kyosei*, interpreted as 'living and working together for the common good'" (Smith 2006, 3). This manual has since become a benchmark for international business best practices and demonstrates his personal commitment to corporate social responsibility.

"Mr. Frits," as he was nicknamed by everyone in his hometown of Eindhoven, was a financially and morally astute business leader. He maintained his family's factories in the midst of a precarious market, while also protecting vulnerable workers through his choices in expansion, use of resources, and courage. Like Oskar Schindler, Frits used the argument that the Jews he employed were indispensable to company production. He never disposed of them, and his self-preservation instincts did not impact his business decisions at the expense of his R2P efforts. Frits' choice to leverage humanitarian impact through the business sector in times of crisis yielded significant long-term business benefits. Through his engagement, the Philips Corporation can be cited as a model of sustainable development all the way through today. When Mr. Frits died at the age of 100 in 2005, he was acclaimed and is sorely missed (Van der Vat 2005).

The Frits/Philips story also illustrated the dilemma many business leaders operating in conflict zones face at some point: whether to stay or to pack up and go. This difficult choice is often calculated in some way or form in pre-ground-breaking risk analysis. However, the implications of staying or going are often not fully comprehended and must be taken under careful consideration. Evacuating senior executives and expat staff not only threatens relations with the community, but it also leaves them in harm's way along with any infrastructure and equipment the company has invested in. If the business decision is to remain active in a conflict zone, it requires significant security measures, long-term planning, and a shift in protection thinking, where R2P becomes paramount.

Hotel des Mille Collines and Paul Rusesabagina

The next case of keeping a business going under extreme duress took place during the 1994 Rwandan genocide against Tutsi and moderate Hutu. The five-star Hotel des Mille Collines became a sanctuary, where the hotel staff and other external actors, including UN peacekeepers, shared a R2P mission.

The shooting down of the plane carrying Rwandan President Juvenal Habyarimana and Burundian President Cyprien Ntaryamira on April 6, 1994 was the spark for the Hutu power militia, Interhamwe, to start the mass violence against Tutsi and anyone who would try to protect them. The movie *Hotel Rwanda* depicts the dramatic events of the period and grants Paul Rusesabagina a leading R2P role that needs to be qualified. Though some survivors have contested his personal contribution and questioned his heroism, underlining his mismanagement, ambiguities, and profiteering (Kayihura and Zukus 2014), there is no doubt that the hotel itself became a refuge against persecution.

Rusesabagina's advanced education, language skills, and family connections granted him a position within the Sabena airlines hotel chain in the country's capital, Kigali (Rusesabagina and Zoellner 2008). He developed refined tastes and shrewdly learned that it often takes luxury items, such as scotch and cigars, to secure what you need and to make sure things run smoothly at a hotel (Lovgren 2004). When the genocide began, Rusesabagina, who was then working at Sabena's other hotel, Hotel des Diplomates, which was occupied by the Rwandan army, moved into the Hotel des Mille Collines, which was protected by a small UN force, under the leadership of Major Stefan Stec (Kayihura and Zukus 2014). As foreign guests were evacuated and the genocide intensified, Rwandan families at risk of assassination fled to the hotel and started occupying rooms and corridors (Banks 2006).

As its general manager, Rusesabagina required that staff delivered bills and services as normally as possible, so that this safe heaven would maintain its standing, keep up with appearances, and not look like a refugee camp. Rusesabagina collected money from the guests during the siege, but he contended that it was needed to restock the supplies from outside the compound. Playing a necessary double game, he continuously bribed his connections in the Rwandan Hutu-led army and the Interhamwe militia for the hotel to be left alone. The staff thought creatively about how to provide for the people staying there, using the hotel pool for drinking water and altering records for protection (Rusesabagina and Zoellner 2008). The small UN protection unit and the UN blue flag also acted as disincentives to attack. All the way through, Rusesabagina urged Sabena headquarters to keep the hotel open – the only chance for guests' survival – while conveying the extreme severity of the situation and urging for international assistance. Maintaining this ongoing phone conversation made it possible, for example, to stop an attack thanks to the intervention of high-level French diplomats in Paris who had been reached through Sabena and got in direct contact with Rwandan government officials. Through a single line, Rusesabagina also invited those at the hotel to contact everyone they knew outside of Rwanda in order to make R2P actionable.

Though witnesses and historians must continue to correct, complete, and discuss some of the above, on June 17 of that year a joint order by the UN, the RPF rebel troops, and the Rwandan army forced the Interhamwe militia to halt in a mass execution after they had already entered the compound, and the hotel was evacuated. Many of the hotel's occupants left Rwanda, including Paul Rusesabagina and his family. The combination of efforts saved 1,268 people from Hotel des Mille Collines from almost certain death.

The commitment that the staff of Hotel des Mille Collines exhibited stands out in terms of responsible leadership, and Paul Rusesabagina played his part as the general manager through the multifaceted nature of his personality and his approach. First and foremost, as a Hutu, because of his connections to the government and army of the time, like Schindler, he had a recognized position in the power circles and continued to leverage it in the subsequent chaos. As refugees poured into the hotel to seek shelter, his early effort to save only family and friends quickly turned into an extended responsibility. Without denying the possibility of self-gain and profiteering, he attempted to continue business as usual for the hotel for as long as possible. By not openly supporting the genocide and not acting out violently, he also realized that he was at risk, as any Tutsi or moderate Hutu was. In that sense, he is an "ordinary man," among many who deserve recognition. Through collective action, the protection that the Hotel des Mille Collines offered to all guests provided an effective response to vulnerability that is rarely found in the chaos of mass atrocities. Like Schindler, whatever his political affinities, Rusesabagina probably never crossed the red line; he shared Schindler's ability to see beyond the surrounding propaganda and came to realize the need to protect those who were most at risk.

What was Rusesabagina's contribution here? We can spot how he responded as the situation unfolded. He took over an entire organization at the beginning of a crisis and kept it running against all odds at a chaotic time; he assumed leadership. He continuously reassessed the circumstances and evolution of resources (human, financial, food, drink, security, external), and, with the support of his staff, mitigated the effects of an increasingly precarious situation. Mobilizing minimum services that a hotel and its staff can provide in such an emergency situation, utilizing them for R2P efforts, he strove to meet the basic needs of hotel "clients," i.e. survival in a sanctuary away from the militia with basic food and drinking water, through his astute access to internal and external resources, including the black market. In some fashion, though he could not confess so for obvious reasons at the time, he transformed the Hotel des Mille Collines into a refugee camp of the private sector within Kigali. Strengthening a coalition of goodwill, even among evil forces, he continually reached out for external assistance that would be crucial in preventing violence at the hotel and in mounting a rescue operation. He thought ahead and used his connections and those of the guests to bring international attention to the situation they faced, with the hopes someone would finally act and deliver them. Being unarmed, he and his hotel staff could not stop the evil outside, but they did their best to contain it with the support of UN personnel. In that sense, Rusesabagina was able to address short-term needs and tactics, mid-term organizational operations and complexity, and to call for more long-term rescue solutions.

At the end, it was not foreign intervention that delivered the guests, it was the progress of the RPF rebel troops on the battlefield, and their humanitarian agreement with the Rwandan army through UN mediation, that became the external saving factors, which of course Rusesabagina could not predict, merely acknowledge. When the UN finally escorted the convoy of "guests" beyond the RPF lines, they were all finally safe. This case shows that immediate protection in and of itself is rarely enough. There had to be external intervention by RPF security forces with the training, resources, and minimum fire power necessary to engage, which were not provided by the international community in this instance, despite urgent requests.

As the Hotel des Mille Collines case demonstrates, as with the previous two cases, standing firm is important and sometimes the only option that is open to the private sector. Addressing the immediate and short-term needs in the midst of chaos, R2P becomes the paramount priority of business leaders and organizations. It trumps business as usual, making the latter a cover-up for something greater, the protection of the basic human right to live. What this case adds is that preparing a safe ending is essential. If the private sector cannot directly provide it, it can communicate its urgency and provoke it indirectly. Business must keep external actors in the loop so that they intervene and replace business with its obvious limitations to face atrocities. Circumstances dictate for the private sector a R2P ongoing double focus on internal containment of present risks and the need for external complementary intervention of urgent rescue. Such double focus helps build solutions that are business savvy and multifaceted, responsibly humanitarian, and the most likely to be successful in prevention, protection, and mitigation efforts.

It is also important to clarify that the examples of business leadership in the above three case studies are not solely due to excellent business acumen and leadership skills. Schindler, Philips, and Rusesabagina were all part of the business elite, had prominent connections with officials and international leaders, and access to funds or high-quality goods that served to ease transactions with perpetrators. Their capabilities as business leaders and those they were able to exercise as members of local elite society are not completely inseparable, but should not be considered one and the same. Schindler was able to remain out of jail and ask for certain concessions for his factory only because of his membership of the Nazi Party, previous loyalty, and access to the black market. His efforts to maintain the Emalia factory, move it to Czechoslovakia, and increase his Jewish workforce would have been unlikely if he had not had the advantages of his affiliation and rank.

Philips may not have been permitted to establish a plant inside the concentration camp at Vught, were it not for his position in society. Likewise, Rusesabagina cultivated friendships with local military leaders and elites, which served his ability to help keep the Hotel des Mille Collines out of harm's way for a time. And these corporate leaders all made significant business decisions again and again amidst chaos and violence to protect the lives of the vulnerable, but the impact and success of those decisions were also dependent on their personal status in society. It is important to distinguish between the abilities of business to wield economic power during R2P situations, and the abilities of individuals due to their relations and place in society. Some of the status and relations may be a natural consequence of business leadership, but it is not a given. This balance must be given due consideration when determining an appropriate response as a business leader in crisis and how best to contain the situation, while awaiting a more comprehensive external intervention.

The Taj Mahal Palace Hotel and Staff Heroism

As the previous case shows, luxury hotels, because of a genuine customer service tradition, can illustrate extreme staff dedication and exemplary behaviors when it matters most. The Taj Mahal Palace Hotel is no exception to this tradition. Though for years it has garnered international recognition, on November 26, 2008 its customer-centric mindset went above and beyond any possible expectations. On that date the hotel counted approximately 500 hotel guests, an additional 600 visiting guests at the restaurants and ongoing conferences, and 600 staff on duty. Around 9pm, ten armed terrorists, most likely belonging to the Islamist Extremist Group Lashkar-e-Taiba, entered the lobby and started shooting (Deshpande 2012). Employees knew every back exit in the hotel. They could have escaped to protect themselves, but none of them left. Instead they blocked access doors to protect the guests, reassured them, and helped them escape the violence as grenades exploded, gun fire rang through the hallways, and the upper floors burned. The telephone operators who were evacuated at the start voluntarily returned to their station in order to keep guests informed and serve as a communication link to the outside world (Spiegel 2011; Deshpande 2012). And the kitchen staff formed a human chain in the dark to lead guests out, ending in the highest number of casualties, all hotel staff, in a single incident during the attacks (Deshpande 2012).

Karambir Singh Kang, the hotel's general manager, conveyed his commitment when he described his mission as the "captain of a ship." As such, he was responsible for everyone in the hotel, even if it put his life in danger (Spiegel 2011). Kang's awareness was instantaneous; he had to shift in full gear to R2P. All his efforts, whatever the personal consequences, had to focus on the guests' survival, with the support of his entire organization. Sadly, he lost his wife and two children in the attack. This case shows that even outside the extreme cases of genocide where there is a legal R2P, some business heroes find the courage to do the right thing against all odds, and extend R2P to the responsibility of any business leader to assist people in danger.

However, the general manager's responsible leadership "at the top" would not have been so successful had it not been seconded by the heroism of the entire staff, by responsible leaders "from below." In a way, the general manager acted as a leader of leaders, who all behaved heroically. A young banquet manager, Mallika Jagad, echoed this sense of personal duty in her account of how she managed to maintain calm and order for guests attending a Unilever dinner that night, helping them all escape the next morning (Deshpande and Raina 2011). She said, "It was my responsibility ... I may have been the youngest person in the room, but I was still doing my job" (Deshpande and Raina 2011). What is amazing is that she calls R2P her job. Even if R2P does not come with the job description, there was no question in her mind that she had to genuinely care for her customers. And how do you best show care to them? By protecting what is most precious to them, their lives, even if meant being in the line of fire. As an incidental, she added that there was a lot of alcohol in the room and it helped boost everyone's courage. Though it looks like a detail, alcohol also played an important role to buy time and goodwill in Schindler's and Rusesabagina's soft approaches to the perpetrators.

In his study of this case, Rohit Deshpande highlights a few reasons to explain the exemplary behavior of the entire staff during the three days of the terrorist attack on the hotel. One of the rationales is the culturally ingrained value system, which asserts guests should be treated like a god (Deshpande and Raina 2011). Another reason stems from the strict religious beliefs of the business owners of the parent company, the Tata Group, which has always put an emphasis on social justice and has been recognized as the eleventh most reputable company in the world (Knealt 2009). Deshpande raises more compelling organizational reasons that are entrenched in the recruitment, training, and reward process at the Taj Mahal Palace Hotel. In a country where excellence is typically measured in grades and achievements, the Taj instead focusses on character in its onboarding system. The Taj hires from small towns and second-tier business schools, an unheard-of practice in such a competitive setting, but one the Taj believes helps find the kindest people with strong character, instead of those primarily motivated by climbing the ladder and getting financial gain (Deshpande and Raina 2011). The hotel also trains its staff for eighteen months instead of the typical six to twelve, and fosters improvisation in meeting the needs of guests instead of a strict, by-the-book policy. It implements a system of regular and quick recognition, ensuring that direct managers recognize positive feedback within forty-eight hours of receiving it from a guest (Deshpande and Raina 2011).

Rohit argues that the hotel staff may have been "performing the behaviors they were selected and trained to perform" (Spiegel 2011). While the private sector in its wide array of business organizations may not be able to create ethical behavior from thin air, the Taj clearly exemplifies that corporations can certainly cultivate and strengthen ethical behavior through corporate design that combines both humanitarian and profitable outcomes. While this last bright spot illustrates an ideal, all four stories offer different levels of involvement, tactics, and methods that can serve as practical inspiration for the private sector in considering its role when faced with dire circumstances.

In the second part of this chapter, building on the lessons of the four cases, we will try to summarize helpers that maximize the chance for R2P to be actionable and effective in business.

Part 2: How Business Leadership and Organization Can Support R2P

In the second part of this chapter, building on the lessons of the four cases, we will try to summarize helpers that maximize the chance for R2P to be actionable and effective in business. After arguing for a clear division of roles between states and business, we will examine how business can prepare for the unthinkable, react in the unlikely event where it must, and extract itself from the situation as fast as it can, while learning lessons for the future.

How Business Can Become an R2P Temporary Substitute for State Intervention

In many ways, business and government work best when they operate in their respective spheres of activities, delivering separately what they can best do. Business likes to avoid state interference, and government does not want to be dominated by business interests. This common avoidance works most of the time, defining liberal states and complementary roles within society. It leaves business as usual alone and also means for example that, through a fair security system, the government holds the primary legal obligation of R2P and should have the necessary means to enforce it justly, within its own territory, and if necessary, outside it, collectively, when interference is deemed necessary by the international community.

However, there are limits to this ideal division of labor between business and government, in particular when the safety and stability of society or important segments thereof – such as groups at risk – are at stake and business as usual is disrupted. In that context, R2P might overcome sectoral differences, requiring a shift in all available resources and community engagement for the sole purpose of people protection. If R2P is an obligation that has been increasingly recognized by, and legally required from, government, it can be complemented by the private sector, as the four cases illustrate, when R2P trumps business as usual. Business can accompany the R2P work of government, and sometimes even intervene while government or international forces mobilize.

Indeed, there are special circumstances where the state is deliberately failing in its R2P duty or temporarily incapacitated in ensuring the security of all or some of its citizens. In such a situation, the business sector might partially fill the gap. When the state apparatus is committing crimes against humanity, such as in the Holocaust during the Nazi regime, or does not prevent it from happening, as in the Rwandan genocide, business leaders can become substitutes at their limited level. Their actions can enter the scene to address the state failing in its duties. They can try to create sanctuaries within oppressive systems. The first three cases demonstrate that possibility and illustrate months or even years of parallel business activities that pretended to be business as usual, but were actually R2P efforts fighting against a corrupt government system.

Sometimes the state security system is just delayed in its response and cannot immediately intervene, as in the Taj Mahal Palace Hotel case. Then again, business needs to jump in to fill in the gap, and do its best to mitigate the risks of mass atrocities. In the latter case, as in the three former ones, it needs to contain the situation, mitigate its most tragic effects, and call for an outside intervention with the necessary resources to end the ordeal, or wait until that happens, like the allied forces in World War II, the RPF in Rwanda backed by the UN, and the special security forces in India.

In a nutshell, business should never be a permanent substitute for state obligation of R2P; it can only act as a temporary auxiliary. But as the cases showed, whether it is five years (World War II), two months (Rwanda), or a few days (India), this provisional R2P intervention of business always looks too long to the victims who are craving for a legitimate intervention of security forces to stop the brutal forces that perpetrate mass atrocities.

How Business Can Adjust to R2P Circumstances

Despite strong rhetoric surrounding R2P discourses, there is often a lack of direction or applicable guidance for follow through. This is in part due to the difficulty of ascribing a cut and dried response when there are so many variables, intertwining roles, and context-specific elements to consider. Given the development and peacebuilding aspects of responding and protecting vulnerable populations during a conflict, related fields have made a more concerted effort to outline possible response protocols and preventive efforts (Uvin 1998; Anderson 1999).

As established through the bright spot cases, the private sector and its leadership, from the bottom to the top, can make significant contributions to R2P efforts. The lack of engagement of the private sector regarding R2P has created a gap in preparedness and existing materials to provide guidance for incorporating R2P practices. Although it may not be possible to specify a predetermined response for the private sector, this chapter will provide a possible framework, with relevant examples, for the private sector for understanding, preparing, and engaging in R2P practices.

Following a similar format used in engaging in responsible negotiations (Lempereur *et al.* 2010; Lempereur 2011, 2012a), we suggest a "3P" framework – addressing the complexity associated with three pillars: the People, the Problems, and the Process – for an adequate R2P response:

- The first aspect concerns the *people*. It is necessary to draw a clear map of stakeholders, determining who needs assistance, against whom, and who is responsible for providing the various aspects of assistance.
- The second aspect concerns the *problems* that R2P faces. Similar problems seem to come up when business is confronted with situations of mass atrocities. We need to identify them, while suggesting some possible solutions. There are so many immediate issues that require actions of containment – seeking a sanctuary, determining how to communicate within it and with the world of perpetrators – while intense communication with potential trusted outside forces or a well-structured intervention can help the final rescue.
- Finally, this framework considers the *process*, or how to go about engaging in R2P efforts with both a short-term and a long-term mindset. For example, engagement with R2P is not always about what to do in response to mass atrocities on the spot, but sometimes about how a business can operate in a society pre-conflict to help prevent them, or how rebuild it post-conflict. It is about the lessons learned from earlier cases, and about integrating R2P into standard operating procedures.

In the vein of the four success stories we have outlined, this three-pillar framework provides a lens for business thinking that fulfills the humanitarian and societal obligation seen in the "duty to rescue" (Glendon

1991), as well as offering a way to maintain practical approaches when R2P trumps business as usual.

How Business Should Handle People Complexity in R2P Situations

Addressing people complexity, business leaders and staff must draw a map of all stakeholders, including who needs assistance, against whom, and who should provide it.

- *Identify who needs assistance.* The four cases we examined designated a category of unarmed people, or group of people, who suffered from illegitimate attacks, open persecutions, and even organized killing. Whether they were targeted because of their religion, ethnicity, nationality, age, gender, sexual orientation, alleged belonging to such or such group, minority or not, or any other discrimination, there was clear and immediate danger to their lives. These people all have in common that they were trying to protect their first human right, the base for all the other rights, the right of survival against major life threats. They were defenseless and often fleeing, and sought an urgent refuge, not only for themselves but sometimes also for their families. They were "people in danger," they needed protection. Today mass atrocities and genocide are outlawed by all civilized nations because international law has universally consecrated R2P as one of the key foundations of *ius gentium* (literally, in Latin, the law of all people) and *ius cogens* (the basic law of all laws). This means the people we are talking about have a right to protection that states and the international community must enforce. But if this right is required from states only, it is hardly enforceable, especially when states are failing or, even worse, perpetrators themselves. When people in need of assistance cannot rely on the immediate support of state security forces to protect them, they have no other choice but to turn to other sources of protection. That is why people in danger naturally look for expedient solutions. As victims on the move, they turn to neighbors, to their goodwill. And the four cases show they might also turn to places of business, such as factories or hotels, which can be considered as temporary sanctuaries, large facilities where they can hide, survive, work, wait, or pay their way through. In factories, current workers from groups at risk or workers who are hired in order to be protected belong to the obvious category of people needing assistance. In hotels, staff and guests who could be targeted for the same reasons we mentioned above also enter this category.
- *Protect against perpetrators and sympathizers.* People in need of assistance could be endangered by the crimes or attempted crimes of armed

people from organized groups that take multiple forms. It could be a terrorist or extremist organization, a militia, a paramilitary group, a revolutionary guard, a mafia, a gang, but it can also take on the appearances of legitimacy, hiding without impunity behind a state apparatus and its institutions. In this case, it becomes a source of extreme danger for its own citizens or a group thereof, whether it terrorizes its population or perpetrates crimes through its secret police, intelligence service, regular army, etc. Whatever the source of danger, organized armed groups promote exclusionary ideologies, which deny the basic human right to live in peace to some people, their family, community, or group. In the four cases we studied, it was easy to identify the perpetrators, and the danger they constituted. Next to perpetrators, however, there is a category of dangerous supporters or radical sympathizers, who are unarmed but share the same ideology of exclusion and might leak information that is potentially dangerous to people at risk, and those who protect them. By conviction or prevarication, they might be ready to denounce those who engage in R2P to armed groups. Because business itself reproduces the fractures of society and its complexity, we should never exclude this sad possibility that insiders within the sanctuary could jeopardize R2P. This risk was lower in the first two cases we examined, where the Jews in danger were acting in solidarity with each other.

• *Provide assistance as business leader or team when necessary.* As we mentioned, the security systems, through the state authorities or, in case of their failure, the international community, should be the primary providers of assistance in R2P. In case of failure of both, people in need of immediate support might turn to any person or organization ready to intervene to mitigate the risks they run. Because of a humanitarian, societal, or moral obligation, leaders of business organization can embrace this "duty to rescue." It might not be the primary motivation of their intervention. For example, Oskar Schindler started Emalia because he saw it as an opportunity to make quick profits. Though he might have started as a profiteer, with the help of his own Jewish team he then found meaning in his unique undertaking. He started drifting away from the Nazi perpetrators to the point of doing everything it took to protect "his" Jews from extermination. Paul Rusesabagina might not have been as extreme as Schindler in his ideology, but whatever his inner motives of change, the results are strikingly similar: more than 1,000 people survived. The Philips and Tata corporations' leadership were more anchored than the two previous cases in humanitarian ideologies from the start, but all the business leaders in the case studies saw the need for R2P efforts when in the midst of crisis. The point here is that leaders might be intrinsically moral or become moral, but does it really matter, as long as R2P is triggered at the right time?

As business leaders, they also need to understand their core mission as human beings. They can make a difference, but alone their actions are limited. Their power lies in the multiplier effect of their entire organization. When R2P is triggered, they need to mobilize their entire organization around the purpose of saving lives. The four success stories we outlined demonstrate that leaders were "leaders of leaders." Many staff from the top to the bottom of the organization bought into R2P and acted accordingly. In the first two cases, Oskar Schindler and Frits Philips could count on their middle management but also their workers and even their families sometimes to strive together in the same direction – for survival. Because Jewish workers were treated well within Emalia and because they were left alone in that sanctuary, they all wanted the organization to work effectively as one. Similarly, guests and staff were dedicated to group preservation at the Taj Mahal Palace Hotel, but the staff exceeded their normal duties when they put their lives at risk to save the hotel guests. The situation was more complex at Hotel des Mille Collines, as the staff probably counted some sympathizers of Hutu power who could be tempted to join the outside world of perpetrators and looters. Paul Rusesabagina must have struggled to keep everyone at their station, and there may have been some defections. We should add that the press and the internal or external protective security systems might be helpers in providing assistance as well. Their intervention might at least delay and hopefully stop mass atrocities. The presence of foreign guests and UN troops constituted some kind of buffer at Hotel des Mille Collines. The mixed role of the Rwandan army, as well as the advancing RPF forces, completes this complex map.

How Business Can Handle the Complexity of Problems in R2P

In exceptional circumstances where R2P plays out, business, because of its human resources, its financial back-up, its various organizational modes, infrastructures, and transportation, can offer protection to people in danger.

- *Establish sanctuaries in case of emergency.* In extreme situations, if business leaders and organizations want to contribute to R2P, above all they must try to set up a refuge, a safer space that is separate from what is going on in the space of mass atrocities. Sometimes there will be negotiations with perpetrators to keep the spaces separate. In both the Emalia and the Philips cases, the SS were asked to remain outside of the camp, to guard it but not to come inside. There could be coalitions involving external actors to put pressure on perpetrators to mind their own business. In the Hotel des Mille Collines case, Interhamwe were kept outside of the hotel perimeter, thanks to the interventions of Rwandan army high-ranked officers and of French high officials. Sometimes quick enclosure protocol kept spaces separate. Restaurant, kitchen and room doors were locked at the Taj Mahal Palace Hotel to limit the space where terrorists could kill at will. In brief, we described four sieges. These are contemporary versions of sanctuaries, the same way Catholic churches often were conceived of in the Middle Ages, places where your worst enemies could not come and grab you.

- *Contain perpetrators through apparent compliance to their rules.* Because outside perpetrators often have the fire power to annihilate these safe havens with overwhelming force, leaders of sanctuaries often learn to navigate a fine line between staving off the outside world while not provoking attacks. Their safe places should never appear for what they are, i.e. refugee camps. Oskar Schindler and Paul Rusesabagina had to put up a facade: the former wore the swastika to show he was a good Nazi, while the latter exhibited signs of allegiance to Hutu power. As long as it took and as hard as it might have been, they had to be efficient negotiators, collaborators with the representatives of evil forces, playing double games, twisting facts to exaggerate their leverage, and creating incentives to prevent perpetrators from doing what they wanted to do. Corporate leaders' art of deception probably put some of their own "refugees" *en garde* or ill at ease, but these tricks, as duplicitous as they were, had to be played for their own sake.

Leaders in these R2P organizations had to look like good friends to the perpetrators, offering them little gifts, drinks, in order to buy their trust or temporarily put them to sleep. Only under these conditions could their businesses continue "as usual" and be tolerated. Both Frits Philips and Oskar Schindler had to pretend they were working hard for the war effort. Schindler had to invent plausible stories to make all his workers, even the youngest ones, indispensable for the war effort. Paul Rusesabagina had to lie that there were still foreign guests at the hotel. Both Schindler and Rusesabagina had to falsify lists. The more their organizations worked as though it was "business as usual" in the perpetrators' eyes and in their apparent interests, the better chance they had to survive in such a hostile environment. Even turning off lights in the rooms at the Taj, locking restaurant doors, or being silent were different ways of pretending, of letting terrorists infer there was no one there and they should go and kill somewhere else, in another room. When business has to react to oppression and fulfill its R2P mission, it has no choice but to be cunning, to play tricks, to make believe. It holds out as long as it can until external support arrives. Even General Bizimungu, from the Rwandan army, guessed that Rusesabagina, who could no longer do him any favors, was just trying to buy time, and somehow it worked. The power of words and tricks is sometimes the only remaining arm to counter fire weapons. During his long voyage, this was also how cunning Ulysses escaped from the worst entrapment situations. There may seem be a lot of hypocrisy, but the end – survival – justifies these extraordinary means that lie outside usual legal and moral realms.

• *Stick to the essentials within the sanctuaries.* The sense of a common purpose – R2P – seems to be the internal guiding light of a more intimate and gentle world, the one that the four stories uncovered behind the veil of oppression, which trumped business as usual. The more the perpetrators behaved badly, the more the leaders and their organizations stuck together and understood the need to cooperate to preserve life and dignity. Rediscovering the fundamentals, such as how much we must love our families and our fellow human beings, is the only way of surviving in hostile environments. Human life prevails over the superficial that can be gained by business as usual. Mass atrocities force a focus on the essentials for survival, both physical – basic food, water, and a safe shelter – and mental – dignity, caring, and respect. Schindler understood that the money he had accumulated was nothing compared with the thousand lives he could save. This bon vivant even found in himself the courage to risk his own life to get back the 300 Jewish women whose train had arrived at Auschwitz. The same holds true for Frits Philips and the Taj staff who also took huge risks. Even the contested Paul Rusesabagina found his way.

The goal is for us to find not perfect people who act perfectly but ordinary people who are put in the most unlikely circumstances and end up doing extraordinary things. Mass atrocities reveal as much the power of evil in those who lose themselves as the power of redemption that any of us can find. Corporations can switch to the latter, as well as all its actors, from the bottom to the top of the pyramid, especially when they constitute a critical mass of people, who make everyday risks, profits, and incentives irrelevant. When we watch righteous heroes who seem so courageous and creative in addressing the problems, we wonder how they achieved the impossible. By sad contrast, we wonder how perpetrators can become so forgetful of their own humanity in wanting to suppress the others'. We might even wonder how we could oppose them when they are super-armed, and still we can, because courage makes ordinary people extraordinary.

- *Seek escape routes to get out of immediate harm.* A place, no matter how hard we try to protect it, might become less and less safe. In that case, another sanctuary needs to be identified, as well as transportation modes to go from one space to another. Schindler used trains to move his workers from a Polish factory to a Czech factory. Rusesabagina helped guests get out of the hotel through convoys that were protected by UN or foreign troops, visas were supplied for some to get out of Rwanda through the airport, and others had to wait until they were transported through enemy lines to join RPF safe space. The staff at the Taj Mahal Palace Hotel directed guests to back kitchen doors so that they could escape, or helped them out of the windows using fire ladders. In each case it was about seeking a (new) safer sanctuary to limit the harm.
- *Dream the future in the present.* People in danger find some relief in remaining in some kind of sanctuary. But they can survive in these limbos only if they project for themselves a better future, a final escape or rescue. *L'espoir fait vivre*: hope makes life. Whether their lives were just an inch away from the arms of the Nazis, the machetes of the Interhamwe, or the machine guns of terrorists, people in need of assistance could dream of a day when their ordeal would cease. Those who unfortunately did not survive would be proud to know that deaths camps were liberated, Nazi Germany was vanquished, and current Germany became a model of democracy within a broader European Union of nations at peace. Similarly, the Rwandan genocide was stopped, the ideology of hatred that the Radio des Mille Collines disseminated was denounced as disastrous, and current Rwanda is in a sustainable development phase, trying to reconstruct and reconcile its communities. The terrorists were neutralized at the Taj Mahal Palace Hotel by security forces; this five-star hotel resumed its business with the staff back at their posts. Current hotel guests are in full admiration of the entire staff of the Taj or Hotel des Mille Collines, who went back to business as usual after the unthinkable happened.

How Business Can Handle the Complexity of Process in R2P

Businesses must not simply face problems head on but must also learn lessons from the past, when R2P trumped business as usual. They can anticipate the worst, reduce the risks of its happening, mitigate its effects through ad hoc standard operating procedures (SOP) in case of danger, etc. If a business policy of zero risk or zero casualty is impossible, corporations, leaders, and staff can extract the good practices from the past and establish a process that is more likely to drive success when it matters most.

- *Assess the risks of mass atrocities.* Because of their nature and because of human madness, risks of mass atrocities cannot be totally eliminated from the surface of the earth at this point in history. Of course, it is hard to predict whether, when, and where businesses will be faced with the terrible cases we outlined in this chapter, and with the ensuing moral duty – R2P. This being said, tools of conflict analysis can help identify countries or regions that are most at risk at a given time. It is part of what business does all the time: risk assessment. Corporations that operate in potential conflict or post-conflict zones should heighten awareness that their leaders, personnel, and clients could face tragic events. Most multinational enterprises (MNEs) already do a fair amount of research and analysis before establishing an international base, but ongoing conflict analysis can provide better insight into how the company is affecting the local society (which can increase or decrease the likelihood of violent outbreaks) and where it might be able to effect change by engaging in R2P efforts. With awareness comes the next step, the need to prepare for the worst.
- *Enhance R2P readiness.* Though nobody wants to be confronted with a plane crash situation, captains, crew members, and passengers must be ready to act in the most effective way if the hard case arises. This preparedness does not mean casualties will disappear, but they can be reduced, because everyone on board more or less knows what to do in the worst case and they are drilled to follow SOPs. The same should happen in a business facing a R2P situation. Taking advantage of conflict risk assessments, corporations need to build robust SOPs, in order to react more appropriately in case of imminent or ongoing mass atrocities. This needs to be more nuanced and responsive than merely an evacuation plan for foreign staff. The same way leaders and staff must know what to do for R2P in case of a fire, they need to be able to create sanctuaries and escape routes. In case of emergency, they must know which numbers to call (local 111, external or internal security, headquarters, standby teams, etc.) or which designated staff to activate (security guards, standby team, crisis unit, etc.). In many ways, such SOPs can serve as a base and mitigate the risks and harm done in a worst case scenario. Leaders and staff might be told what to do if there are explosions, for example, which evacuation routes to favor, which doors to lock, etc.

- *Build a fair, inclusive organization.* Organizations are first made of people and then processes. This means that corporations that want to be R2P ready must care about people first, their own people – staff – but also their stakeholders. The more a corporation is fair and inclusive in its hiring, ongoing training, daily treatment, and promotion, the more it will look like a "shared society," where nobody feels discriminated against and everyone feels welcome. Good HR policies, as the Taj Mahal Palace Hotel demonstrates, is the best life insurance to prepare for the worst. Everyone remembers the recruitment policy of the Tata Group, its search for the kindest people, and not necessarily the smartest people. Staff should also become more conflict sensitive and be introduced to R2P questions and practicalities. Building diversity, solidarity, and interdependence within the corporation and upholding high standards of caring is the best guarantee that everyone will stick together and help each other in cases of emergency, including R2P in business.
- *Integrate into the community around to support all local stakeholders.* Risk management analysis and strategies may measure the likelihood of violence or reliability of a workforce, but active engagement by the business with the community, in both conflict preventive and mitigation measures, can go much further to ensure profitable longevity for all corporations. Organizations should not be closed systems, living separately from the community that surrounds them. Leaders of companies and staff should do everything possible to support ties with the community and a transformation process that brings the community to a higher purpose of inclusivity, avoiding pockets of exclusion. What does such an engagement mean concretely? The company must be a good citizen, devote some of its human and financial resources to support fair services around, be it the schools, hospitals, crèches or any other way of committing to sustainable development toward all stakeholders, and not simply generating profits for shareholders in a hit-and-run policy. Businesses should engage in fair ways with the community leaders so that they are empowered and encouraged in the transformation process that makes R2P in its worst version unlikely, and makes R2P in its most gentle positive version a communal duty for everyone. This view of corporate social responsibility means for corporations not to wait until it is too late to contribute to community members striving for positive common goals, instead of running risks of reverting to divisions and their potentially dangerous side effects. Corporations need to be part of community strengthening. Corporations might do all of the above to behave responsibly – by promoting a CSR approach – or even to secure their investments – by promoting a utilitarian economic

approach – and still there is no certainty that success will be there, thus the other means that we outline below.

- *Develop an early warning system.* Whatever companies do, for example getting all the best people on board, and engaging the community to build a more inclusive society, it might not be enough to maintain peace and coexistence. This is why companies need to develop early warning systems. They should develop ways of disseminating information from and to all the levels of the pyramid. Everyone should be encouraged to communicate risks to the system in order to prevent collapse. The earlier the signal, the easier and the milder the intervention. People tend to wait until it is too late to intervene. If local staff notice troubles happening on the ground, and if they are rewarded to tell the truth, they will make it possible to develop effective ways of coping. In the past, it was not clear that early warning systems existed or that early warning signals were taken seriously; it is important that changes occur here to prevent mass atrocities from happening whenever possible. Companies, like all the other actors, can utilize mechanisms like this to develop strong preventive roles to nip dangers in the bud.

- *Intensify contacts with corporate headquarters in case of incident.* When incidents occur, even if they look minor, they should be properly reported in order to reinforce cohesion and security measures, which will protect staff and other stakeholders. Headquarters should be ready to put in place crisis management units, which should always be on stand-by. Some specialized agencies exist to support corporations in this task, and the private sector can engage these organizations to assist them in R2P efforts if needed.

- *Carefully assess whether the company should stay or go.* If incidents intensify or reoccur, leaders have a responsibility to weigh the risks of staying or leaving. For sure, the presence of expats could make the situation more dangerous for them or the local staff, but it can also have a reversed effect of protection. The fact that Hotel des Mille Collines continued its business "as usual" during the genocide meant that it could offer a sanctuary, which would have disappeared if the Sabena owners had decided to stop activities. The fact that European guests left made the situation more perilous for local people at risk. In a situation such as this, R2P needs to be thought through holistically. Everyone involved should be protected, not simply expats or western guests. This is also what Taj Mahal Palace Hotel staff proved: they did not discriminate against any of their guests; they protected everyone. This is a lesson that we all need to learn from.

- *Keep information flow running in case of grave incident.* When serious incidents have occurred that trigger immediate awareness of a need to intervene to assist people in danger, companies need to address that situation in responsible ways. They must leverage the SOPs that we outlined earlier and that they have developed. At the same time, they must adjust these SOPs to circumstances and improvise, as the situation dictates. Next to these direct intervention strategies companies must keep communication channels open. For example, the Taj Mahal Palace Hotel staff used SMS to alert each other. What is striking in the first two cases is the fact that both Schindler and Philips were quite alone in their efforts, trying to do the right thing in their corner, whereas both hotel cases show that managers and staff needed to quickly resort to the support of external authorities, who are (or should be) in charge of security matters. Those efforts may also be complemented by the role of the press, which alerts the public to the seriousness of what is going on, holds the government responsible for R2P implementation, and calls for intervention, whether local or from the international community. Though contacting the state authorities and the press and keeping them in the loop does not make them necessarily efficient on the ground immediately, it creates an environment of urgency where the burden shifts from private containment to public engagement.

- *Involve a protective security system and government authorities, as well as the press.* It is never easy to know who to turn to for intervention when major risks of mass atrocities exist, or when mass atrocities have actually been reported. It is important at that time to identify who is part of a security system that can be trusted and act through an unbiased and just intervention to protect vulnerable populations. The chaos that prevails in such situations requires strong vigilance. Among the legitimate authorities that corporations need to involve there might be representatives of local, national, or consular authorities from democratic states, the UN, or the Red Cross, i.e. people in charge of ensuring R2P and restoring security for all citizens. Whether the latter will have the capacity or will to intervene is not always guaranteed. Again corporate leaders and staff need to be ready to wait, i.e. to contain the situation until everyone is finally rescued. As we mentioned, the press is an important actor, and its involvement can be critical in alleviating rather than escalating the situation. However, in the Taj Mahal Palace Hotel attack, the fact that some guests communicated to the BBC, gave details of the situation that the leader of the terrorists watched, made it more dangerous rather than less for the hotel guests and staff. We should never underestimate how much external communication should be closely monitored in order not to worsen the situation of people at risk. We recall the damage that Radio des Mille Collines did. The new risks that social media create can also make things worse, as it becomes natural for everyone to communicate freely through their mobile phones without much forethought about the possible negative, unintended consequences of their messages.

- *Keep the pressure high to protect your workers and other protected stakeholders.* Corporations, their leaders, and staff need to act intensively in private to make things happen, and heighten the sense of urgency so that ad hoc authorities take seriously workers and other stakeholders in danger. In case of inaction or procrastination, the threat of going public and bringing the press into the conversation should be contemplated, with a careful assessment of the risks of this approach. The pressure on legitimate authorities to exercise their R2P should not be reduced until a final rescue takes place.
- *Apply lessons learned.* Unfortunately, each situation of potential or real mass atrocities requires a close debriefing within the organization. The four cases we detailed show we need a structured approach for all leaders here. As R2P is integrated in business as usual, in their SOPs, it will be possible to refine the framework, and for the private sector to be more effective at R2P efforts.

Conclusion

As demonstrated in the case studies, business heroes leveraged their resources and access to protect vulnerable people who faced mass atrocities. They found these resources in themselves, not necessarily in ideology, high morality, or the law, but in the simple awareness that everyone's life and dignity must be an utmost priority. They were able to mobilize the resources of their entire organizations, making everyone a leader of R2P, whatever their role was. As "leaders of leaders," they invented ways of coping with the worst, building sanctuaries, escape routes, lying to perpetrators when necessary, but also rediscovering the true essentials of what makes life worth living. They knew the limitations of their actions, and served as a necessary, yet temporary, substitute awaiting external intervention and rescue.

Oskar and Emilie Schindler, Frits Philips, Paul Rusesabagina, and Karambir Singh Kang impressed us as leaders, and so did all the other lesser known leaders of their organizations who made it possible to save thousands of lives in times of crisis. Their courage was not the exception but should be the rule for all modern business leaders. Their actions single out possibilities for everyone in business – be it owners, senior executives, managers, and staff, or even clients and guests – but also in governments, the public security sector, and the press. These innovators who opened the possibility of R2P ways in business make it possible for everyone to know a little better what to do to protect people in danger, to circumvent the perpetrators, to respond responsibly in case of emergency, but also to establish SOPs that reduce the risks in such cases.

R2P can look foreign to businesses operating "as usual," a concept out of business leaders' and organizations' comfort zones. The point is that human-centered decisions can be business decisions that make a difference when it matters most, when R2P trumps business as usual, when innocent lives can be saved by the private sector.

References

Adams, Susan. 2014. "The world's most reputable companies 2014." *Forbes Magazine*, April 8. Accessed September 29, 2014. www.forbes.com/sites/susanadams/2014/04/08/the-worlds-most-reputable-companies/

Anderson, Mary B. 1999. *Do No Harm: How Aid Can Support Peace – or War.* Boulder, CO: Lynne Rienner Publishers.

Banks, David. 2006. "Paul Rusesabagina, No 'ordinary man.'" *NPR News and Notes*, April 6. Podcast audio. www.npr.org/2006/04/06/5324187/paul-rusesabagina-no-ordinary-man

Books LLC. 2010. *Dutch Righteous Among the Nations.* General Books LLC.

Burkeman, Oliver and Ben Aris. 2004. "Biographer takes shine off Spielberg's Schindler." *The Guardian*, November 25. Accessed September 20, 2014. www.theguardian.com/world/2004/nov/25/germany.film

Business & Human Rights Resource Centre. 2013. "UN Working Group on the Use of Mercenaries." *Business-humanrights.org.* Accessed September 20, 2014. http://business-humanrights.org/en/conflict-peace/special-initiatives/un-working-group-on-the-use-of-mercenaries

Call, Charles T. 2012. *Why Peace Fails.* Washington, DC: Georgetown University Press.

Cheadle, Don and John Prendergast. 2005. "Rwanda's lessons yet to be learned." *Boston Globe*, January 8. Accessed September 20, 2014. www.crisisgroup.org/en/regions/africa/central-africa/rwanda/rwandas-lessons-yet-to-be-learned.aspx

Crouch, Gregory. 2005. "Frederick Philips dies at 100; businessman saved Dutch Jews." *The New York Times*, December 7. Accessed September 20, 2014. www.nytimes.com/2005/12/07/business/07philips.html

Crowe, David M. 2004. *Oskar Schindler.* Cambridge, MA: Westview Press.

Deshpande, Rohit. 2012. "The ordinary heroes of the Taj Hotel." Filmed November 20. TED video. www.youtube.com/watch?v=vQGz1YRqBPw

Deshpande, Rohit and Anjali Raina. 2011. "The ordinary heroes of the Taj." *Harvard Business Review*, December. Accessed September 20, 2014. http://hbr.org/2011/12/the-ordinary-heroes-of-the-taj/ar/1

Duffield, Mark. 2014. *Global Governance and the New Wars*. London: Zed Books.

George, Terry and Keir Pearson. 2004. *Hotel Rwanda*. DVD. Directed by Terry George. Lion's Gate Entertainment. Released by Metro Goldwyn Mayer.

Glendon, Mary Ann. 1991. *Rights Talk*. New York: Free Press.

Holocaust Research Project. 2008. "Oskar Schindler." Accessed September 20, 2014. www.holocaustresearchproject.org/survivor/schindler.html

Institute for Human Rights and Business. 2013. *Corporate Responses to Hate Speech in the 2013 Kenyan Presidential Elections, Case Study: Safaricom*. Digital Dangers Series. London: Institute for Human Rights and Business.

Kayihura, Edouard and Kerry Zukus. 2014. *Inside the Hotel Rwanda*. Dallas, TX: BenBella Books.

Keneally, Thomas. 1982. *Schindler's List*. New York: Simon & Schuster.

Knealt, Klaus. 2009. "World's most reputable companies: The rankings." *Forbes Magazine*, May 6. Accessed September 29, 2014. www.forbes.com/2009/05/06/world-reputable-companies-leadership-reputation-table.html

Lempereur, Alain. 2011. "Responsible negotiation: Caring for people, problems, and processes." *Human Capital Review*, November. http://ssrn.com/abstract=1949528

2012a. "Responsible negotiation: Exploring the forest beyond the tree." *Journal of Global Responsibility* 3 (2):198–207.

2012b. "Becoming a more responsible negotiator." *Negotiation* 15 (4):8.

Lempereur, Alain, Aurelien Colson, and Michele Pekar. 2010. *The First Move: A Negotiator's Companion*. Hoboken, NJ: Wiley.

Lovgren, Stefan. 2004. "'Hotel Rwanda' portrays hero who fought genocide." *National Geographic News*, December 9. Accessed September 20, 2014. http://news.nationalgeographic.com/news/2004/12/1209_041209_hotel_rwanda.html

Mallaby, Sebastian. 2001. "New role for mercenaries." *Los Angeles Times*, August 3. Accessed September 20, 2014. www.globalpolicy.org/nations-a-states/private-military-a-security-companies/pmscs-and-the-un/40931-new-role-for-mercenaries.html

Mwau, Cornelius. 2012. "Political texts to be vetted." *The Star*, October 24. Accessed September 20, 2014. http://allafrica.com/stories/201210240707.html

The New York Times. 2001. "Emilie Schindler, 93, dies; saved Jews in war." *The New York Times*, October 8. Accessed September 20, 2014. www.nytimes.com/2001/10/08/world/emilie-schindler-93-dies-saved-jews-in-war.html

Page, Ludmilla. 1992. "Oral history." Filmed March 11. Video. United States Holocaust Memorial Museum. Accessed September 20, 2014. https://ushmm.org/wlc/en/media_oi.php?ModuleId=10005787&MediaId=3213

Pham, Phuong N. and Patrick Vinck. 2012. "Technology fusion and their implications for conflict early warning systems, public health, and human rights." *Health and Human Rights* 14 (2):106–117.

Poblet, Marta. 2011. *Mobile Technologies for Conflict Management*. Dordrecht: Springer.

Puttnam, David. 2013. "Does the media have a 'duty of care'?" Filmed June. TED video. www.ted.com/talks/david_puttnam_what_happens_when_the_media_s_priority_is_profit

Roberts, Jack. 1996. *The Importance of Oskar Schindler*. San Diego, CA: Lucent Books.

Rusesabagina, Paul and Tom Zoellner. 2008. *An Ordinary Man*. Thorndike, ME: Center Point Publishing.

Search for Common Ground. 2014. "Search for common ground: understanding differences; acting on commonalities." www.sfcg.org

Seemungal, Martin. 2014. "Mobile phone usage explodes in Africa, spurring innovation." *PBS NewsHour*, February 15. Podcast Audio. www.pbs.org/newshour/bb/mobile-phone-usage-explodes-africa-spurring-innovation/.

Sen, Amartya. 1999. *Development as Freedom*. New York: Knopf

Smith, Mike. 2006. "Frederik ('Frits') Philips, 1905–2005." *Initiatives of Change UK*. www.uk.iofc.org/frits-philips

Spiegel, Alix. 2011. "Heroes of Mumbai's Taj Hotel: Why they risked their lives." *NPR, All Things Considered*, December 23. Podcast audio. www.npr.org/2011/12/23/144184623/mumbai-terror-attacks-the-heroes-of-the-taj-hotel

Thompson, Bruce. 2002. *Oskar Schindler*. San Diego, CA: Greenhaven Press.

US Holocaust Memorial Museum. 2014. "Fulfilling a responsibility to protect: What will it take to end the 'Age of Genocide'?" United States Holocaust Memorial Museum, Speakers and Events, May 4. www.ushmm.org/confront-genocide/speakers-and-events/all-speakers-and-events/fulfilling-a-responsibility-to-protect

Uvin, Peter. 1998. *Aiding Violence: The Development Enterprise in Rwanda*. West Hartford, CT: Kumarian Press.

Van der Vat, Dan. 2005. "Frits Philips: Dutch industrialist who nurtured his company and its staff." *The Guardian*, December 6. Accessed September 30, 2014. www.theguardian.com/news/2005/dec/07/guardianobituaries.mainsection1

Yad Vashem. 2014a. "Philips Family." *Db.yadvashem.org*. Accessed September 20, 2014. http://db.yadvashem.org/righteous/family.html?language=en&itemId=4043449

2014b. "Schindler Family." *Db.yadvashem.org*. Accessed September 20, 2014. http://db.yadvashem.org/righteous/family.html?language=en&itemId=4017377

2014c. "Schindler, Emilie." *Db.yadvashem.org*. Accessed September 20, 2014. http://db.yadvashem.org/righteous/righteousName.html?language=en&itemId=4017376

Zallian, Steven. 1993. *Schindler's List*. DVD. Directed by Steven Spielberg. Universal Pictures.

4   The Responsibility to Prevent, Inc.: The Missing R2P–Business Link: An Anomaly in International Affairs

Jonas Claes[1]

As the global governance infrastructure further solidifies, states and international organizations continuously create avenues for unconventional actors, including business enterprises, to become involved in the various facets of international affairs. Driven by external encouragement, and its own strategic compass, the private sector plays a growing role in efforts to address global climate change, advance human rights, or support sustainable development. "Far more funding for development today comes from private investment capital than from bilateral, government-to-government aid, or multilateral aid through the UN and other IGOs" (Karns and Mingst 2004, 20). Assessing the actual or potential role of this heterogeneous sector in the prevention of mass violence, a core objective of this volume, is no easy task. The private sector includes a wide array of organizations, from small and medium-sized local enterprises, to large transnational corporations, including financial institutions and mass media. Corporate leadership similarly varies, from ordinary citizens to powerful CEOs.

The potential of the corporate world in international norm development, through virtue of the influence and resources at its disposal, has been demonstrated on various occasions. In 1999, Secretary-General Kofi Annan announced the UN Global Compact as a way to convene world business executives alongside the leadership of different UN agencies and Member State representatives. Among the nine principles agreed to by its signatories, the UN Global Compact assured that businesses "should support and respect the protection of internationally proclaimed human rights and ... make sure that they are not complicit in human rights abuses" (UN Global Compact 1999). The development of the Extractive Industries Transparency Initiative (EITI), officially

---

[1] The author wishes to recognize Ian Proctor, former program assistant at USIP's Center for Applied Research on Conflict, for his invaluable input and research assistance.

launched in 2003 by a coalition of extractive industries, representatives of governments, and non-profit leaders, further illustrates the ability to bridge economic interests with normative concerns about resource predation, corruption, and conflict into an actionable agenda.

The perceived responsibility of private actors in peacebuilding similarly advanced, beyond their traditionally assigned role as natural culprit. While business is still more frequently regarded as part of the problem, conflict analysts increasingly recognize their potential as a source of local resilience with significant leverage to strengthen domestic capacity, invest in post-conflict repair, or even facilitate conflict resolution. The expectations from business actors have exceeded the low threshold of "doing no harm" to include a series of active responsibilities. The focus on corporate social responsibility[2] illustrates this transcendence beyond responsibilities of omission in peacebuilding.

As established fields of theory and practice, human rights promotion and peacebuilding attracted considerable engagement from the business community. Corporate engagement in realizing the Responsibility to Protect, a nascent political norm that aims to reduce the frequency and impact of mass atrocities or the four so-called R2P-crimes (UN General Assembly 2005)[3], has not followed this trend. The limited private sector commitment does not necessarily reflect a lack of interest on their end, but rather an underappreciation of shared interests and general disregard within the atrocities prevention community. Such is evident in the legal frameworks and other formative documents examined below: private sector actors are seen merely as bystanders, or contextual players acted upon. The same 2005 World Summit Outcome Document that formalized the global commitment of heads of state and government to the R2P principle in Articles 138–140 seeks to "encourage responsible business practices, such as those promoted by the Global Compact" in Article 17. Unfortunately, more than ten years after the formal inception of the principle, the R2P–business nexus has moved little beyond a few tangential references. The normative development of the R2P principle, and the attitude of its advocates, explains this anomaly in international affairs a great deal, as R2P steadily continues its transition from an aspirational principle to a realized norm in international affairs.

---

[2] "Corporate social responsibility" is a concept whereby companies integrate social and environmental concerns in their business operations and in their interaction with their stakeholders on a voluntary basis (Commission of the European Countries 2006, 2).

[3] The 2005 World Summit Outcome Document, unanimously endorsed by heads of state and government, defines the scope of the Responsibility to Protect as narrowly focussed on the crimes of genocide, ethnic cleansing, war crimes, and crimes against humanity.

This chapter will assess the potential of corporate actors in advancing the preventive ambitions of the R2P principle. The first section identifies three core explanations for the missing R2P–business link: the state-centric focus in the conceptualization and strategizing around R2P, the perception of corporate actors as a spoiler, and the principle's association with the use of military force. The second section highlights the potential for private sector engagement in early warning and early prevention. The conclusion considers the effect of active corporate engagement on the development of R2P as an international norm.

The Missing R2P–Business Link: Key Explanations

Corporate actors are mostly unfamiliar with the R2P narrative and the inferred responsibilities that sprout from their presence in countries at risk of mass violence. Upon initial scrutiny, corporate managers may regard atrocities prevention or peacebuilding as irrelevant to their operations, or even a distraction from their core business (Zandvliet 2005, 2). However, individual business leaders have significant economic, legal, and moral incentives to engage in atrocities prevention, as Alain Lempereur and Rebecca Herrington demonstrate in their chapter of this volume. Mass violence presents security challenges to staff and infrastructure, and maintaining a significant presence in areas facing extreme conflict or mass atrocities, or the association with perpetrators of mass violence, could lead to significant reputational costs (Nelson 2000; Albright and Cohen 2008, 100). Above all, widespread political instability scares potential investors, creating enormous risks to commercial activity. Through early warning coordination and exchange, business actors may acquire higher-quality assessments to inform their own investment decisions, and develop stronger business relations with government actors who regulate their activity, enforce corporate laws, or purchase their goods and services. When considering the expense of relocation, advanced security requirements, or the sunk costs related to previous investments, early prevention presents itself as a more cost-effective option to larger corporations than crisis management. Corporate involvement in atrocities prevention makes good business sense, as it reduces the risk to commercial activity, while offering a more conducive investment climate.

So far these incentives have not been sufficient to connect those international and civil society organizations that constitute the atrocities prevention or R2P community with private sector actors. The R2P narrative, its framers and its advocates, have contributed to this lacuna in three important ways.

1.   Normative Development for States, through States

Since its inception, the framers of the Responsibility to Protect have elevated sovereign states as the dominant players in atrocity prevention, assigning a complementary role to non-state entities such as multinational corporations or small businesses. This state-centric approach in the early development of the R2P principle is natural, since the foundational documents guiding R2P's conceptual framework and strategy sought to generate state buy-in and overcome a widespread concern that the more intrusive forms of R2P practice would erode national sovereignty.

As a normative principle, the Responsibility to Protect reminds states of legal responsibilities and moral commitments that predate the 2005 World Summit, most notably the 1948 Convention on the Prevention and Punishment of the Crime of Genocide. Above all, the Responsibility to Protect remains a political instrument that, upon its invocation, ought to create a sense of urgency and pressure heads of state, senior diplomats, and other government officials to consider the wide array of policy instruments at their disposal. The toolbox for atrocities prevention features economic, diplomatic, legal, and military instruments, ranging from coercive elements such as sanctions or condemnations, to "softer" approaches such as fact-finding missions or security sector reform. While some measures can be applied by the state apparatus within the country at risk, most R2P tools present supportive or coercive steps that external governments and inter-governmental organizations can take. To this end, the founding documents mention the private sector mostly in reference to the need for broader coordination, and rarely offer concrete suggestions for business sector involvement.

The International Commission on Intervention and State Sovereignty, which first coined the principle in 2001, was mandated by the Canadian government to identify whether "it is appropriate for *states* to take coercive – and in particular military – action, against another state for the purpose of protecting people at risk in that other state" (ICISS 2001, vii). The members of the Commission did recognize the potential of business actors to steer impending chaos away from violence, early on in the prevention phase: "Effective conflict prevention depends on disparate actors working together strategically. States, the UN and its specialized agencies, the international financial institutions, regional organizations, NGOs, religious groups, the business community, the media, and scientific, professional and educational communities all have a role to play"

(ICISS 2001, 25–26). The ICISS report, however, did not specify concrete contributions corporations were able to make.

While offering valuable conceptual contributions, the seventy-four-page ICISS report does not present a general consensus about the scope and application of the R2P principle by any means. The Commission's ambition exceeded the political zeitgeist of that time, by advocating a right to intervene against "large-scale loss of life" and a softening of the UN Security Council prerogative to authorize military force, both taboos until today. It was not until the endorsement of R2P by heads of state and government in the 2005 World Summit Outcome Document that the core tenets underlying the principle were formally agreed upon.[4] Articles 138–140 of the Outcome Document refer to the protection responsibilities of "Each individual State," and "The international community," an ill-defined entity that variably alludes to the UN General Assembly, the UN Security Council, or the United States and its allies (Chomsky 2002). The strategic guidance for non-state entities with significant leverage and preventive tools at their disposal, including diaspora, youth, community leaders, or business actors, remained scant.

The 2009 report by the UN Secretary-General on "Implementing the responsibility to protect" was the first in a series of annual documents to further conceptualize the principle, and confirmed the primary role states play in the protection of populations at risk: "That responsibility ... lies first and foremost with the State," which comes from "the nature of State sovereignty and from the pre-existing and continuing legal obligations of States" (UN General Assembly 2009, 8–9). The report highlights the need for coordinated capacity building and assistance by all members of the international community, including the corporate world: "To assist states in meeting those obligations ... it [Pillar two] seeks to draw on the cooperation of Member States, regional and subregional arrangements, civil society and the private sector, as well as on the institutional strengths and comparative advantages of the United Nations system (UN General Assembly 2009, 9). However, the majority of recommendations address state-to-state capacity building, donor and development assistance programs of state-based agencies, and dispute resolution mechanisms by local communities. When the report specifically mentions the private sector, it is under Pillar III's response mandate, only to say: "Less well known is the role of individuals, advocacy

---

[4] State sovereignty implies responsibilities, and the primary responsibility for the protection of its people lies with the state itself. For more details about the conceptual development of the principle, see "The Responsibility to Protect and Peacemaking" (Williams and Claes 2012).

groups, women's groups and the private sector in shaping the international response to crimes and violations relating to the responsibility to protect" (UN General Assembly 2009). Additionally, "[f]oreign direct investment, cultural exchanges, and tourism" are expected to suffer from atrocities, which cause great reputational damage, and may lead individual and private investors to "impose an embargo," independently of the Security Council (UN General Assembly 2009, 26).

The Secretary-General's July 2014 report on international assistance and R2P went further than any previous conceptual or strategic UN document in describing concrete pathways for business sector engagement. Private sector actors can help mitigate risk "by strengthening local economies and employing a workforce inclusive of all social groups," and infuse their expertise into national measures "through public-private partnerships" (UN Security Council 2014, 7). At the same time, the Secretary-General acknowledges the traditional understanding of the private sector's role as explicit or implicit perpetrator, or antipathetic bystander. The 2014 annual update marks a swift departure from previous reports, characterized by scant recognition of the contributions the private sector can make.

2.   Self-constraint by the R2P Community

Those civil society organizations and scholars that drive the conceptual development of R2P and organize the advocacy around atrocities prevention similarly hamper the inclusion of the business community as a central actor in the implementation of R2P. The R2P community is dominated by advocacy organizations with a thematic focus on human rights, peace, or development. In light of their mandate these organizations traditionally demand action from government and inter-governmental organizations in support of local civil society; in countries at risk of mass violence, large corporate actors are commonly regarded as an obstacle or spoiler, not the solution. Business and peace are often understood as opposing concepts: "There has been considerable research on how business can cause or heighten conflict, and the literature describes businesses as one major source of strife, particularly in resource-rich countries" (Forrer *et al.* 2012, 2). Corporations rarely get credit for good efforts and receive an abundance of criticism when they are perceived as doing the "wrong" thing (Zandvliet 2005).

The scholarly debate on the comprehensiveness of the responsibility to prevent similarly leads to self-constraint. A common disagreement relates to the starting point of R2P initiatives, and the utility of invoking the principle early on in the escalation toward mass violence. Maximalists maintain that R2P is applicable as soon as the first risk factors emerge, allowing preventive efforts to address the root causes of mass violence well in advance; minimalists urge for prioritization, in favor of short-term initiatives where mass atrocities are imminent, and strategic use of R2P invocations where the political instrument is likely to generate a sense of urgency (Williams and Claes 2012, 430). Those who define R2P's prevention role narrowly, to concentrate on crisis management, are wary of conceptual overstretch, and urge to "[a]void the blurring of the lines between R2P and the 'right to development'" (Bellamy 2009, 101). Minimalists rightly fear that R2P's political panache could suffer from an expansive view of its application. However, this pragmatic view risks excluding relevant actors, such as the business sector, that have a sustained presence in unstable environments and a comparative advantage in the early prevention of widespread political instability and massive human suffering.

3.   R2P's Association with the Authorization of Military Force

A third explanation for the missing R2P–business nexus is the common association of R2P with the 2011 military interventions in Libya and Côte D'Ivoire, or the absence thereof in Syria (at the time of writing). For casual observers, R2P appears on the radar only when prevention has failed, and the response options beyond military and diplomatic coercion, or humanitarian relief, have become limited. This linkage stems from the continued misconception that the invocation of R2P automatically allows for the use of military force, even without Security Council authorization. Apart from the diplomatic efforts by former Secretary-General Kofi Annan to quell the 2008 post-election violence in Kenya, rarely is any non-military action to prevent the escalation to mass violence prominently labeled as R2P. The authorization of US President Barack Obama in August 2014 to "prevent a potential act of genocide" (Obama 2014) against the Yazidi population in northern Iraq illustrates the level of escalation that is required until R2P appears in foreign policy analysis (Milne 2014; New Statesman 2014). This association with military force limits the space for a constructive consideration of the role for business actors, as their potential lies primarily in early preventive engagement, prior to the eruption of mass violence.

In addition to the aforementioned challenges, other impediments to enhance private sector engagement remain. The lack of commitment is an important hurdle facing any type of preventive engagement, including the meager recognition of the problem, or the difficulty in demonstrating success by measuring a counterfactual: how do we know our efforts effectively prevented something? Early prevention typically implies lower confidence levels that the identified risks will result in a full-blown mass atrocity situation. The occurrence of R2P crimes is rare, whereas the presence of risk factors is much more frequent. "Human beings naturally resist paying certain costs today, even if small, to protect against uncertain future costs" (Albright and Cohen 2008, 22). This counts for business actors as well.

In a context of latent risk, private actors may question the distinction between upstream atrocities prevention and ongoing commitments toward corporate social responsibility or the Global Compact, conflict-sensitive business practice, human rights promotion, or sustainable development. This challenge is mirrored by the conceptual and operational confusion between atrocities and conflict prevention in the peacebuilding field. In the early prevention phase, the overlap between atrocities and conflict prevention instruments is significant. "Of 103 episodes of mass killing observed since 1945, 69 cases (67%) occurred within, and 34 cases (33%) occurred outside, a context of armed conflict" (Bellamy 2011, 2). Since atrocities frequently occur in conflict situations, conflict prevention is considered a prime avenue for effective atrocities prevention. However, atrocity situations also occur outside a context of ongoing violent conflict, and therefore merit a distinct focus from any actor that operates in areas at risk.

Paradoxically, the scant consideration of private sector engagement in atrocities prevention is partly driven by those NGOs, scholars, and casual observers that help sustain the momentum around R2P and aim to broaden international commitment to prevent mass atrocities. However, these hurdles toward greater business engagement in atrocities prevention should not lead to defeatism, as the opportunities for future engagement are multiple. It is imperative to cultivate an active partnership with private sector actors and identify avenues for voluntary engagement and positive contribution. Enhanced corporate involvement, in line with their strategic interest, is particularly promising within the realm of early or upstream prevention, a practice that receives much lip service but remains heavily underutilized.

The Missing R2P–Business Link: Avenues for Involvement in "Upstream Prevention"

Mass atrocities rarely present a spontaneous event but result from extended processes that generally require planning by the instigator and the mobilization of perpetrators. The phased nature of atrocities mobilization and execution offers opportunities for timely intervention, well before the killing erupts. Those actors with a sustained presence in countries that experience regular cycles of political instability, including development donors, regional organizations, human rights organizations, but also business actors, have a keen eye on local dynamics long before large-scale violence breaks out, and are therefore well-suited contributors to the commitments embedded within the R2P principle.

Preventive efforts taken at the earliest stage, commonly referred to as "upstream prevention," include the communication of early warning signs and timely engagement to address risk factors once they become apparent. Upstream prevention deals with the underlying causes of mass atrocity crimes rather than their immediate manifestation. The objective is to enhance the state capacity to prevent atrocities committed by non-state perpetrators while reducing the risk that state actors become complicit or engaged in heinous crimes themselves. Upstream prevention is preferable on moral, economic, and strategic grounds, given the likelihood of saving more civilian lives in a less costly and more effective manner. "If underlying risks and evolving dynamics can be recognized and described accurately in advance of or at the early stages of a crisis," Albright and Cohen clarify, "the full panoply of policy options will still be open" (Albright and Cohen 2008, 17–18).

Corporate contributions can certainly be made to advance the cessation of mass violence, protect civilians from ongoing atrocities, or facilitate post-atrocity healing and repair. However, once the situation escalates into ongoing mass violence, business actors will be more constrained in their options. Companies have more leverage or bargaining power early on in their investment and production cycle (Zandvliet 2005, 5). The conditions for local investment, in terms of trade openness, the respect for human rights, workforce education, and other dynamics that may affect risk levels, are better raised prior to funding decisions, as opposed to after considerable financial commitments have been made.

The relevance of business actors in the realization of the R2P principle becomes clear when considering the upstream instruments within existing R2P or atrocities prevention toolboxes presented in scholarly work and policy guidance. It is difficult to envision how these instruments can be realized without corporate involvement. While developed as a blueprint for US government decision-makers, the Genocide Prevention Task Force Report by former Secretaries Madeleine K. Albright and William S. Cohen identifies two components of a preventive strategy that are particularly conducive to business engagement: early warning and early prevention. The remainder of this chapter illustrates several instruments and tools businesses can apply within these broad strands of preventive action.

1. *Early Warning*

Early warning presents the cornerstone of a comprehensive and effective system to prevent mass violence. The timely prevention of R2P crimes implies a reliable process to acquire knowledge, identify risk, and communicate actionable findings to state and non-state actors able to mitigate risk and reach the people in need of protection. In times of shrinking foreign affairs budgets and new communication technologies, effective early warning allows for prioritization, in terms of both time and location. However, expectations need to remain realistic, since early warning does not allow for exact predictions of where and when genocide and mass atrocities will occur (Albright and Cohen 2008, 19).

Cooperation on early warning between governments, regional organizations, and humanitarian organizations, such as Human Rights Watch and Amnesty International, let alone the business community, remains underdeveloped. This gap results from the sensitive nature of information about the risk of political instability, as well as a general coordination failure within this peacebuilding domain. An additional challenge is the tendency to report on developments in urban areas and overlook more remote areas (Albright and Cohen 2008, 20). Existing risk assessments and intelligence gathering by state actors and non-profit organizations would benefit from the complementary data collected by multinational corporations engaged in short- and long-term risk analysis for investment purposes. Financial actors already have access to robust data collection mechanisms, but interact infrequently with government stakeholders to assess the risk of political instability. The growth of risk analysis and management in the private sector in determining new markets has the potential to contribute to a much more minute understanding of the political dynamics in areas at risk of violence. The credibility of warnings increases when the information is derived from multiple sources. Ideally, the information offered by corporate actors would feed into existing early warning systems. Smaller business actors are well positioned to monitor and analyze identified high-risk situations in rural areas and communicate sudden risk increases. Such information networks would allow traditional peacebuilding actors, larger business actors, or even their own employees to apply the early prevention or self-protection – instruments that are most needed.

Effective early warning requires awareness of those factors that are strongly associated with the risk of future mass violence, including leadership instability, non-violent protest, or state-led discrimination (Harff 2003, 57–73). A local mining company may have better insights than the most sophisticated government intelligence unit on the systematic exclusion of minority groups, the stockpiling of weapons, or evidence of sporadic but intensifying levels of violence or human rights abuses. The communication of early warning signs by business actors has the advantage that it offers an additional incentive to those government representatives with an interest in sustained business activity to take the required preventive measures. Coordinated engagement in early warning will serve businesses well, beyond their broader interest in a stable work environment. A formalized exchange with state actors and intergovernmental organizations, through public–private partnerships, will serve to triangulate and improve the quality of data already available to larger and mid-size businesses. Coordinated data exchange also formalizes their ties with political officials, and advances their public image in pursuit of a moral objective. One mechanism easily appropriated into early warning systems and already in practice is industry groups, effective in other areas of global governance, peacebuilding, and economic management. Crocker *et al.* cite the involvement of the Baltic and International Maritime Council (BIMCO) as one of three coordinating bodies[5] that enable collective conflict management (CCM) in the realm of piracy off the Horn of Africa. In addition to protecting commercial interests by checking the safety and security of routes and supplies, "CCM participants seek an innovative and effective yet voluntary response that brings some measure of governance to an anarchic zone" (Crocker *et al.* 2015, 281–282).

Early warning of imminent violence is rarely considered a crucial missing piece in the prevention puzzle, but rather it is the lack of automated response mechanisms that is a key failing. The question of how to translate warning signs into a commitment to act is the single most pressing dilemma in relation to the responsibility to prevent (Bellamy 2011, 54). However, given the wealth of data large business actors acquire to justify investment decisions even in the most hostile or remote environments, useful contributions can surely be made to fine-tune existing early warning systems. Business assessments that are sensitive to the risk of mass violence should have access to the existing alert channels of the peacebuilding community, and feed into the analysis conducted by the UN Office on Genocide Prevention and the Responsibility to Protect, which is mandated to collect information and act as an early warning mechanism to the UN Secretary-General, and through him to the UN Security Council (UN General Assembly 2010, 2). Improved

---

[5] The other listed bodies are the International Association of Independent Tanker Owners (INTERTANKO) and the International Maritime Bureau of the International Chamber of Commerce.

information exchange will not only enhance the assessment quality but also allow for better coordinated preventive action that includes the business community.

2.   Early Prevention

Early prevention calls for action prior to the onset of mass violence, and requires a multifaceted strategy to address the risk factors or underlying drivers of atrocity crimes, together with a more targeted focus on the motives and means of individual leaders to mobilize their followers (Albright and Cohen 2008, 36–37). Businesses have an interest and the ability to engage in both. Early prevention strategies can "successfully obviate the need for a much more difficult crisis response," and differ from crisis management, conflict mitigation, or other peacebuilding measures tied to a later phase in the conflict cycle. Those cases for early prevention where the broader international community may not be paying adequate attention, i.e. those high-risk–low-attention situations like Sri Lanka, Kyrgyzstan, Bangladesh, and the "northern triangle" in Central America, appear more conducive to business sector involvement than cases of imminent or ongoing mass violence, such as the Central African Republic, Syria, or Iraq (Steinberg 2013).

Promoting horizontal equality is one suggested way in which larger transnational corporations can actively address a key risk factor early on. The role of poverty and inequality as a driver of conflict or mass violence remains under scrutiny. The lack of consensus on the proposition that inequality increases the risk of conflict is due to errors of measurement, Stewart argues. Studies finding no effect usually look at vertical inequality, while inequalities among culturally defined groups or relative deprivation do increase the risk of violent conflict (Stewart 2008).

In his work on the psychological dimensions of violent conflict, Horowitz confirms Stewart's findings. "The sources of conflict reside, above all, from the struggle for relative group worth" (Horowitz 1985, 143). Rather than a driver of conflict or atrocities, horizontal inequalities serve as a risk factor that may increase the likeliness of mass violence, particularly when embedded in local narrative or manipulated by the political elite (Claes 2013, 3). By ensuring inclusiveness and non-discrimination in hiring practices, and promoting tolerance in the workspace, corporations may increase the actual and perceived equity in the distribution of assets, income, and opportunity between groups. Relative equality between identity-based groups is commonly prioritized as a structural objective to prevent mass atrocities, including the 2001 ICISS report and the 2009 Genocide Prevention Task Force report. The adoption of the New Economic Policy in Malaysia following the 1969 racial riot exemplifies the potential involvement of the private sector in government initiatives to reduce inter-ethnic resentment and inequality through an inclusive economic policy. While government regulated, this long-term economic planning effort required close coordination with corporate leadership over a period of two decades to increase domestic ownership of businesses and drive down socio-economic disparities.

The Task Force also highlighted the importance of positive inducements, such as the promise of future investment and the provision of new infra-structure, and negative inducements, including investment conditional-ity, to steer opportunistic leaders away from a strategy of mass violence (Albright and Cohen 2008, 42–43). While some multinational corporations remain largely indifferent to the threat of mass atrocities, except with regard to their own personnel, more responsible companies recognize how their current and future investment plans can offer leverage over governments to promote more responsible behavior (Albright and Cohen 2008, 100). A country like Bangladesh, where the risk of mass atrocities is more latent than imminent, would benefit from business sector involvement in early atrocities prevention, particularly around the election period. The January 2014 presidential elections saw several hundred casualties in what was the most violent period in Bangladesh since independence. As they are known to support the ruling Awami League party, minority communities suffer disproportionately from repression and attacks committed by the political opposition. Major economic forces, such as the garment industry, missed a clear opportunity to pressure political leaders in the run-up to election day, as they clearly suffer from the recurrent political chaos. The intensely vio-lent labor strikes or mass protests, known as *hartals*, bring public life and the nation's economy to a halt for extended periods. Unfortunately, the largest business sectors remain wary of raising their voices, as they are intensely politicized, and often split between the ruling party and the opposition.

At times, however, business actors do apply their leverage and exert pressure. During the 2001–2002 standoff between India and Pakistan, when both countries amassed troops along the Line of Control (LoC) in Kashmir, large US corporations resorted to the diplomatic channels at their disposal. As a result, the US government issued an advisory note to the Indian ambassador in Washington, DC, warning about a US and UK business exodus in case the conflict escalated. The Indian government was presented with a choice, "between business and war,"[6] a message which rapidly reached the presidential office in Delhi. Within days, mili-tary action was taken to de-escalate the confrontation.

---

[6] Interview with former diplomat, Dhaka, Bangladesh, July 2014.

Table 4.1 *"Upstream" prevention toolbox for business actors*

	Early warning	Early prevention
Tools for the private sector	• Coordinating risk assessment networks, through public–private partnerships or industry groups • Supporting free and responsible media • Information exchange • Joint analysis • Do no harm assessments • Providing early warning to prevention actors, and potential victims	• Promoting inter-communal economic ties • Encouraging/practicing Fair Labor Practices • Horizontal equality promotion (e.g. through employment and safety net programs for marginalized populations, or non-discrimination in hiring practices) • Advancing the employment of youth and women • Promise or use of economic incentives and other positive inducements, such as infrastructure commitments • Threat or use of negative inducements, like investment conditionality or relocation • Workforce education and training • Support for effective regulation of extractive industries • Social campaign 'branding' • Publicly underwriting, and complying with, relevant international norms and principles

Beyond these illustrative examples, the business sector has a multifaceted toolbox at its disposal for upstream engagement in early warning and early prevention. The options include both supportive and coercive measures, with immediate or long-term effect. See Table 4.1.

Active engagement in early warning and early prevention, through the measures presented above, will help overcome the current disconnect between R2P and the private sector, and contribute to the realization of R2P as an international norm.

Conclusion: Toward an Effective Normative Framework

A strong normative framework, solidified through corporate engagement, is a critical component of atrocities prevention strategies, as it guides the behavior of other relevant players within the international community. Martha Finnemore defines norms as "observable patterns of behavior for actors which can prescribe future actions" (Finnemore 2012, 263–264). As their acceptance grows, norms are said to be emerging, moving along a continuum from aspirational to effective, as hopes and verbal commitments transform into law, institutions, and practice (Williams 2015, 84).

Given the inconsistent practice of states and non-governmental entities in the face of heightened risk, or even ongoing atrocities, the R2P principle is still nascent in its trajectory toward an established norm. The principle has advanced through the creation of new positions and institutions. In fact, R2P may present one of the most important normative developments in this field since the adoption of the 1948 Genocide Convention, keeping the need to protect innocent civilians high on the political agenda, and broadening the belief that mass atrocities prevention presents one of the most urgent security challenges of our time (Albright and Cohen 2008, 98). However, a more automated consideration of available policy options in the face of risk, by state entities and business actors alike, is required to move the normalization of R2P forward. Through consistent early warning and early prevention, business actors help create expectations, and encourage other members of the international community to act accordingly.

Corporate enterprises have both an interest and the capacity to strengthen local resilience, and mitigate the risk of atrocity crimes early on in the escalation phase. As noted, strategic documents identify numerous instruments corporate actors can apply to advance the Responsibility to Protect through early warning and early action. However, clear incentives so far have not been able to bridge the gap between the R2P and business communities. It is imperative that private sector actors are included as valuable contributors in strategic efforts to realize prevention commitments. Global governance actors and R2P advocates must articulate the incentives, including "the much greater cost of acting once a crisis occurs and the social and economic devastation facing countries that experience atrocity crimes" (UN Security Council 2014, 18). Clear data-based evidence on the translatable effects for the private sector, presented by the sunken investments of having to cut and run, additional associated costs of exiting and re-entering a context of mass violence, and the lost opportunities during the crisis, will likely resonate in the corporate world.

There are limits to what the private sector could and should do. Its geographic reach and commercial presence are often linked to the presence of natural resources, a cheap workforce, or important consumer markets. We cannot ask businesses to assume a leading role in peacebuilding. What we can do is work with businesses to identify how the goals of atrocities prevention and successful enterprise align and bolster cooperation in some of the mutually beneficial early warning and early prevention activities presented in this volume.

References

Albright, Madeleine K. and Cohen, William S. 2008. *Preventing Genocide: A Blueprint for U.S. Policymakers.* Washington, DC: The United States Holocaust Memorial Museum, The American Academy of Diplomacy, and the Endowment of the United States Institute of Peace.

Bellamy, Alex J. 2009. *Responsibility to Protect: The Global Effort to End Mass Atrocities.* Cambridge: Polity Press.

    2011. *Mass atrocities and armed conflict: Links, distinctions, and implications for the Responsibility to Protect.* Policy Analysis Brief for the Stanley Foundation. Muscatine, IA: The Stanley Foundation.

Chomsky, Noam. 2002. "The crimes of 'Intcom.'" *Foreign Policy*, September.

Claes, Jonas. 2013. *Atrocity prevention at the state level.* U.S. Institute of Peace, Peace Brief 144. Washington, DC: United States Institute of Peace Press.

Collier, Paul. 2009. *Wars, Guns, and Votes: Democracy in Dangerous Places.* New York: HarperCollins Publishers.

Commission of the European Countries. 2006. "Implementing the partnership for growth and jobs making Europe a Pole of excellence on corporate social responsibility." Communication from the Commission to the European Parliament, the Council, and the European Economic and Social Committee. Brussels, Belgium. http://eur-lex.europa.eu/LexUriServ/LexUriServ.do?uri=COM:2006:0136:FIN:en:PDF

Crocker, Chester A., Fen Osler Hampson, and Pamela Aall. 2015. "The piccolo, trumpet, and bass fiddle: The orchestration of collective conflict management," in *Managing Conflict in a World Adrift.* Washington, DC: United States Institute of Peace Press, 271–291.

Finnemore, Martha. 2012. "Constructing norms of humanitarian intervention." In *Conflict After the Cold War: Arguments on Causes of War and Peace*, 4th Edition, edited by Richard K. Betts. Upper Saddle River, NJ: Pearson Education, Inc., 236–251.

Forrer, John, Timothy Fort, and Raymond Gilpin. 2012. *How business can foster peace.* US Institute of Peace, Special Report 315. Washington, DC: United States Institute of Peace Press.

Harff, Barbara. 2003. "No lessons learned from the Holocaust? Assessing risks of genocide and political mass murder since 1955." *American Political Science Review* 897:57–73.

Hoeffler, Anke and Marta Reynal-Querol. 2003. *Measuring the costs of conflict.* Report from the Centre for the Study of African Economies and The World Bank. Oxford University.

Horowitz, Donald L. 1985. *Ethnic Groups in Conflict.* Berkeley, CA: University of California Press.

International Commission on Intervention and State Sovereignty (ICISS). 2001. "The Responsibility to Protect." Ottawa, Canada: International Development Research Centre.

Karns, Margaret P. and Karen A. Mingst. 2004. *International Organizations: The Politics and Processes of Global Governance.* Boulder, CO: Lynne Rienner Publishers.

Kolk, Ans. 2001. "Multinational enterprises and international climate policy." In *Non-state Actors in International Relations,* edited by Bas Arts, Math Noortmann, and Bob Reinalda. Burlington, VT: Ashgate Publishing Limited, 211–255.

Kuper, Leo. 1981. *Genocide: Its Political Use in the Twentieth Century.* New Haven, CT: Yale University Press.

Kwok, Chuck and Solomon Tadesse. 2006. "The MNC as an agent of change for host-country institutions: FDI and corruption." Working Paper 882. Ann Arbor, MI: The William Davidson Institute.

Lin-hi, Nick. 2008. "Corporate social responsibility: An investment in social cooperation for mutual advantage." Discussion Paper for the Wittenberg Center for Global Ethics. Leipzig, Germany: Wittenberg Center for Global Ethics.

Martin, Jena. 2010. "What's in a name? Transnational corporations as bystanders under international law." West Virginia University College of Law Working Paper Series. Morgantown, WV: West Virginia University.

Milne, Seumas. 2014. "Another war in Iraq won't fix the disaster of the last." *The Guardian,* August 13. www.theguardian.com/commentisfree/2014/aug/13/war-in-iraq-yazidis-aid-military-intervention

Nelson, Jane. 2000. *The business of peace: The private sector as a partner in conflict prevention and resolution.* Report for International Alert, Council on Economic Priorities, The Prince of Wales's Business Leaders Forum. London: Folium Press.

New Statesman. 2014. "Leader: We have a responsibility to protect the Yazidis of Iraq." *The New Statesman,* August 14. www.newstatesman.com/politics/2014/08/leader-we-have-responsibility-protect-yazidis-iraq

Obama, Barack. 2014. "Statement by the President." Office of the Press Secretary. Published August 7. www.whitehouse.gov/the-press-office/2014/08/07/statement-president

Rowlands, Ian H. 2001. "Transnational corporations and global environmental politics." In *Non-state Actors in World Politics,* edited by Daphne Josselin and William Wallace. New York: Palgrave, 133–149.

Seyle, D. Conor. 2013. *Business Participation in the Responsibility to Protect.* Broomfield, CO: One Earth Future Foundation.

Steinberg, Donald. 2013. "Remarks by Donald Steinberg, President and CEO, World Learning, at the U.S. Institute of Peace." World Learning Press Room. Published July 22. www.worldlearning.org/pressroom/speeches/responsibility-to-protect-in-the-real-world-a-tale-of-two-countries

Stewart, Frances. 2008. *Horizontal Inequalities and Conflict: Understanding Group Violence in Multiethnic Societies.* New York: Palgrave Macmillan.

United Nations General Assembly. 2009. *Implementing the Responsibility to Protect: Report of the Secretary-General,* A/63/677 (January 12). www.unrol. org/files/SG_reportA_63_677_en.pdf

——— 2010. *Early Warning, Assessment and the Responsibility to Protect: Report of the Secretary-General,* A/64/864 (July 14). www.responsibilitytoprotect.org/N1045020(1).pdf

——— "2005 World Summit Outcome," Document A/Res/60/1, October 24, 2005. www.un.org/womenwatch/ods/A-RES-60-1-E.pdf

United Nations Global Compact. 1999. www.unglobalcompact.org/about

United Nations Security Council. 2014. *Fulfilling Our Collective Responsibility: International Assistance and the Responsibility to Protect: Report of the Secretary-General,* A/68/947 (July 11). http://responsibilitytoprotect.org/N1446379.pdf

Williams, Abiodun. 2015. "The changing normative environment for conflict management." In *Managing Conflict in a World Adrift,* edited by Chester A. Crocker, Fen Osler Hampson, and Pamela Aall. Washington DC: United States Institute of Peace Press, 83–100.

Williams, Abiodun and Jonas Claes. 2012. "The Responsibility to Protect and peacemaking." In *Peacemaking,* edited by Susan Allen Nan, Zachariah Cherian Mampilly, and Andrea Bartoli. Santa Barbara, CA: Praeger, 420–437.

Zandvliet, Luc. 2005. *Opportunities for Synergy: Conflict Transformation and the Corporate Agenda.* Berlin, Germany: Berghof Research Center for Constructive Conflict Management.

5   The Kenyan Private Sector's Role in Mass Atrocity Prevention, Cessation, and Recovery

Patrick Obath and Victor Odundo Owuor

> Kenyans have turned their inequalities into local folklore & perfected exclusiveness.
>
> Politicians leverage these narratives into political ammunition during election campaigns, & pit one exclusive group against another.
>
> When Kenya gets into a crisis, we try & solve it from within our divisions, rather than across them.
>
> Karuti Kanyingi[1]

Introduction

In 2008 Kenya experienced post-election violence on a scale that was unprecedented in its history as a nation. During this time, the private sector organized multiple interventions that led to the start of a process that eventually culminated in the formation of a coalition government. In the tenure of the coalition government a new constitution was promulgated that would transform the political landscape of the country but that was felt could also create a platform for political violence if the transformation was not handled correctly. The next general elections were due at the end of 2012 and the private sector in Kenya was concerned about the possibility of events of 2008 repeating themselves. So members arranged an exploratory meeting in August 2011 to examine ways of preventing politics from escalating into some form of violence, as had been the case in almost all elections in Kenya from independence.[2] At the start of 2012 an all-inclusive campaign dubbed "Mkenya Daima" was crafted, and launched at the end of January that year (Mkenya Daima 2013). Loosely translated, the Kiswahili words "Mkenya Daima" mean "My Kenya Forever." The initiative sought to create leadership

---

[1] The Karuti Kanyingi quote is from a PowerPoint presentation he made to the Kenyan private sector in the aftermath of the 2008 post-election violence.

[2] This phenomenon is not unique to Kenya – the periodic elections on the African continent are almost without exception accompanied by active conflict. See "Election-Related Violence in Africa" (Atoubi 2008).

that represented the aspirations of Kenyans who in 2010 had promulgated the new constitution.

The campaign objective was therefore to promote peace and inclusiveness and inspire all Kenyans toward peaceful elections and prosperity. Essentially, the Mkenya Daima campaign was an extension of the engagement the business community had in promoting the reform agenda following the 2007–2008 post-election violence. This chapter provides an analysis of the circumstances around these interventions, much of which has not previously been documented. The analysis is a continuation of the main argument of this book that private sector institutions and collective business groups have economic interests in the support of peace and prevention of mass atrocities. The case of Kenya during this period provides a concrete example of how the private sector as a whole can come together to address potential R2P violations. The lead author of this chapter was, by virtue of his position in the Kenya apex business association, thrust into the middle of the events analyzed in this chapter.[3] The chapter will therefore describe the interventions by the private sector in the resolution of the 2008 post-election violence, the thinking behind them, and the design of the Mkenya Daima campaign, and the results it achieved. It will also look at the lessons learned and the success factors of the private sector interventions.

Historical Background

In order to fully appreciate the circumstances in which the interventions occurred, a review of Kenya's profile is in order. In addition to forty-two tribes, Kenya has a significant number of citizens with South Asian heritage, as well as many Caucasian descendants of the British colonial legacy. The country of 42 million has Christianity at 82.5 percent of its population and Islam at 11.1 percent as the main religions. Kenya's segment of the population of twenty-four years and under stands at 50.8 percent. The country's economy is the largest in east and central Africa (*The World Factbook* n.d.). Apart from serving as a regional headquarters for a plethora of multinationals such as Citigroup, AIG, Total, Siemens, General Electric, BBC, General Motors, CNBC, Barclays Bank, Old Mutual Group, Lafarge, Standard Chartered Bank, Airtel, Huawei, Google, Stanbic Bank, Coca-Cola, Diageo, Samsung, LG, and Microsoft, to mention but a few, Kenya is host to the United

---

[3] Patrick Obath is a former chairman of the Kenya Private Sector Alliance and is currently vice chairman of the KEPSA Foundation. He served as chairman during much of the period under discussion in this chapter.

Nations Office at Nairobi (UNON).[4] UNON is the headquarters for the United Nations Environmental Program, the United Nations Human Settlements Program, and all the other African regional programs in the United Nations system.

On the political front, Kenyan politics was for a long time characterized by a single-party system. This form of government began soon after independence when the two prominent parties, Kenya Africa National Union (KANU) and Kenya African Democratic Union (KADU), combined to form one party, KANU. The first president of the republic, Mzee Jomo Kenyatta, ruled under this one-party state until he passed away in his sleep on August 22, 1978 (Aseka 2001). He was succeeded by his vice-president, Daniel Arap Moi, through a constitutional process. Daniel Arap Moi oversaw single-party rule for a period, until after sustained domestic and international pressure he permitted multiple parties in early 1992. Daniel Arap Moi subsequently presided over two multi-party elections during his rule, one in 1992 and the other in 1997, both of which he was declared the winner, despite allegations of extensive election malpractices. Although he agreed to multi-party democracy, President Moi did not accept the idea that through this he might lose the presidency. Thus, it was in this period in the 1990s that violence became institutionalized during national elections (Stiftung 2001). In short, violence became a means of securing political power and winning elections.[5]

Fast forward to the year 2002, when the third multi-party elections were held. Unlike the two previous iterations, these elections were relatively violence free. Two issues had a bearing on these elections. First, the incumbent was not contesting, having served out his two-term constitutional limit. Moi's chosen successor in these elections was Uhuru Kenyatta, Jomo's son. Second, both leading contenders – Uhuru Kenyatta (from Moi's KANU) and Mwai Kibaki of the opposition – were Kikuyu. Mwai Kibaki, who represented a diverse coalition of ethnic groups, handily defeated Uhuru Kenyatta and formed the NARC (National Rainbow Coalition) government.

The Kenya Private Sector, 2002–2007

After the elections in 2002, the new NARC government was anxious to partner more closely with the private sector as a central pillar of its

---

[4] UNON is led by a Director-General, a position equivalent to the UN Under-Secretary-General: www.unon.org/.

[5] In doing this Moi created a system similar to those documented in the EISA Policy Brief No. 1 (EISA 2009).

economic recovery strategy.[6] At a meeting in early 2003, the government ministers made it very clear that they saw the private sector as uncoordinated and divided into several competing groups and confessed they did not know who to talk to. Prior to 2002, the private sector consisted of separate business interests that each had an agenda specific to the sector that it presented. There were several key business associations, such as the Kenya Association of Manufacturers, the Kenya Flower Council, the Federation of Kenya Employers, and several financial sector bodies representing bankers, insurers, accountants, and the like. Individual corporations also carried out their own advocacy with government. This proliferation of private sector umbrella bodies created major confusion within government, among donors, and in the private sector itself. What would have been considered as the major and most representative private sector organization, the Kenya National Chamber of Commerce and Industry, was moribund. There was clearly a need to have an apex body that all the other disparate groups could belong to and that could dialogue with the NARC government.

After a series of meetings and consultations between the various existing "umbrella" private sector organizations, it was agreed to form the Kenya Private Sector Alliance (KEPSA).[7] More than 200 associations declared their support for the new umbrella body, making it the first and only inclusive, diverse, and representative voice of the private sector that all had dreamed of. On March 12, 2003, KEPSA was formally launched. The vision of KEPSA was to create a strong, unified, proactive, and results-focussed private sector with values that espoused low ego, mutual respect, and non-confrontational engagement. KEPSA was readily accepted by the government and the development partners as the voice of the private sector. It started engaging in advocacy on issues dear to business within and across a wide spectrum of sectors.

KEPSA also worked continuously to develop the sector federations where there was no strong subject matter representation. The first key pillars of KEPSA were policy and advocacy, sector development, resource mobilization, and communications and public relations. During this time KEPSA further aligned the older and better-established private sector organizations behind its initiatives, to the extent that bodies such as the FKE (Federation of Kenya Employers), KAM (Kenya Association of Manufacturers), Media Owners Association (MOA), ICPAK (Institute of Certified Public Accountants of Kenya), and others became members

---

[6] The NARC government was a coalition of two Kenyan political parties (the Liberal Democratic Party and the National Alliance Party) from 2002 to 2005 when it fell apart.
[7] See Kenya Private Sector Alliance, "About," www.kepsa.or.ke/.

and regularly sent their representatives to meetings, as well as participating in joint advocacy programs on various sectorial and cross-sectorial issues.

As the 2007 elections approached, conversations in all sectors and in the media became heavily politicized. The two coalitions vying for government, the Orange Democratic Movement (ODM), led by Raila Odinga, and the Party of National Unity (PNU), led by incumbent Mwai Kibaki, were strongly ethnically aligned, with ODM relying mainly on Luo, Luhya, and Kalenjin voting while PNU support came predominantly from the Kikuyu, Meru, and Embu voting. The third party, ODM-Kenya, led by Kalonzo Musyoka, mainly coalesced around the Kamba community while also hunting for votes in other parts of the country.

This was the first election since KEPSA was formed and there was no clear agenda within KEPSA on how it would get involved in the process. Indeed, the values that were driving KEPSA's vision were such that it would have been wrong for KEPSA to get actively involved in the electioneering process. In the lead up to the national elections in December 2007, the country's development partners as well as various diplomatic representatives began to voice their concerns about the bias the government and the staff of the Electoral Commission of Kenya (ECK) were exhibiting in the preparation of the elections – especially the space and resources allowed to the opposition parties. The development partners and the diplomatic representatives were viewed by the Kibaki administration as supporting the opposition, and the government tried to stop them from going round the country, ostensibly because it could not guarantee their security and also because it deemed that they needed government permission to travel outside the capital city.

Non-governmental, faith-based, and other civil society organizations also became actively involved in the election processes. It did not escape attention that quite a few of them became partisan in their relationship with the opposition and the outgoing government. The media houses were by and large even-handed in their coverage of the electioneering process. However, as the ruling party had the most "newsworthy" individuals in the form of sitting ministers, heads of state-owned enterprises as well as most of the public institutions, it got most of the coverage by default. This gave the perception that the media was biased toward the government. This perception was to become an important factor in the period immediately after the announcement of the election results and during the period of post-election violence.

With ethnic tensions at fever pitch, the turnout of more than 70 percent was the highest recorded in any national elections in the country. On December 30, 2007, the chairman of the ECK declared Mwai Kibaki the winner and he was hastily sworn in as president a few hours later (ICR2P 2015). The opposition parties all rejected the results on the basis that the elections had been rigged. This stand by the opposition and subsequent pronouncements by the leaders of the main political parties were instrumental in fanning the already volatile situation, triggering widespread violence that resulted in more than 1,300 deaths and the displacement of more than 650,000 civilians (Gettleman 2007).

The 2008 Post-election Situation

The first two months of 2008 were to prove the most traumatizing for the nation. The chronology of events is telling.

The declaration of Kibaki as the winner of the elections by the ECK after two tense days of disputed vote tallying, and his hurried swearing in on the same day, precipitated violent protests, mainly in opposition strongholds. Raila Odinga's opposition ODM won the majority seats in the parliamentary election and this numerical advantage was expected to translate into presidential victory as well. The debate around this added fuel to the already acerbic rhetoric going around the country. The leaders began blaming each other's followers as the cause for the violence spreading. In the first week of January, Mwai Kibaki, the incumbent president, agreed to a re-run of the election if ordered to do so by the Supreme Court, and at the same time offered to form a government of national unity. The opposition rejected this offer and calls for mass protests continued. Within a day the protests were called off after intervention by a special envoy from the United States. The incumbent president formed a cabinet immediately and the opposition supporters responded by escalating the violence.

The violence started almost spontaneously on January 1 when youths in the slums of Nairobi and Kisumu started looting government buildings and the shops and houses of those they perceived to have been supporters of the ruling party. The worst event was when a mob set fire to a church in the town of Eldoret, killing thirty people from the incumbent president's tribe (Gettleman 2008).[8] Some of the violence was due to positions taken by various political parties before the election that could be viewed as setting the stage for violence in the event that the election did not go the way that was expected by the respective political parties. This started the second wave of violence. The third wave of violence was in reprisal attacks that were reportedly organized by the government and police, either using excessive force or choosing not to prevent violence.

---

[8] These deaths have remained etched in the Kenyan conscience (Gettleman 2008).

The human costs of this violence were traumatic. Most estimates place the number killed between late December 2007 and February 2008 at a minimum of 1,300, with another 650,000 people being displaced.[9]

In addition to the tragedy of human costs described above, the 2007–2008 post-election violence delivered massive economic damage to Kenya.[10] The country's GDP growth rate in 2007 was 7.1 percent, while the 2008 rate plummeted to 1.7 percent and did not return to higher growth rates until 2010 (Miriri 2013). Tourism, Kenya's main source of foreign exchange, took a big hit (Holland 2008). During the post-election violence, many supply and transport routes to and from Nairobi and other urban centers, especially leading into the Rift Valley and the western part of the country, were barricaded by the perpetrators of the violence, and as quickly as the police and law enforcement agencies responded by removing the barricades, others were erected. The result was that essential commodities such as fuel, mobile telephone airtime, and some items of food could not reach many parts where violence was being perpetrated. Milk, vegetables, and other perishable foods and inputs could also not be evacuated from the farms or collection centers to get to the main towns, which were the consumption centers, or to plants for processing and packing (Shaba 2008). Public transport was also seriously curtailed and the many Kenyans who had traveled to their rural homes over the Christmas period could not return to their places of work once the holiday season was over.

The lockdown on transport also affected imports and exports for landlocked Uganda and Rwanda, which use the northern road transport corridor to get the bulk of their goods to and from international markets. Rail transport was not spared either, as several sections in Nairobi and to the west of the country were uprooted by marauding youths, effectively cutting off the only alternative to road transport. All these actions meant that many Kenyan businesses, and to a lesser extent those in Uganda and Rwanda, began to suffer as a result of the disruption of the supply routes. Goods could not get to market and raw materials could not be obtained, so production had to be curtailed. The Kenyan flower industry, a key source of foreign exchange, came to a standstill (Ksoll et al. 2009). The town of Naivasha, where many of the major flower concerns base their operations, became a no-go zone,

---

[9] Other estimates have suggested the number killed to be as high as 5,000. Michela Wrong reports that 5,000 inquests from this electoral violence sit unprocessed in the Office of the Director of Public Prosecutions (Wrong 2013).

[10] A synthetic model of what these changes portended for Kenya is depicted by the 'before-and-after' study "Measuring the Economic Cost of the 2007/08 Post-Election Violence in Kenya" (Guibert and Perez-Quiros 2013).

especially for the horticultural workers with origins in areas linked to Raila Odinga.[11] Nairobi and the neighboring urban centers were not spared either. Schools that traditionally open in the first week of January remained closed as teachers were not at their stations, either through fear of victimization on a tribal basis or because they could not get there thanks to a crippled transport system.

Private Sector's Role in the Start of Cessation and Recovery from Post-election Violence

With the goings on in the first week, the private sector – especially the more prominent members of KEPSA – became increasingly concerned about the direction of two key developments in the country. The first was the closure of the supply routes and its impact on business. The second was the political gerrymandering that was fueling the violence without any progress toward a resolution of the stalemate caused by the disputed election results and the positions taken by the various political protagonists (African Union 2008).

On the first count, the private sector, through KEPSA, joined hands with the bureaucrats in government as well as the police and other disciplined forces to craft a way of getting supplies into the violence-hit areas (Lumsdaine et al. 2013).[12] The first action was to slowly secure the supply routes starting from the major cities – Nairobi, Mombasa, and Kisumu – and radiating in all the required directions. This allowed all the suppliers to start resuming supply slowly without the need of convoys, though due to the higher risk associated with human transportation at the time, convoys were created for passenger transport operations. Daily coordination meetings were held to review progress and plan new actions based on intelligence reports from the affected areas. Within a week distribution routes in Kenya were stabilized and attention shifted to serving the landlocked nations. Transport to these areas took the best part of two weeks to get started and the resumption of full operations took almost a month. The private sector (through KEPSA) was instrumental in identifying key actions to be taken, developing the implementation plans for

---

[11] See a description of the revenge killings in Naivasha in "Revenge Killings Stoke a Violent Cycle in Kenya" (McCrummen 2008).

[12] A recurring theme in literature on preventive actions for violence in the 2013 elections was the extent of coordination between government bodies, international institutions, NGOs, business, and other local actors who suffered great financial losses as a result of the 2008 PEV to bring normalcy to various communities. KEPSA was at the forefront of these efforts. See "Keeping the Peace: Lessons Learned from Preventive Actions towards Kenya's 2013 Elections" (Lumsdaine et al. 2013).

the agreed actions and then rapidly organizing logistics as and when the security organs had secured the routes.

On the second count, the private sector (through KEPSA) formed a small working group that met to strategize on how it could help break the political stalemate that was threatening to plunge the country into anarchy. The main concerns were many. The violence that had started in the regions outside of Nairobi was now springing up in small pockets in the settlement areas in Nairobi and threatening to fully flare up. The regular security forces were largely disjointed along tribal lines and were feared to be ineffective in the event any major security operations were required. The use of the military to quell the unrest and maintain peace was considered, but using the army to contain violence in Nairobi could have led to major strife and probably full anarchy.

Traditionally, mediation between the protagonists would have been started by either civil society or faith-based organizations. However, as many of the stronger organizations had become partisan during the electioneering period, none of the protagonists trusted them to mediate in this case. The African Union made frantic efforts to craft a way forward but initially was unable to make headway, and there was no major representation from the diplomatic corps in the country to start any form of dialog. The protagonists would not have listened to the diplomatic corps anyway – some of these representatives had vilified the incumbent administration and were therefore seen as either supporting the government or the opposition as a result of their pronouncements during the campaign period. With few credible actors left in the country, the private sector realized it had to take the leadership role and help bring back some semblance of normalcy.

The private sector's immediate initiative was to present a united front in any intervening action and also craft a strong and direct common message to the three principals – Kibaki, Raila, and Kalonzo – urging them to come together as "statesmen" and put the nation ahead of their political ambitions. Private sector members close to the principals made initial approaches behind the scenes to explore the possibility of them formally meeting with a larger, representative private sector group as a form of starting mediation. By mid-January all the principals had agreed to the requested meetings and the private sector chose January 18, 2008 to meet each of them separately, starting with Kibaki in the morning, Raila in the middle of the day, and Kalonzo in the afternoon.

As this private sector mediation was building up, the chairman of the Africa Union, Ghanaian President John Kuffor, arrived in the country to mediate. He did not make any headway but got the protagonists to agree in principle to work toward finding a solution with an African panel headed by former UN Secretary-General Kofi Annan. While waiting for this to happen the crisis continued, with the opposition holding protest rallies across the country and the government trying to take control of the situation. As planned, a private sector group under the banner of KEPSA, and consisting of representatives of the major business organizations and large and medium-sized corporate heads, met with teams from the government and the opposition, led by Kibaki and Raila respectively at different times on January 18.

The message from KEPSA to the two principals sought to express business concerns regarding the effects of the current chaos – loss of jobs, disruption of agricultural activities, transportation, education, tourism, etc. – and the impact this continued to have on the economy. The message also expressed that the private sector was not seeking to craft a political solution but that it expected the three leaders to put the country ahead of their individual political ambitions. It would further stress the concern that the private sector had about the violence in Nairobi escalating to looting of public and government facilities, business premises, and private homes. In the absence of a committed police force with strong leadership, it was feared that these forces would not respond to the escalation and that anarchy would then descend on the nation. It was clear that the government and the opposition had not anticipated that the chaos would continue for this long, or take the form it had taken.

During the meeting with the government, KEPSA delivered the strong written message that had been crafted on the key principles outlined above. A lengthy discussion took place, with the government seeking to understand the basis of KEPSA's message. It also gave the KEPSA members an opportunity to give detailed examples of how the violence was affecting businesses, the employees, their families, and extended families. Some of the members gave personal testimony of the impact the post-election violence had on their families and employees, including fatalities and injuries. In response, the government offered to institute measures to cushion businesses from the impact of the violence and had already started by paying contractors it had engaged and those who had arrears. It instructed the Kenya Revenue Authority (KRA) to speed up the refund of money owed to businesses.[13] KEPSA was requested to outline the areas of support that the business community needed to recover from the impact of the post-election violence. It was also evident that the president's priority was resettlement of the displaced

---

[13] See Kenya Revenue Authority, the country's revenue agency, available at www.revenue. go.ke/.

people in the Rift Valley and finding the perpetrators of the worst cases of violence, especially the torching of a church in Eldoret that resulted in thirty deaths.

At the end of the meeting, KEPSA requested that as a matter of urgency Kibaki meet Raila, and he agreed to the proposal. During the meeting with the main opposition party, ODM, the same written message as crafted for the government was delivered. The only change was the addressee. A similar lengthy discussion took place, with the private sector giving similar testimony to strengthen the message. In response, the opposition agreed fully with the KEPSA prognosis of the possible direction that the post-election violence could take. They expressed their wish that Kibaki's stay in office should be viewed as an extension of his previous term while alternatives on the way forward were explored. This was more or less to state that the election result should be nullified. Their demand was that one of the following options be exercised:

- The president steps down and Odinga assumes the presidency.
- Fresh elections are held.
- A power-sharing arrangement be entered into.

The opposition also required that long outstanding issues such as land ownership, equity in distribution of wealth and jobs, and so forth be discussed fully.[14] At the end of the meeting KEPSA requested Odinga to meet Kibaki and he agreed, but only in the presence of mediators. Following the meetings, Kibaki set up a committee to dialog with the opposition team, but the team would not meet with the Kibaki committee.

In subsequent meetings with both the government and the opposition teams, KEPSA requested and the parties delivered the following:

- Both the government and opposition were to issue statements appealing for an end to the violence and mass demonstrations and follow this up with similar positive actions from the leadership at all levels.
- Security in the up-country areas were to be beefed up and improved as there was a lot of tension, fear, and mistrust among the communities. This was in parallel with the actions being taken to restore supplies to the violence-hit areas so that the security apparatus could have fuel and communication capabilities to effectively contain the violence. (Private security companies in the hot spots volunteered material support as well as offering their personnel to work alongside the state security organs.)

[14] See the state of land-related grievances in "The Report of the Truth, Justice and Reconciliation Commission, Vol. IIB" (Kenya Transitional Justice Network 2013).

KEPSA also increased its actions in several areas:

- It held several press conferences jointly with the Central Organisation of Trade Unions (COTU), with a strong message to the protagonists to influence their supporters to stop violent encounters, as well as appealing to them to engage in dialog to break the impasse, and to seek ways to resolve it.[15] The communication reminded them that the total numbers that KEPSA and COTU represented were more than the total number of votes that were cast for the three presidential candidates during the recently concluded elections.
- It engaged members of parliament from both sides at a personal level and identified business and social groups that would work with the members of parliament in their constituencies.
- It started work on promoting healing and reconciliation among employees in its membership through the relevant bodies, such as COTU, the Federation of Kenya Employers, the Micro and Small Enterprises Federation, etc. This was in response to the realization that tribal sensitivity and rivalries had percolated into workplaces as a result of the electioneering activities and the post-election violence.
- It engaged its media members who agreed to put a ban on live coverage of events to avoid spontaneous actions or pronouncements that could foment violent action elsewhere. Certain important events would be covered live but broadcast on short tape delay to allow for removal of offending language or action.

Kofi Annan arrived in the last week of January and held a series of meetings with many stakeholders, including several with KEPSA and its sector organizations. He quickly got the two sides to agree to mediation and they formed teams to do so. KEPSA had requested and Kofi Annan agreed to provide a daily briefing on the progress of mediation through their secretariat. KEPSA and its members continued to consult and engage widely, and got good insights into the underlying issues that could contribute to the cooling off of the political standoff. It shared these insights with the negotiation teams.

A National Accord and Reconciliation Agreement (the Agreement) was finally signed on February 28, 2008.[16] KEPSA and COTU issued a

---

[15] COTU is the umbrella workers' body representing all other Kenyan worker unions: http://cotu-kenya.org/.

[16] The Kenya National Dialogue and Reconciliation Accord was signed by Mwai Kibaki, President, and Raila Odinga, Prime Minister, in the presence of Kofi Annan, the lead negotiator representing the African Union Panel of Eminent African Personalities (Kenya National Accord and Reconciliation Act 2008).

joint statement in its support on February 29. The Agreement had four key agenda items:

- One: to stop violence and restore fundamental rights and liberties.
- Two: to address the humanitarian crisis that involved resettlement of internally displaced persons (IDPs).
- Three: to resolve the political crisis.
- Four: to examine and address constitutional, legal, and institutional reforms, poverty and inequality, youth unemployment, and land reforms.

KEPSA in the Lead Up to the 2013 Elections (Mass Atrocity Prevention)

Following the signing of the Agreement, the coalition government set about running the country and implementing the agreed agenda items. The key step that the government undertook, and which was probably the most difficult in the view of the private sector, was that of completing agenda item four. The main plank of this was the constitutional, legal, and institutional reforms. A "Committee of Experts" was formed to harmonize the various drafts made in the journey of the Constitution review and release one document. This was completed and subjected to stakeholder reviews and the parliamentary process. A referendum was conducted on August 4, 2010 and the draft Constitution approved by 68 percent of those who voted. On August 27, 2010, President Mwai Kibaki of Kenya promulgated the country's new Constitution (Constitution of Kenya 2010). This was the culmination of a journey that had begun more than two decades previously when the first attempt was made to reform the constitutional order that Kenya had inherited from Britain, its former colonial power, in 1963.

In 2011, concerned that the progress toward implementing the Agreement was slowing down, KEPSA convened a series of meetings with subject matter experts and representatives from various statutory commissions involved in implementing the Agreement and concluded as follows:

- Political violence had reduced and illegal groups fizzled out. However, members of these illegal groups had not been demobilized and these groups could very easily be mobilized at will.
- The government had made great efforts to resettle the many categories of the internally displaced persons (IDPs) due to the 2007/8 PEV (post-election violence). Some IDPs had been resettled while others

had not. Ethnic biases had also emerged in the resettlement process, with some communities turning away IDPs perceived to be from other communities.

- The coalition government had held together despite numerous challenges. There was heightened inter- and intra-political party rivalry and competition, as well as mistrust and suspicion, which collectively had resulted in reduced government efficiency and service delivery, leading to weakened confidence in the government. Over time, the relations between the president and the prime minister had improved, but the image of this improved partnership was not evident among the principals' supporters and to the wider public.
- The Constitution implementation process was underway, with a number of the constitutional implementation institutions already in place and others still under formation.
- Fault lines that caused the 2007/8 PEV had not yet been fully addressed. There was a danger of a recurrence of violence and chaos at the next general elections.
- The two parties in the coalition government had demonstrated limited focus on reforms as there was now growing attention on strengthening positions for the next general elections.

The emerging issues related to the 2013 elections were also identified. First, Kenya was witnessing the crisis of two publics, with the majority of Kenyans not able to crystallize the contribution of the state to their welfare. This possibly explains why ethnicity remains entrenched in Kenya and people turn to ethnic networks for their welfare support.[17] Second, the electoral system lacked mechanisms to prevent politicians from mobilizing and exploiting the masses using ethnicity. Third, the devolved government/county system would likely create tribal fiefdoms and further polarize the country.[18] Fourth, importantly, was that there was no evidence of any common values that held Kenyans together. There was, therefore, a need to develop a set of supra-national values and a supreme national identity more powerful than ethnicity. Fifth was that the faith-based organizations had seriously compromised their position, as did the judiciary, due to accusations of taking sides in the 2007 general elections.

---

[17] To understand how ethnicity affects the whole fact of citizenship and identity, which are central to development in Kenya, see "Ethnicity and Development in Kenya: Lessons from the 2007 General Elections" (Yieke 2010).

[18] See David Ndii's commentary on the role of devolution in enabling "distributional grievances" in "Devolution is a Success Story Despite Hitches" (Ndii 2014).

KEPSA saw this as an opportunity to galvanize the country to create a viable united Kenya with strong national values and identity. The
private sector had to become the beacon of hope for Kenyans. In order
to achieve this, the private sector sought to create certainty around the
dates of the elections, address the feeling of hopelessness among the
youth, reduce the likelihood of sabotage of the national constitution
implementation process, attack the continued show of impunity from the
political class and reduce their ability to ignite fear and tension, improve
the effectiveness of civic education, monitor and attack migration of vot-
ers, campaign against the re-emergence of organized militia, and finally
disassociate itself from private sector organizations and companies that
directly supported ethnically oriented leaders.

The private sector also sought to accentuate the positives that would
create a rallying point of hope for Kenyans. This involved messaging that
would urge Kenyans to be resilient, pool together, and remain united,
look for transformational and honest leadership, work to jointly secure
their security, seek civic education, and ensure that they were part of
creating peaceful elections. In order to effect this, KEPSA developed
a national integration campaign called Mkenya Daima, its main focus
being to promote national integration and cohesion through a superior
national value system and bringing people of opposing views to share a
common platform and counter ethnicity threats. The campaign would
inspire peace to avoid a repeat of civil disorder, nurture patriotism
among Kenyans, and be steered by KEPSA but intimately involve faith-
based organizations, civil society organizations, the National Cohesion
and Integration Commission, Vision 2030 Secretariat, and the media,
legislature, and judiciary.[19]

The campaign was launched on January 30, 2012 and run up to mid-
2013. Phase I of the campaign ran from March to June 2012, with the
sub-theme "My Kenya is … ." It was intended to create a wave of positive feeling about "the power of the people" in Kenya, and to show that
people throughout the country had strong views about "what is Kenya"
and were not afraid to express them. Without being specific about the
upcoming elections it would also start seeding messages about non-
violence, tolerance, brotherhood, progress, etc.

Phase II started in July 2012 and ran until October of the same year.
Its focus was on "Tushangilie Kenya," i.e. celebrating Kenya, and hand-
ling the negatives that divided Kenyans with the sub-theme "My Kenya

---

[19] The National Cohesion and Integration Commission was created by an act of Parliament
on December 24, 2008 to encourage national cohesion and integration by outlawing discrimination on ethnic grounds (NCIC 2008).

is not ... ." It had a strong emphasis on media participation and direct activities such as town hall meetings, faith-based forums, county meetings, music and theater, community radios, and mainstream TV and radio. This phase began to deal with behavior and attitude change. It also saw the launch of "Tushangilie Kenya," the campaign's theme song. There were messages that would be continuously delivered through all the activities on what the public should expect of leaders. This was that:

- all leaders must make sense;
- all leaders must inspire peace;
- we must speak truth to power – tell them respectfully, firmly, and assertively what needs to be done;
- leaders must be conversant with issues;
- all leaders must be non-partisan.

Phase III of the campaign ran from November 2012 until April 2013. It was to cover the period from when the election date was announced and end two months after the election. This would allow for run-offs or appeals following the announcement of the election results. This phase would be a continuation of behavior and attitude change. The key message was that rights come with responsibilities. The sub-theme for this phase was "My Kenya will be ..." It was to emphasize that each Kenyan was responsible for their country; it was "my Kenya and I would do my best for the country to ensure we achieve the best outcome for the benefit of each Kenyan." This would include choosing leaders that believe and have demonstrated that Kenya comes first (Kenya "kwanza") in whatever they have done and stand for.[20]

Phase IV, which was to build on conflict mitigation capacity and application, would run concurrently with phase III while focussing on conflict-prone areas, with a view to resolving existing disputes before the elections. There were some of the key events during the Mkenya Daima campaign that shaped the style and outcomes experienced. The first was meetings with Inter Religious Council of Kenya (IRCK). This is an umbrella organization for all the faith-based organizations in the country. During these engagements, IRCK agreed that each of the faiths (Christian, Muslim, and Hindu) would craft common messages that would be used in the various religious services and meetings convened by their membership. It agreed to carry out pilots and then spread the experience once the pilots were completed.

The Media Owners Association (MOA) was engaged as part of the Mkenya Daima campaign and agreed to moderate its messaging during

---

[20] "Kwanza" is Kiswahili for first.

the campaign period as well as before, during, and after the election date. It also led to MOA conceptualizing and arranging the first ever series of live debates featuring all the presidential candidates. This was carried live by all the media houses and was an important step in moving voter discussion away from personalities and ethnicity to focussing on issues and manifestos.[21] Held just before election day, it helped to calm the rhetoric immediately prior to the election.

Several meetings were held between the Mkenya Daima campaign team and the sitting parliamentarians, the executive, and institutions involved in national peacebuilding, civic education, and cohesion or management of the election process. The main objective was again to share the messaging of the Mkenya Daima campaign and to push for inclusion in the communications and actions of these organs of government. The outcome was that as the electioneering period progressed, the emphasis on peace and accountability could be seen during political campaigns and also in the activities that these important organs were carrying out.

Community-based activities and grass-roots campaigns which were being carried out by NGOs as well as development agency projects were enrolled through meetings with the development partners, who agreed to share the Mkenya Daima messaging with staff involved in projects that they funded. They also provided some funding toward the campaign secretariat. KEPSA and its membership contributed to the messaging through engagement of employees, suppliers, service providers, and agents.

A media campaign was launched with messaging developed by the secretariat. This consisted of advertising, radio and TV interventions, jingles, and road shows, which were intentionally left "sponsor-less" but attributed purely to Mkenya Daima. This was done to avoid any of the partners from KEPSA, FBOs, NGOs, development partners, and the media being targeted as a backlash against the messaging.

The impact of all these activities was that the campaign period was relatively calm, even as the political temperatures rose in the typical personality attack rhetoric that defines the campaign style of most Kenyan politicians.[22] During the voting there were small pockets of violence, but none directly associated with the election process. When results were announced, there were some skirmishes, but these were quickly brought

---

[21] This holding of the first ever set of presidential debates in Kenya helped address some of the issues raised in "The Role of Ethnic Identity and Economic Issues in the 2007 Kenyan Elections" (Gutierrez-Romero 2007).

[22] See "Choosing peace over democracy" (Long *et al.* 2013).

under control. The elections were a close call, and the opposition ODM party challenged the results in court, as provided for in the Constitution (Long *et al.* 2014).[23] The Supreme Court upheld the election results.[24]

Key Success Factors in KEPSA Involvement

KEPSA played an important role in the 2007/8 PEV cessation as well as in the road to recovery from the PEV. It also played a catalytic role in promoting the relatively peaceful elections in 2013. The four key factors that contributed to KEPSA's ability to play the role it did were as below.

First, KEPSA's advocacy platform is one based on non-confrontation. Its way of working involves dialog with all parties seeking to come to a common ground that will be acceptable to all parties, even if there are some areas of divergence. This common ground is then strongly promoted. KEPSA is strictly non-partisan and has always worked with all players in both political and socio-developmental issues. This engagement with all parties and their inclusion in decision-making has created a strong bond of trust with all stakeholders that KEPSA deals with.

Second, the ability of the private sector to contribute to conflict prevention is considerably enhanced both when the private sector acts in a collective and coordinated fashion typical of well-run business associations, and when it joins with other spheres of society to strengthen its message. KEPSA leveraged this particular strength by building on existing institutional structures and past efforts to promote the public good in Kenya. The fact that KEPSA had been in existence for a decade, during which it engaged in promoting the interests of the private sector as well as actively pursuing reduction in hostilities during two election cycles, only helped it gain more credibility with political actors.

Third, in a country like Kenya, key political actors have private sector interests, many of which are part of KEPSA. The actors are therefore able to communicate with other businesspeople about these common interests, sharing a language of needs and interests that helps the actors see the economic importance of political stability. This was even more apparent in the 2013 election cycle, where the two leading candidates

---

[23] An exit poll conducted by US academics argues that the winning presidential threshold was allegedly not met and that there was no winner in the first round of presidential voting; see "Uhuru didn't get 50% in 2013 – US academics" (Oruko 2014). Also see "Voting Behavior and electoral irregularities in Kenya's 2013 election" (Long *et al.* 2014).

[24] See the detailed discussion of the elections and the issues prevailing immediately after in "Kenya after the elections" (International Crisis Group 2013).

came from families with vast business concerns in Kenya and the wider East Africa region.

Fourth, KEPSA is viewed as an organization with high integrity and transparency – a rare commodity in Kenya. KEPSA has not had any scandals associated with the organization from its inception. There have been attempts to tar its image, yet each time parties questioning any activity in KEPSA have been invited to examine all documentation and have recanted their accusations. KEPSA's membership is mainly business organizations that cut across all sectors of the economy, from large multinationals to the micro, small, and medium enterprises. The decade-old existence of KEPSA has been characterized by clarity of vision, an appreciation of who its clientele are, what its needs are, how the association satisfies those needs, and how governance, programs, finance, and staff are organized on a multi-year basis.[25] In its many activities, KEPSA has used its convening power as an effective foundation for bringing stakeholders to the table rather than for seeking political accommodation and favor.

In conclusion, KEPSA was able to play an important role in preventing violence during the 2013 elections due to the Mkenya Daima campaign that it crafted and then engaged a large cross section of stakeholders.[26] It was also instrumental in stemming the slide to anarchy in the country during the 2008 PEV period, as well as laying a foundation for the conciliation agreement discussions when it crafted an early, frank, and open engagement with the principals of the main political parties involved. All these interventions were possible only because KEPSA has been the one body that has stood out as a frank, non-partisan, non-confrontational, and transparent home-grown organization. KEPSA has also had a strong convening power and acted with integrity in all these interventions.

References

African Union, Office of the African Union Panel of Eminent African Personalities. 2008. "Back from the brink: The 2008 mediation process and reforms in Kenya." www.knchr.org/Portals/0/GeneralReports/back-FromBrink_web.pdf

Aseka, Eric Masinde. 2001. *Mzee Jomo Kenyatta*. Nairobi, Kenya: East African Educational Publishers.

---

[25] These attributes determine the long-term health of business associations; see *The Executive's Handbook of Trade and Business Associations: How They Work, and How to Make Them Work Effectively for You* (Mack n.d.).

[26] See a comprehensive report of this and other interventions: "The role of Kenya's private sector in peacebuilding: The case of the 2013 election cycle" (Owuor and Wisor 2014).

Atoubi, Samuel Mondays. 2008. "Election-related violence in Africa." *Conflict Trends.*

Constitution of Kenya [Kenya]. August 27, 2010. Accessed August 29, 2015. www.refworld.org/docid/4c8508822.html

Central Organization of Trade Unions (COTU). http://cotu-kenya.org/

Electoral Institute of Southern Africa (EISA). 2009. "When elections become a curse: Redressing electoral violence in Africa." Paper presented at the Electoral Institute of Southern Africa's 4th annual symposium Preventing and Managing Violent Election-Related Conflicts in Africa: Exploring Constructive Alternatives, November 17–18. www.content.eisa.org.za/pdf/pb01.pdf

Gettleman, Jeffrey. 2007. "Disputed vote plunges Kenya into bloodshed." *The New York Times*, December 31. www.nytimes.com/2007/12/31/world/africa/31kenya.html

2008. "Mob sets Kenya church on fire, killing dozens." *The New York Times*, January 2. www.nytimes.com/2008/01/02/world/africa/02kenya.html?pagewanted=all&_r=0

Guibert, Laura and Gabriel Perez-Quiros. 2013. "Measuring the economic cost of the 2007/08 post-election violence in Kenya." https://editorialexpress.com/cgi-bin/conference/download.cgi?db_name=CSAE2013&paper_id=75

Gutierrez-Romero, Roxana. 2007. "The role of ethnic identity and economic issues in the 2007 Kenyan elections." University of Oxford Department of International Development, CSAE WPS/2010–6. www.csae.ox.ac.uk/workingpapers/pdfs/2010-06text.pdf

Holland, Hereward. 2008. "Post-poll violence halves Kenya Q1 tourism revenues." *Reuters*, May 2. www.reuters.com/article/2008/05/02/idUSL02261502

International Coalition for the Responsibility to Protect (ICR2P). 2015. "The crisis in Kenya." www.responsibilitytoprotect.org/index.php/crises/crisis-in-kenya

International Crisis Group (ICG). 2013. "Kenya after the elections." International Crisis Group Africa Briefing No. 94. www.crisisgroup.org/-/media/Files/africa/horn-of-africa/kenya/b094-kenya-after-the-elections.pdf

The Kenya National Accord and Reconciliation Act, Law No. 4 of 2008, http://kenyalaw.org/kl/fileadmin/pdfdownloads/Acts/NationalAccordand ReconciliationAct_No4of2008.pdf

Kenya Private Sector Alliance (KEPSA). 2013. "MKenya Daima Report." January/April, www.kepsa.or.ke/MKENYA_DAIMA_REPORT_January_April_2013_(Full Report).pdf

Kenya Transitional Justice Network. 2013. "Report of the Truth, Justice and Reconciliation Commission, Vol. IIB." www.acordinternational.org/silo/files/kenya-tjrc-summary-report-aug-2013.pdf

Ksoll, Christopher, Rocco Machievello, and Ammeet Morjaria. 2009. "Guns and roses: The impact of the post-election violence on flower-exporting firms." University of Oxford Department of Economics, CSAE WPS/2009-06. www.csae.ox.ac.uk/workingpapers/pdfs/2009-06text.pdf

Long, James D., Karen Ferree, and Clark Gibson. 2014. "Voting behavior and electoral irregularities in Kenya's 2013 election." *Journal of East African Studies* 8:1. http://dx.doi.org/10.1080/17531055.2013.871182

Long, James D., Karuti Kanyinga, Karen E. Ferree, and Clark Gibson. 2013. "Choosing peace over democracy." *Journal of Democracy* 24 (3):145.

Lumsdaine, Benjamin, Trixie Akpedonu, and Aminata Sow. 2013. "Keeping the peace: Lessons learned from preventive actions towards Kenya's 2013 elections." Geneva Peacebuilding Platform, Paper No. 10, 11–19. www.gpplat-form.ch/sites/default/files/PP 10 Kenya – Keeping the peace.pdf

Mack, Charles S. n.d. *The Executive's Handbook of Trade and Business Associations: How They Work, and How to Make Them Work Effectively for You.* Westport, CT: Quorum Books.

McCrummen, Stephanie. 2008. "Revenge killings stoke a violent cycle in Kenya." *The Washington Post*, January 29. www.washingtonpost.com/wpdyn/content/article/2008/01/28/AR2008012800849.html

Miriri, Duncan. 2013. "Kenyan city fears violence re-run ahead of tight vote." *Reuters*, February 2. www.reuters.com/article/2013/02/27/us-kenya-elections-economy-idUSBRE91Q08420130227

National Cohesion and Integration Commission. 2008. *National Cohesion and Integration Act No. 12 of 2008.* http://kenyalaw.org/kl/fileadmin/pdfdown-loads/Acts/NationalCohesionandIntegrationAct_No12of2008.pdf

Ndii, David. 2014. "Devolution is a success story despite hitches." *Daily Nation*, April 9. www.nation.co.ke/news/politics/Devolution-is-a-success-story-despite-hitches/-/1064/2272742/-/5apyltz/-/index.html

Oruko, Ibrahim. 2014. "Uhuru didn't get 50% in 2013 – US academ-ics." *The Star*, February 12. www.the-star.co.ke/news/article-154815/uhuru-didnt-get-50-2013-us-academics

Owuor, Victor Odundo and Scott Wisor. 2014. *The role of Kenya's private sector in peacebuilding: The case of the 2013 election cycle.* Research Report. Broomfield, CO: One Earth Future Foundation. http://oneearthfuture.org/sites/oneearthfuture.org/files//documents/publications/kenyaprivatesector-policybrief_1.pdf

Shaba, R. A. 2008. "Effects of the 2007/8 post-election violence on milk marketing systems: A case of smallholder farmers in Uashin Gishu, Kenya." HBO Kennisbank. Student paper prepared for Hogeschool VHL University of Applied Sciences. www.hbo-kennisbank.nl/en/page/hborecord.view/?uploadId=vanhall_larenstein%3Aoai%3Alibrary.wur.nl%3Ascriptiesvhl%2F1897133

Stiftung, Friedrich Ebert. 2001. "Political and electoral violence in East Africa." Center for Conflict Research Working Papers on Conflict Management, No. 2. http://library.fes.de/pdf-files/bueros/kenia/0138.pdf

United Nations Office in Nairobi Kenya (UNON). n.d. www.unon.org/

The World Factbook. n.d. "Kenya." Washington, DC: Central Intelligence Agency. Continually updated. www.cia.gov/library/publications/the-world-factbook/geos/ke.html

Wrong, Michela. 2013. "Indictee for President!" *The New York Times*, sec. Latitude, March 11. http://latitude.blogs.nytimes.com/2013/03/11/being-prosecuted-by-the-i-c-c-helped-uhuru-kenyattas-chances-in-kenyas-election/

Yieke, Felicia A. 2010. "Ethnicity and development in Kenya: Lessons from the 2007 general elections." *Kenya Studies Review* 3 (3):5–16. http://kessa.org/ yahoo_site_admin/assets/docs/p8_20_Felicia_A_Yieke_Kenya_Studies_ Review_KSR-december_2011.351102108.pdf

6   R2P and the Extractive Industries

Jill Shankleman

Summary

The starting point for this chapter is that Responsibility to Protect is not a concept currently understood or embraced by oil, gas, and mining businesses. The chapter explores whether and how this might change.

It looks at the relationship between extractive industry activities and R2P from several perspectives, starting from an exploration of why R2P might be relevant to this industry, and the potential interfaces between systems for risk management, corporate social responsibility, and respect for human rights found within the extractive industries and the concept of R2P. It then describes the significant barriers to the engagement of extractive industry companies in R2P and presents conclusions about what proponents of business engagement in R2P might do to overcome these barriers.

The chapter argues that the extractive industries (oil, gas, mining) are often present in conflict states and hence more likely than many other sectors of business to find themselves facing situations in which atrocities (genocide, war crimes, ethnic cleansing, and crimes against humanity) have taken place or might take place – for example, in 2014, oil companies in South Sudan and Libya, mining companies in the Central African Republic or Democratic Republic of the Congo. Extractive companies to a greater or lesser degree (depending on their size and experience) have anticipatory security and emergency response plans designed to protect their people and physical assets in the event of violent conflict that affects them directly. These plans focus on securing the perimeter of business sites and evaluating expatriate staff. However, extractive companies are also under external pressure to include respect for human rights in their corporate social responsibility programs as a consequence of the recent soft law definition of business responsibilities in the United Nations Guiding Principles on Business and Human Rights, and mechanisms such as the Organisation for Economic Co-operation and Development (OECD) Guidelines for Multinational Enterprises.

The combination of security risks associated with operating in conflict-prone locations and the reputational and soft law pressures to be sensitive to human rights issues suggests that it might be in the interest of extractive industry companies to consider risks of R2P events and, where relevant, to develop appropriate prevention and response plans. This could lead, for example, to greater efforts to protect local workforces in the event of violent conflict. However, it is unlikely that there will be any substantive extractive industry involvement in international efforts to promote R2P in the absence of documented cases where a failure to engage has damaged businesses, or where positive engagement in R2P has benefited business performance or reputation. Those seeking to promote extractive industry engagement in R2P should consider reframing Responsibility to Protect as "responding to risks of atrocities," and use risk-based terminology that fits within the business logic of emergency response planning and human rights due diligence.

Introduction

This chapter presents a case study of one business sector – the extractive industries – and discusses the potential relevance of R2P to this sector, the various processes and management tools into which R2P issues might be inserted, and the barriers to doing so. The chapter starts with an introduction to the sector, exploring the ways in which its activities are relevant to R2P. The next section reviews the various processes that have been established to address societal risks associated with oil, gas, and mining, and the international management systems that are adopted by some, by not all, companies to address these problems. The chapter then explores the significant barriers to extractive industry businesses, including R2P within their risk management and corporate social responsibility frameworks. The chapter suggests a number of practical ways in which aspects of prevention, response, and rebuilding might be incorporated into extractive industry processes, and concludes with an assessment of how likely this is in practice.

The chapter is based on more than twenty years' experience working with extractive industry companies and the World Bank's political risk insurance arm, the Multilateral Investment Guarantee Agency (MIGA), on corporate social responsibility and human rights at the head office and operational level, and on research carried out under fellowships with the United States Institute of Peace and the Woodrow Wilson International Center for Scholars (Shankleman 2007, 2009).

R2P

The R2P doctrine ("Core Documents: Understanding RtoP" n.d.) has been developed this century under the aegis of the United Nations in response to violent civil conflict leading to mass atrocities in Bosnia, Rwanda, and Cambodia at the end of the twentieth century that the international community failed to prevent. The doctrine defines responsibilities in relation to situations of acute human rights abuse, i.e. genocide, ethnic cleansing, crimes against humanity, and war crimes in circumstances where the state is unable or unwilling to intercede, or is itself a perpetrator. The basic propositions are that the international community should encourage and assist states to exercise their responsibility to protect their populations, and where the sovereign state is unable or unwilling to act to prevent atrocities, the international community has the responsibility to intervene through diplomatic, humanitarian, or peaceful means, or by using military force. Intervention is understood as including prevention and post-violence rebuilding as well as reaction to situations of violent abuses.

Consistent with the focus of the book, this chapter examines the scope for voluntary and non-military interventions by extractive industry companies in R2P, including prevention and post-violence rebuilding as well as reaction to situations where atrocities are being perpetrated.

Why Is R2P Relevant to the Extractive Industries?

Structure of Extractives Sector Operations

The extractive industries have several attributes that make the concept of R2P potentially relevant to companies in the sector.

One critical factor is that upstream[1] oil, gas, and mining businesses locate themselves where the resources are found, in contrast to many other sectors in which businesses have more freedom to determine where to base themselves. Many resources, such as oil, gas, and minerals (such as copper, gold, and coltan), are located in fragile and conflict-prone states. For example, there are extractive industry businesses carrying out exploration or producing resources in every one of the sixteen states identified in the Fund for Peace 2014 Index of Fragile States as "Very High Alert," "High Alert," i.e. most fragile ("The Fragile States Index"

---

[1] Upstream: the searching for potential underground or underwater crude oil and natural gas fields, drilling of exploratory wells, and subsequently drilling and operating of the wells that recover and bring the crude oil and/or raw natural gas to the surface.

2014).[2] Oil produced by a mix of national and international businesses is the basis of the economy in Libya, Iraq, South Sudan, and Nigeria, all of which are experiencing violent conflict giving rise to atrocities. For the first decade of the twenty-first century, there was a marked expansion in oil and gas production in fragile states driven by high global demand and prices. However, the geography of oil and gas production is now changing fast toward a greater share of production in developed countries, notably the United States as a result of the fracking revolution, with the USA now the largest producer worldwide.[3] This geographic shift means that in contrast to a decade ago, oil companies are increasingly focussed on business risks in developed countries, risks such as political and public opposition to fracking in European countries such as the UK that are believed to have substantial resources that could be developed were opposition overcome.

A second reason why R2P is potentially relevant to the extractive industries is that investment in oil or mining exploration and production is capital intensive, fixed in place – often literally "sunk," e.g. buried pipelines or underground mines – and long term. (In contrast, much of the downstream processing and refining of oil and minerals consists of industrial processes for which the facilities can be dismantled and set up in alternative locations.)[4] Most mines or oilfields are expected to be producing for decades. Extractive industry companies, therefore, have a strong interest in the locations where they operate remaining peaceful. However, a corollary of the long-term nature of upstream extractive industry investment and the revenues it generates for governments is that in most cases warring parties take care not to damage extractive industry facilities since the wealth they generate benefits whoever controls that area. Thus, during Sudan's long civil war, oil production started and continued unaffected in the border area between what is now Sudan and South Sudan, with South Sudan then gaining most of the oil fields with independence in 2011. This pattern may be changing – in the South Sudan civil war that started in December 2013, oilfield areas are being heavily contested and oil production facilities have been damaged,

---

[2] The "Very High Alert" states are: South Sudan, Somalia, Central African Republic, Democratic Republic of the Congo, Sudan; the "High Alert" countries are: Chad, Afghanistan, Yemen, Haiti, Pakistan, Zimbabwe, Guinea, Iraq, Ivory Coast, Syria, Guinea Bissau.

[3] In 2013, the United States produced 11 percent of global oil compared with 9 percent from all of Africa, whereas in 2010 the positions were reversed (US 9 percent, Africa 12 percent) (BP 2013).

[4] See for example of a company that trades in used oil refineries, www.used-refinery.com/index.php?id=refineries0 and an example of one of many sites that advertise used mining equipment for sale, www.nelsonmachinery.com/.

leading to a fall in output and urgent investment by the government to execute repairs (Gridneff 2015). In Libya, conflict has seen oil wells largely undamaged, but vital ancillary facilities such as terminals and worker camps mined or looted (Blas 2011).

Alongside the clear business interest in peace and stability where it operates, the extractive industry faces the challenge that its presence in states with weak institutions and poor governance can itself contribute to conflict, e.g. by generating wealth that becomes contested between elite groups or regions, generating funds that can be used to finance conflict, acquiescing to extortionary "revolutionary taxes" or in-kind "gifts" that support human rights violators, or if pollution or poor management by the industry destroys livelihoods and established social structures.[5] From publication of the seminal paper on "Greed and Grievance in Civil War" (Collier and Hoeffler 2004), academic research and analysis of the policy implications of structural links between resource extraction and conflict by organizations such as the World Bank (McNeish 2010) and non-governmental organizations such as International Alert, has generated controversy and argument about the conditions under which extractive industry presence and violent conflict are linked, but has also created conditions under which extractive companies are becoming "conflict sensitive." This is reflected in a trend toward participation by extractive industry companies in various multi-stakeholder initiatives to try to avoid or reduce damaging impacts of extractive industry presence in fragile states. These initiatives, such as the Kimberley Process, the Extractive industries Transparency Initiative, the Voluntary Principles on Security and Human Rights, and more recently involvement in consultation to develop the Guiding Principles for Business and Human Rights (discussed below), provide points of reference and frameworks within which R2P could potentially be raised for discussion by extractive companies.

Where extractive companies focus on conflict, the primary concerns are localized disputes and violent conflict in the areas where they operate, especially risks of company–community conflict that could affect business operations, for example through damage to property, interrupted production, or loss of asset value. A study by the mining industry association, the International Council on Mining and Metals (ICMM), found that mining companies have been experiencing an increasing number of

---

[5] Conflict associated with resource extraction is an aspect of the wider phenomenon of "resource curse." For a good survey of the literature on the resource curse and the factors that make a country more or less likely to suffer the curse, see "Natural Resources: Curse or Blessing?" (Van der Ploeg 2011). For a detailed description of the mechanisms by which corporate behavior can exacerbate or reduce conflict, see "Conflict-Sensitive Business Practice: Guidance for External Industries" (2005).

local conflicts since 2002. Disputes are commonly about displacement of people from lands ceded by governments to extractive companies, damage to essential resources such as water, and who gets the available job opportunities. The form of conflict ranges from demonstrations and roadblocks to threats to people and property, to involving national and international NGOS in advocacy, and sometimes using litigation to press for a change in business behavior or extraction rights. Such conflicts can affect business operations, occasionally they force the shutdown of an operation, but they are rarely associated with the acute violence that R2P concepts are focussed on (ICMM 2015; Mensah and Okyere 2015).

A third important factor that makes R2P potentially relevant to extractive businesses is that because states own sub-surface resources in most countries (except the United States), businesses involved in exploration and production of sub-surface resources always operate under some sort of contractual agreement with government. Because the value of resources is usually high, these contracts are very important to the economy. Hence upstream oil and gas businesses generally have high-level and ongoing contact with governments. This is a factor that on the one hand puts extractive companies in a position of potentially being able to influence governments, and on the other hand, because of the centrality of the relationship with government to business success, can make companies reluctant to raise sensitive issues that could destabilize this essential relationship with government (Shankleman 2007).[6]

Differentiating between Types of Extractive Industry Company

Although the factors of location, longevity, and relations with government are common to the industry as a whole, the businesses in the extractives sector are far from homogenous and have differing capabilities, risk profiles, and management systems. These differences influence the extent to which extractives sector companies are currently seeing, and are likely in future to see, R2P as relevant.

There are four principal categories of company in the extractives sector. Many people are familiar with the large western companies that operate worldwide, and, in the case of oil, have integrated businesses running from upstream to retail gas stations. In most cases, the majority of raw material production by these companies is from outside the

---

[6] Note that the power in the relationship between governments and extractive companies typically shifts according to the stage of a project. At the exploration stage and before a company has invested in production, companies have more influence than after they have sunk the costs of production and governments know that they are unlikely to leave.

"home" country, with refining and other processing carried out in end-market locations. These "majors" tend to have substantial corporate political memories, sophisticated risk management systems, large numbers of employees, and a long time horizon that includes the expectation that the company will be working in each production location for decades, through from initial exploration to the end of commercially viable production. Examples include Exxon and Shell in the oil and gas sector, Rio Tinto and BHP in mining. Within the sector, it is the western majors that have been most involved in multi-stakeholder initiatives to address above-ground risks.

Another category is the large Asian part-state-owned companies that are recent entrants to the international scene and have become prominent over the past ten to fifteen years through rapid international expansion that has included acquisition of small western companies, buying into exploration and production fields operated by other companies, and securing licenses from governments in their own right. These companies are operating in several fragile and conflict states, such as South Sudan, Myanmar, the Democratic Republic of the Congo, as well as in developed countries such as Canada and Australia. However, unlike the western majors, they still undertake the majority of their production in their "home" countries while engaging in global expansion. Examples are China National Petroleum Corporation (CNPC), Petronas (Malaysia), and Aluminum Corporation of China (known as Chinalco). These companies have less developed risk management systems than the "majors," less international experience to draw on when operating in fragile states, and their management approaches are still primarily based on the ways in which they run their home country business (Shankleman 2009). Asian extractive companies have to date not been involved in initiatives to address resource and conflict issues, although the People's Republic of China is a government participant in the Kimberley Process.

A third important category of extractive industry companies in the context of operations in fragile states and R2P is those known in the oil sector as "independents" and in mining as "juniors." These are smaller companies than the majors or the Asian part-state-owned businesses and focus on exploration to find resources; the business aim of many is to sell the concession or the company itself if exploration proves successful. Key characteristics of this set of companies include being active risk takers, since exploration is inherently risky, with many exploration wells in both the oil and mining sector proving "dry," having small corporate staffs with a concentration of people working in the exploration field, and generally a short time horizon for activities in any one location. Independents and junior companies are often short lived themselves compared with the majors.[7] Some of these companies do participate in extractive industry conflict-related initiatives, but most do not.

Finally, in the oil sector most countries, except the United States and the United Kingdom, that have an oil or gas production industry have a national oil company (NOC) involved in production. In some countries, for example Norway, the NOC plays a minor role in overall production; in other countries, production is dominated by the NOC, for example Saudi Arabia where Saudi Aramco dominates oil and gas production and refining, producing more oil each year than any other oil company worldwide. Though national oil companies dominate production in the Middle East, in most countries new to oil and gas national companies are usually small, inexperienced, and passive partners. National companies are rare in the mining sector. A few national oil companies, notably Norway's Statoil, Malaysia's Petronas, and Brazil's Petrobras, are involved in international oil industry initiatives, but most are not.

Risk Management and Corporate Social Responsibility (CSR)

Risk management is central to extractive industry businesses. Exploration and production carry risks to workers and to the environment; commerce in oil and mining products is highly vulnerable to commercial risks arising from price volatility; worldwide, companies face political risks from governments ranging from sudden imposition of extra taxes to recall of production concessions. Typically extractive companies regularly conduct a range of technical, commercial, environmental, health and safety, and governmental risk analyses of their operations. Risks are often expressed in their potential financial costs, for example from delayed production or the need for additional security systems. Extractive industry risk assessment focusses primarily on risks to the business.

Project risk assessment systems examine all aspects of risk associated with a project as part of step-by-step decision-making on whether to progress from exploration to oil field or mine development. Experienced extractive industry companies identify above-ground risks, including political, social, and environmental factors, as a distinct risk category and devote considerable attention to this. Note, however, that small companies (particularly those operating in conflict areas but with little experience of these environments) can fail to recognize the category of above-ground risk at all. "We will operate just like we do in Australia."[8]

---

[7] The trade press is a good source of information about exploration, trade in extractive industry concessions, and extractive industry companies. For example, www.rigzone.com/news/ and www.mining.com/.

[8] Personal communication, mining executive, Democratic Republic of the Congo.

CSR provides another framework within which extractive companies are involved in understanding the wider social impacts of business. Over the past decade, the idea of corporate social responsibility has taken root in much of the extractives sector – especially within the larger companies. There is large variation about what this means in practice, and in the terminology used by companies, which may focus on communities, corporate citizenship, philanthropy, etc. In essence, CSR comprises voluntary spending by business on activities that benefit people who are not employees or shareholders but who may be, or may represent or influence, the communities in the countries where companies operate. Corporate CSR activities range from small-scale financial support for charitable endeavors to very large-scale and long-term community development projects and partnerships between businesses, between business and civil society, and with governments. Almost all extractive industry companies have corporate social responsibility programs and use their websites to publicize their activities. Industry organizations such as IPIECA for the oil industry and ICMM for the mining sector, and the United Nations Global Compact, facilitate networking around CSR by businesses and the development of common practices and approaches.

Advocates for extractive industry companies paying attention to issues not conventionally considered as "core," for example human rights, gender equality, or LGBT issues, typically seek to construct a business case that combines a statement of risks/costs with a statement of benefits. Thus, a 2014 paper advocating greater attention by mining companies to avoiding conflict with the local community focusses on evaluating the costs to business of conflict and the potential benefits of avoiding conflict in terms of access to investment capital. "The most frequent costs were those arising from lost productivity due to temporary shutdowns or delay. For example, a major, world-class mining project with capital expenditure of between US$3–5 billion will suffer costs of roughly US$20 million per week of delayed production in Net Present Value (NPV) terms, largely due to lost sales" (Davis and Franks 2014).

Extractive Industry Engagement with R2P

Overview

The corporate functions where R2P potentially lies within extractive industry companies are risk management and corporate social responsibility.

R2P is currently wholly absent from extractive industry risk management or corporate social responsibility concepts and vocabulary. It is not a concept discussed by corporate executives or their security, risk management, or corporate social responsibility advisers, nor an idea that the leading non-governmental organizations that advocate for more responsible behavior by extractive industry companies are promoting.[9] For example, a Harvard Kennedy School study on mining companies and conflict, based on researching multiple cases of mining and conflict, does not include any reference to responsibility to protect; nor does a comprehensive set of analyses about business, violence, and conflict published by the Red Cross (Bernard 2012).

The response of extractive industry companies to violent conflict that cannot be contained and affects business activities (including access to international airports) is generally to shut down temporarily and evacuate expatriate staff to the closest safe haven. For example, oil fields in Libya have been repeatedly shut down and reopened due to the ongoing conflict within the country, and companies including ENI and Total have evacuated expatriates (Faucon 2014). Similarly, in South Sudan, when conflict flared in late 2013, the Asian oil companies CNPC, Petronas, and ONGC shut down parts of their operations.[10] Often, however, violent conflict does not directly affect business operations. An example was the continuation of gold production in Mali during conflict over 2012–2013 because violence did not affect business operations or supplies (Desert Gold Ventures Inc. 2013; *Marketwired News* 2013).

There are some corporate actions that could be seen as reflecting R2P, but these are not labeled or understood as such. For example, tire company Firestone provided shelter in its camps to civilians during the Liberian war (Peel 2004); some oil companies provide human rights training for police and military forces in, for example, Azerbaijan and Cameroon; oil companies have intervened directly with the Burmese military to prevent use of forced labor on their projects. These activities are always analyzed in terms of human rights, corporate social responsibility, or corporate risk management, and never as reflecting R2P (Rosenau *et al.* 2009).

As well as a very small number of reported actions by extractive industry companies that could be construed as examples of R2P in practice although not conceptualized as such by the businesses involved, there is a range of overlapping regulations, multi-stakeholder processes, and voluntary performance standards for the extractive industries that are relevant to R2P. These provide, variously, examples of obligations on

---

[9] Organizations such as Global Witness, Amnesty International, Oxfam.

[10] See, for example, "ONGC Videsh Temporarily Shuts Down Its Oilfield Operations in South Sudan" (Desert Gold Ventures Inc. 2013).

companies, fora into which discussion of R2P could perhaps be inserted, and models for awareness raising and standards creating processes in the extractive industry that could potentially be drawn on to try to engage business in R2P.

Regulations

Legally binding regulations are beginning to come into force or are being drafted to increase transparency about extractive industry operations on issues where links have been made between extractive industry activities and conflict, corruption, or poor governance. These follow after more than a decade of pressure from non-governmental organizations and voluntary initiatives (discussed below). In the United States, provisions in the 2010 Dodd–Frank Financial Reform Act (Dodd–Frank Wall Street Reform and Consumer Protection Act 2010) require companies to disclose information about minerals sourced in the Democratic Republic of the Congo or neighboring countries (the "Conflict Minerals Rule"), and to disclose information on annual payments made to each government where the company has exploration or production activities.

In the European Union countries, oil, gas, mining, and timber companies will be required from 2016 to disclose information on payments to governments,[11] and the European Union is considering a conflict minerals rule.[12] The "conflict minerals" regulations apply to companies using specified minerals in their products; financial disclosure regulations apply to most extractive industry companies with upstream operations and either listed with the United States' Securities and Exchange Commission (SEC) or registered as businesses in the European Union. These regulations are indirectly relevant to R2P – the key point is that they recognize that voluntary approaches to securing changed behavior across the industry are limited because not all extractive companies choose to adopt them. However, although these regulations apply to companies within the relevant jurisdictions, in general they do not apply to state oil companies or Asian part-state-owned companies, except where these have SEC listed (in the US) or EU registered arms. For example, China's largest oil company, China National Petroleum Corporation (CNPC), has a United States listed arm, Petro China,

---

[11] "New Disclosure Requirements for the Extractive Industry and Loggers of Primary Forests in the Accounting (and Transparency) Directives," MEMO/13/54, December 6, 2013, http://europa.eu/rapid/press-release_MEMO-13-541_en.htm.

[12] "EU Proposes Responsible Trading Strategy for Minerals from Conflict Zones," European Commission, IP/14/218 May 3, 2014, http://europa.eu/rapid/press-release_IP-14-218_en.htm.

and this is covered by Dodd–Frank requirements, whereas operations under the CNPC arm (including CNPC businesses in Sudan and South Sudan) are not included.

A quasi-legal international instrument governing the behavior of multinational companies is the "Guidelines for Multinational Enterprises" (OECD 2011) issued by the OECD (n.d.).[13] The guidelines establish a broad set of responsibilities for OECD-based companies that operate abroad on issues such as environmental management, human rights, labor, technology transfer, and business practices. Each OECD member government is required to establish a "national contact point" where complaints about the behavior of multinationals seen as breaching the guidelines can be made, and must be investigated. The importance of the guidelines is that they provide a mechanism for applying the standards derived from multi-stakeholder initiatives such as those discussed below.

Multi-stakeholder Processes

The early 2000s saw three important multi-stakeholder initiatives launched to address specific problems related to extractive industries, conflict, corruption, and governance. Each was launched following collaboration between large western extractive companies, large western NGOs, and the United States and European governments, and the number has subsequently grown to embrace a wider set of participants.

The Kimberley Process Certification Scheme has set up a system for tracking the provenance of rough (unfinished) diamonds and excluding diamonds produced in conflict areas from end markets (Kimberley Process n.d.). Countries can choose to join, and the Kimberley Process secretariat reports that as of September 2014, members covered 99.9 percent of global production of rough diamonds as well as the main importing countries, including the United States, European Union Member States, China, and India. Companies and civil society organizations participate in the process as observers. Most diamond traders and processors are involved; however, Global Witness, one of the original NGO participants that was key to the establishment of the process, has since withdrawn due to concerns about ineffective controls on diamonds from countries such as Zimbabwe (Gooch 2015). In terms of R2P, the Kimberley Process allows for prohibition on trade in unprocessed diamonds from countries with active conflict – for example, in 2014 trade in rough diamonds originating from the Central African Republic was

---

[13] The "club" of developed countries with market-based economies.

banned (Kimberley Process n.d.). This could be construed as a response to atrocities.

The US and UK governments and a group of extractive industry companies and international NGOs established the Extractive Industries Transparency Initiative in 2000 (EITI 2013). This focusses on reducing the potential of government revenues from extractive industries to be misused through corruption or in financing conflict, and on alleviating producing country concerns that companies are not paying to governments all that is due under their contracts. Under the EITI process, governments choose to join. If they join, then they must ensure that a national EITI committee is set up that includes representatives of government, extractive companies, and civil society. This committee must manage a process by which all extractive companies report the payments they make to government, and this is reconciled with information from government about what is received. Any discrepancies are investigated and resolved, and the resulting reports made public. As of September 2014, forty-six countries with oil, gas, or mining production were members (twenty-nine "compliant" with the EITI standard having produced EITI reports consistent with the requirements of EITI, seventeen "candidate" members that have satisfied the organizational requirements of EITI but not yet produced a compliant report). After a slow start in 2000, EITI has expanded to include membership from both developed countries such as the United States and fragile and conflict-prone states such as the Democratic Republic of the Congo. However, some countries have been suspended from membership: Gabon, Equatorial Guinea, and Central African Republic. As with the Kimberley Process, there is a range of businesses and NGOs that are formal supporters of EITI, though this comprises principally western extractive companies and NGOs. Although EITI is not directly relevant to R2P, the regular meetings of the participating governments, companies, and NGOs might provide a forum for discussion of R2P, and the model of country-based, tri-sectoral commissions is potentially relevant to engaging business systematically in post-conflict reconstruction.

The Voluntary Principles on Security and Human Rights (VPSHR) are another voluntary initiative established by largely the same group of organizations as EITI, also in 2000 (Voluntary Principles on Security and Human Rights 2000). The VPSHR are more directly relevant in their content to R2P than the Kimberley Process or EITI. They concern the way in which security is provided to extractive industry facilities such as mines, pipelines, and oil wells, and set out a code of practice for companies designed to ensure that the security of facilities is not provided in a way that compromises the security or human rights of communities. The VPSHR require that companies conduct comprehensive security risk assessment, including identifying any risks that security provision might present to communities, set standards for the use of private security contractors, including restrictions on the use of force and provision of human rights training, and try to work with government security forces (which usually have the right to provide security to extractive industry operations) to ensure that similar standards are applied. The membership of the VPSHR is growing slowly: as of September 2014, nine governments had joined – these represent countries with extractive industries and/or the home of major extractive industry companies. Twenty-six extractive industry companies participate – these are all western companies, mostly large businesses – and eleven NGOs. As with the Kimberley Process, there has been some withdrawal by leading NGOs originally involved. The relevance of R2P to VPSHR is that risks of, and responses to, atrocities are not generally considered in VPSHR risk assessments, yet a case can be made that in fragile and conflict states, risk should be evaluated. There are frequent meetings and workshops organized directly by the VPSHR secretariat or by human rights or extractive industry organizations where it would be relevant to introduce R2P issues.

Risk and Impact Management Systems

Environmental and social impact assessment (ESIA) and corporate systems to implement the UN Guiding Principles on Business and Human Rights (Business & Human Rights Resource Centre 2015) are tools that are being used more and more frequently by extractive industry companies to influence the way in which they operate in different locations.

Before exploration or production starts at a location, ESIA looks at the social and environmental context, identifies ways in which the project could affect the context and the way in which the context could affect the project, and develops risk mitigation strategies accordingly. In most parts of the world, the impact assessment focusses on environmental impacts, and is driven by national regulations on environmental impact assessment (EIA). However, since 2006, when the private sector lending arm of the World Bank, the International Finance Corporation (IFC), first issued its Social and Environmental Performance Standards (IFC PS) (revised in 2012), the scope of impact assessments undertaken by many companies in the extractives sector has widened to include an understanding of the social context and assessment of potential social impacts (International Finance Corporation 2015). These standards have been adopted by many other banks that finance projects as well as by companies as part of their internal risk management policies.

The IFC standards indicate where appropriate impact assessment should include consideration of conflict risks – both from the perspective of how conflict or instability might affect a project and how the project might exacerbate conflict.[14] However, doing so is not yet common practice. One reason is that impact assessments are often submitted for approval to governments – and discussing conflict risks is seen as treading on sensitive ground that many governments regard as intrusive and inappropriate for foreign investors to opine on. Based on the assessment of impacts, businesses develop a social and environmental management and monitoring plan (SEMMP) that defines their commitments to the community and to avoiding environmental damage, and the resources that will be deployed to implement these commitments. One specific component of these plans is an "emergency response plan." There are examples where businesses have started to identify "human conflict or violence" as a type of emergency, although without any specific measures to address this in the response plans.[15] The IFC PS are potentially relevant to R2P in two ways. First, IFC undertakes periodic, consultative reviews of the standards after which revised standards are issued. For the next review (not yet scheduled but likely around 2017) the R2P community could become involved and present specific recommendations about when and how R2P issues should be addressed. Second, the R2P community could make the case to individual extractive industry businesses starting new projects in locations where there is a risk of violent conflict

---

[14] "For larger operations or those in unstable environments, the review will be a more complex and thorough risks and impacts identification process that may need to consider political, economic, legal, military, and social developments, any patterns and causes of violence, and potential for future conflicts. It may be necessary for clients to also assess the record and capacity of law enforcement and judicial authorities to respond appropriately and lawfully to violent situations. If there is social unrest or conflict in the project's area of influence, the client should understand not only the risks posed to its operations and personnel but also whether its operations could create or exacerbate conflict. Conversely, if the client's operations involving the use of security personnel are consistent with Performance Standard 4, they may avoid or mitigate adverse impacts on the situation and contribute to the improvement of security conditions around the project area. Clients should consider security risks associated with the entire range and all stages of their operational activities, including personnel, products, and materials being transported. The risks and impacts identification process should also address negative impacts on workers and the surrounding communities, such as the potential for increased communal tensions due to the presence of security personnel or the risk of theft and circulation of firearms used by security personnel."

[15] Digby Wells Environmental, "ESIA Update for the New Liberty Gold Mine in Liberia: ESHS submission and update of specialist reports," March 2014. http://aureus-mining.com/investors/technical-reports.

that the companies' impact assessments and emergency response plans should include consideration of the risks of conflict leading to atrocities, and of how the company would respond, for example, if one section of the community came under violent threat from another, or violent militia threatened the community.

The UN Framework for Business and Human Rights (Business & Human Rights Resource Centre 2015) issued in 2008, and the Guiding Principles for its implementation by business (UNGPs) issued in 2011 (Business & Human Rights Resource Centre 2015), have put the question of business impacts on human rights on the corporate agenda. Many large extractive industry companies participated in the consultation process leading to the Framework and the Guiding Principles. The central argument in the Framework and Guiding Principles is that while governments have the primary responsibility for ensuring protection of human rights, businesses have a responsibility to respect human rights and to remedy abuses of human rights linked to their activities. To discharge their responsibilities, businesses should have in place policy commitments regarding respect for human rights, conduct human rights due diligence on their activities to identify and remedy any risks to human rights related to their business, and have processes to remedy any abuses of rights they commit or contribute to. The UNGPs discuss the role of business in conflict areas, but focus on the business responsibility to avoid infringing human rights (complicity) without addressing the responsibilities of business where others commit abuse of rights in an area where an extractive company is operating during a conflict.

Some extractive industry companies are beginning to develop human rights policies consistent with the UNGPs. The process is most advanced in large western companies; there is little evidence that the Asian part-state-owned companies, independents, or wholly state-owned companies (with a few exceptions[16]) are yet taking steps to implement the UNGPs.[17] However, industry corporate responsibility organizations such as IPIECA (the global oil and gas industry association for environmental and social issues) and the International Council for Mining and Metals, as well as the multi-sectoral Global Compact, are providing advice to members on human rights, and it is to be expected that more extractive industry companies will develop human rights policies. The focus of extractive

---

[16] Exceptions include Statoil (Norwegian).

[17] A rapid review on October 14, 2014 of the websites of the top ten oil and gas companies (measured by market capitalization by HIS) found that four (Exxon, Shell, BP, Total) make clear statements about the UNGPs on their websites, one refers to the Universal Declaration of Human Rights (Chevron n.d.), two use the phrase "human rights" but provide no commitments or substantive discussion (Petronas, Sinopec), and three make

industry human rights policies is on identifying ways in which corporate actions might damage human rights, and putting in place systems to avoid this. The main issues identified by companies are labor rights, land acquisition, and security.

To date there is little discussion within the industry or the human rights community of ways in which businesses might contribute to the wider respect of human rights, or how extractive businesses could, or should, respond to atrocities unconnected to their activities but in locations where they operate. However, since the right to life and security is a central human rights tenet, expressed in Article 3 of the Universal Declaration of Human Rights as "everyone has the right to life, liberty and security of person,"[18] it is wholly consistent with the UNGPs that companies should consider in their human rights policies and due diligence how they would respond to the risks or actuality of violence and conflict in locations where they operate leading to threats to life, liberty, and security of persons.

Using Links with Governments

One way in which extractive businesses respond to violent conflict in the locations where they operate is by encouraging their home governments (i.e. the governments of the state within which the company has its head-quarters) to play a role, whether diplomatic or military. Such interventions are not publicized and take place below the radar, so are hard to document with certainty, but it is noticeable, for example, that China is deploying more troops to the United Nations Mission in South Sudan (UNMISS) than to any other UN peacekeeping operation, and it is claimed that China was instrumental in expanding the UNMISS mandate to include protection of civilians in the vicinity of oil facilities (Zhou 2015).

Other Factors that Could Enable Business Engagement in R2P

One important attribute of extractive companies is a workforce that is generally well educated, well paid, and comprises a mix of local people

---

no reference to human rights at all (Schlumberger, Gazprom, PetroChina). See "Firms with Investment in North American Liquids Plays Rewarded by Stock Market in 2013" (*Oil and Gas Journal* 2013), "Respecting Human Rights" (Exxon n.d.), "Respecting Human Rights" (Shell n.d.), "Human Rights Policy" (BP n.d.), and "Respecting Human Rights in our Sphere of Operations" (Total n.d.).

[18] United Nations, Universal Declaration of Human Rights, 1948, see www.un.org/en/documents/udhr/.

and expatriates. In addition, extractives companies usually have high-quality IT, communications, and logistics capabilities. These factors mean that in the context of violence and mass atrocities, companies have the potential to link into communities and out to the international community, as well as drawing on good IT, communications, and logistical resources. There were news reports about the 2014 Ebola outbreak suggesting that businesses based in Liberia, for example, were able to draw on these resources to address this emergency effectively in the areas where they were located (Beaubien 2015).

Barriers to Extractive Industry Engagement in R2P

As discussed above, R2P is not included in extractive industry risk or impact management and response frameworks at the level of individual corporations or industry organizations, although there exists a range of processes and frameworks into which R2P could potentially be inserted with benefit to people exposed to risks of atrocities as well as to corporate reputation. However, there are significant barriers to changing this and getting extractive industry involvement in R2P. The barriers derive from corporate culture, from gaps in awareness and understanding of R2P concepts, but principally from the weakness of the business case supporting engagement.

The barriers within corporate culture to incorporating R2P concepts into human rights and risk mitigation systems are twofold. First, the phrase "responsibility to" is itself a major problem. Corporate lawyers play a large role in determining what kind of corporate social responsibility commitments companies engage in, and find terminology such as "responsibility," which imply an absolute requirement, unacceptable because of the fear that they could lead to litigation if the responsibility is not discharged, or not considered by litigants to have been discharged. Adopting any commitment not required by law that exposes the business to litigation risk, even a small risk, is generally seen as unnecessary and to be avoided. In addition, at the level of operations in any given location, corporate managers often have limited understanding of tensions within the society where they operate and are reluctant to countenance conflict scenarios.

In terms of barriers deriving from weaknesses in corporate awareness and understanding of R2P, the extractives business community thinks of R2P, if at all, as a doctrine permitting military intervention by states, for example military intervention in 2011 in Libya. The wider concept of R2P as including diplomatic, humanitarian, and peaceful interventions, and interventions to prevent and rebuild as well as to respond to crimes against humanity, etc., is not well understood. Extractive companies are very reluctant to employ any concepts or terminologies that link them to military action.

The most significant barrier to extractive industry companies adopting approaches to R2P in terms of contributing to prevention, humanitarian response, and rebuilding is that the business case for using resources to understand and engage in R2P is not strong. Situations of mass atrocity are rare; for any individual business, the likelihood of coming close to a R2P situation is very low.

The core of extractive industry risk management lies in identifying risks, the extent to which each risk can be reduced/managed by the corporation, and the scale of potential impact on the business. While it can be argued that extractive companies should consider human rights risks because there are several ways in which these exist in many countries, and there are now quasi-legal instruments that mandate recognition of human rights as a business issue, the risk to businesses of being implicated in abuses on the scale that trigger R2P issues is low, and the potential for a business having a positive impact may also be low. So what effort should be devoted to R2P risks beyond existing procedures for evacuating and protecting company staff and property?

Nevertheless, what is seen as a business case can change swiftly when new risks appear, or previously recognized risks are seen as more "risky." An example is the increased attention paid by extractive companies to avoiding oil spills since the BP spill in the Gulf of Mexico in 2010, which caused environmental damage and damage to BP as a business.[19] Similarly, the swift development of extractive industry responses to the Ebola crisis in parts of West Africa, for example, the collaboration of multinational companies operating in Liberia in the Ebola Private Sector Mobilization Group (EPSMG). EPSMG is a good example of the type of contribution that extractive companies are generally willing to provide in the face of an external crisis that also has potential impacts on their activities, i.e. assisting governments and others to respond, providing essential assets and resources, acting as a clearing house to match responders' needs with corporate giving, to learn from the outbreak and work with others in support of a stronger healthcare system in the future, to raise international awareness and advocate for a larger global response and for open trade and humanitarian corridors (Golden Veroleum Liberia n.d.).

---

[19] See, for example, the Global Industry Response Group recommendations on avoiding and responding to oil spills produced by the International Association of Oil & Gas Producers, www.iogp.org/Our-library/management-committee/mutual-aid-framework.

Conclusions

The possibility that extractive companies will embrace the concept of R2P is low. However, it may be possible to persuade some extractive companies to incorporate some of the substance of R2P in their risk management systems. Encouragement would involve explaining why such action is important to society and to the business. Assertions of moral responsibility are unlikely to have traction.

For example, in terms of prevention, extractive industry companies might be encouraged to use corporate social responsibility funds for projects building community capacity to manage conflicts, assert rights, etc., and where they operate in conflict zone to use their linkages into the community and outward to host and home governments to channel information about rising tensions. Where companies have good security and community relations systems, they should be in a position to identify rising tensions at an early stage. In addition, there is potential value to companies as well as to people potentially affected from including consideration of the risks of, and company response to, ethnic cleansing or other crimes against humanity in risk mitigation and emergency response plans. For example, how would the business respond in circumstances where violent ethnic tensions lead to large numbers of people seeking shelter in their camp? Other practices that are developing as part of corporate social responsibility and human rights programs that can also be conceptualized as making a contribution to R2P include transparent, equitable, and non-discriminatory recruitment, employment, promotion, and community investment in locations with ethnic divisions and tensions. A deliberate effort to establish a workplace culture that is tolerant, non-discriminatory, and combats stereotyping would make a preventive contribution, as would monitoring tensions and incidents in the workforce and community that could lead to, or reflect, ethnic, religious, or other inter-communal tensions. Another effort would be to apply the highest environmental, social, and safety standards to avoid the damage to local communities and livelihoods that might contribute to violent conflict.

In terms of reacting to atrocities, there are also actions that extractive companies could be encouraged to take and to include in their emergency planning. For example, providing information to relevant national and international bodies – sometimes extractive industries operate in remote locations otherwise inaccessible – including protection of workers' families and neighboring communities in emergency response plans, providing shelter and evacuation or emergency medical transportation if other external (i.e. government) systems fail, making company clinics and logistics facilities available to victims, and preventing company facilities, equipment, materials, and workers from being commandeered by combatants.

The stage of rebuilding post atrocities is rather less difficult for extractive companies to engage in. Depending on the situation, maintaining their operations and the related employment may be an important support for the community during conflict: in most cases restarting operations quickly to create employment and income opportunities will be a positive step. Then, in a post-conflict environment, the preventive tools become important, too.

In order for extractive companies to consider these steps, the R2P community will need to reach out to businesses, extractive industry organizations, and influential standard-setting bodies such as the International Finance Corporation and make the case. Doing so will require country-specific case studies and examples. Extractive industry buy-in to R2P will probably also need an amended terminology – for example, "responding to risks of atrocities" is a terminology more likely to secure a positive response than "responsibility to protect."

Absent a real example where an extractive company is faced with the build-up to, or fact of, atrocities on its doorstep, and is either celebrated for an effective response or decried and denounced for failing to act, R2P is unlikely to get onto the corporate agenda. If R2P becomes relevant, then the established approach of reaching out to NGOs and international organizations, collaboration between companies, and voluntary standard setting and information exchange could be expected to start. Overall, although there could be some benefits to extractive industry companies from awareness of responsibility to protect, and some benefits to the R2P community from engagement by business, such benefits are likely to be marginal to all players.

References

Beaubien, Jason. 2015. "Firestone did what governments have not: Stopped Ebola in its tracks." *NPR.org.* Accessed May 7. www. npr.org/blogs/goatsandsoda/2014/10/06/354054915/firestone-did-what-governments-have-not-stopped-ebola-in-its-tracks

Bernard, Vincent, ed. 2012. *International Review of the Red Cross: Business, Violence and Conflict*, Issue 887. *International Committee of the Red Cross.* www.icrc. org/eng/resources/international-review/review-887-business-violence-conflict/index.jsp

Blas, Javier. 2011. "War damage to hit return of Libya crude." *Financial Times*, September 6. www.ft.com/cms/s/c382946a-d7b5-11e0-a06b-00144feabdc0,Authorised=false.html?_i_location=http%3A%2F%2Fwww. ft.com%2Fcms%2Fs%2F0%2Fc382946a-d7b5-11e0-a06b-00144feabdc0. html%3Fsiteedition%3Duk&siteedition=uk&_i_referer=#axzz3MzUfhee9

BP. 2013. "Statistical review of world energy 2013." www.bp.com/content/dam/
    bp/pdf/statistical-review/statistical_review_of_world_energy_2013.pdf
    n.d. "Human rights policy." www.bp.com/en/global/corporate/sustainability/
    society/human-rights/implementing-the-UN-guiding-principles.html
Business & Human Rights Resource Centre. 2015. "UN 'Protect, Respect and
    Remedy' Framework and Guiding Principles." Accessed May 7. http://
    business-humanrights.org/en/un-secretary-generals-special-representative-
    on-business-human-rights/un-protect-respect-and-remedy-framework-and-
    guiding-principles
Chevron. n.d. "Search results." www.chevron.com/search/?k=human%20
    rights&text=human%20rights&Header=FromHeader&ct=All%20Types;
Collier, Paul and Anke Hoeffler. 2004. "Greed and grievance in civil war." *Oxford
    Economic Papers* 56:563–595.
"Conflict-sensitive business practice: Guidance for external industries." 2005.
    International Institute for Sustainable Development. Research Report.
    www.iisd.org/pdf/2005/security_conflict_sensitive_business.pdf
"Core Documents: Understanding RtoP." 2008. International Coalition for the
    Responsibility to Protect. www.responsibilitytoprotect.org/index.php/publi-
    cations/core-rtop-documents
Davis, Rachel and Daniel Franks. 2014. "Costs of company–community con-
    flict in the extractive sector." Harvard Kennedy School. www.hks.har-
    vard.edu/m-rcbg/CSRI/research/Costs%20of%20Conflict_Davis%20%20
    Franks.pdf
Desert Gold Ventures Inc. 2013. "Desert Gold's Mali operations ongoing and
    unaffected by conflict in the north." www.desertgold.ca/news/PR_FEB_
    4.pdf
EITI. 2013. "Extractive industries transparency initiative." https://eiti.org/
ExxonMobil. n.d. "Respecting human rights." http://corporate.exxonmobil.com/
    en/community/human-rights/respecting-rights/approach?parentId=f1d5
    e90f-1506-4002-a9f4-b379a23f26ba
Faucon, Benoît. 2014. "Eni, Repsol expatriates evacuated from Libya."
    The Wall Street Journal, July 20, sec. Business. www.wsj.com/articles/
    eni-repsol-expatriates-evacuated-from-libya-1405893922
"Firms with investment in North American liquids plays rewarded by stock mar-
    ket in 2013 says IHS." 2013. *Oil and Gas Financial Journal*, March 13.
Golden Veroleum Liberia. 2014. "Ebola private sector mobilization group
    formed to fight ebola." http://goldenveroleumliberia.com/index.php/
    2014-06-20-14-21-57/latest-news/270-ebola-private-sector-mobilization-
    group-formed-to-fight-ebola
Gooch, Charmian. 2015. "Global witness leaves Kimberley Process, calls for dia-
    mond trade to be held accountable." *GlobalWitness*. Accessed May 7. https://
    www.globalwitness.org/archive/global-witness-leaves-kimberley-process-
    calls-diamond-trade-be-held-accountable/
Gridneff, Ilya. 2015. "South Sudan hires ex-Blackwater chief to restore war-hit
    oil." *Bloomberg.com*. Accessed May 5. www.bloomberg.com/news/articles/
    2014-12-18/south-sudan-hires-ex-blackwater-chief-to-restore-war-hit-oil
The International Council on Mining and Metals (ICMM). 2015. "International
    alert and ICMM collaborate to explore conflict between mining companies

and local communities." Accessed May 5. www.icmm.com/news-and-events/news/international-alert-and-icmm-collaborate-to-explore-conflict-between-mining-companies-and-local-communities

International Finance Corporation. n.d. "Sustainability at IFC." www.ifc.org/wps/wcm/connect/Topics_Ext_Content/IFC_External_Corporate_Site/IFC+Sustainability/Our+Approach/Risk+Management/Performance+Standards/

"The Kimberley Process." n.d. www.kimberleyprocess.com/en

Kimberley Process. "Administrative decision on ensuring that diamonds from the Central African Republic are not introduced into the legitimate trade." www.kimberleyprocess.com/en/2014-administrative-decision-car

Marketwired News. 2013. "Business as usual at Mali mines." Accessed May 5. www.marketwired.com/press-release/business-as-usual-at-mali-mines-lse-rrs-1745372.htm

McNeish, John Andrew. 2010. *Rethinking Resource Conflict.* Report 62052. The World Bank. http://documents.worldbank.org/curated/en/2010/09/14297302/rethinking-resource-conflict

Mensah, Seth Opoku and Seth Asare Okyere. 2015. "Mining, environment and community conflicts: A study of company–community conflicts over gold mining in the Obuasi municipality of Ghana." Accessed May 5. www.academia.edu/9771420/Mining_Environment_and_Community_Conflict_A_Study_of_Company-Community_Conflicts_over_Gold_Mining_in_the_Obuasi_Municipality_of_Ghana

Oil and Natural Gas Corporation Limited. 2013. "ONGC Videsh temporarily shuts down its oilfield operations in South Sudan." www.ongcindia.com/wps/wcm/connect/ongcindia/home/media/press_release/ongc-videsh-temporarily

Organisation for Economic Co-operation and Development (OECD). 2011. "Guidelines for multinational enterprises." www.oecd.org/corporate/mne/

n.d. "Members and partners." www.oecd.org/about/membersandpartners/

Peel, Michael. 2004. "Some day good, some day bad." *Financial Times,* July 28. www.ft.com/intl/cms/s/05b182e4-e04a-11d8-9c9c-00000e2511c8, Authorised=false.html?_i_location=http%3A%2F%2Fwww.ft.com%2Fcms%2Fs%2F0%2F05b182e4-e04a-11d8-9c9c-00000e2511c8.html%3Fsiteedition%3Duk&siteedition=uk&_i_referer=#axzz3AZNIEB4F

Rosenau, William, Peter Chalk, Renny McPherson, Michelle Parker, and Austin Long. 2009. "Corporations and counterinsurgency." Product page. www.rand.org/pubs/occasional_papers/OP259.html

Shankleman, Jill. 2007. *Oil, Profits, and Peace.* Washington, DC: United States Institute of Peace Press.

2009. *"Going Global: Chinese Oil and Mining Companies and the Governance of Resource Wealth."* Washington, DC: Woodrow Wilson International Center for Scholars.

Shell Oil. n.d. "Respecting human rights." www.shell.com/global/environment-society/society/human-rights.html

"The Fragile States Index." 2014. Fund for Peace. http://fsi.fundforpeace.org/

Total. n.d. "Respecting human rights in our sphere of operations." www.
total.com/en/society-environment/ethics-and-values/areas-focus/
respecting-human-rights-our-sphere-operations?xtmc=human%20
rights&xtnp=1&xtcr=4

United States. 2010. *Dodd–Frank Wall Street Reform and Consumer Protection
Act: conference report (to accompany H.R. 4173)*. Washington, DC: US GPO.
www.sec.gov/spotlight/dodd-frank.shtml

Van der Ploeg, Frederick. 2011. "Natural resources: Curse or blessing?" *Journal
of Economic Literature* 49 (2):366–420.

Voluntary Principles on Security and Human Rights. 2000. "The Voluntary
Principles." www.voluntaryprinciples.org/

Zhou, Hang. 2015. "Testing the limits: China's expanding role in the South
Sudanese civil war." The *Jamestown Foundation*. Accessed May 7. www.james-
town.org/programs/chinabrief/single/?tx_ttnews%5Btt_news%5D=42945

7   Information Technology, Private Actors, and the Responsibility to Protect

Kirsten Martin

> The Internet is no longer just an essential channel for commerce, entertainment and information. It has also become a stage for state control – and rebellion against it.
>
> Markoff 2009

The UN's Responsibility to Protect focusses attention on the responsibilities of the global community to intervene and prevent human rights violations. Introduced in 2001 and gaining in popularity, the Responsibility to Protect suggests two sets of responsibilities: "(1) the responsibility of a state to protect its citizens from atrocities, and (2) the responsibility of the international community to prevent and react to massive human rights violations" (Payandeh 2010).

While the focus of R2P has rightfully been on sovereign states both to protect their citizens and to prevent and react to human rights violations in other states, the role of private actors has been underexamined. Obvious examples are where communities hold firms responsible for providing weapons to brutal regimes, or ignoring the plight of the vulnerable in local communities. More generally, firms, as private actors within the international community, create responsibilities within R2P based on the consequences of their actions and their roles within the local communities: firms may engage in communities in conflict where human rights abuses occur and voluntarily take on a role as a member of the local community.

This chapter seeks to better understand how private actors can contribute to the prevention, cessation, and aftermath of R2P events such as the violation of human rights. Specifically, it focusses on firms in the information and communication technology industry (ICT), such as telecommunication and Internet communication technology, which provide products and services normally provided by state actors and that impact the ability of human rights abuses to occur.

The goal of this chapter is to develop a framework for the ethical analysis of global information technologies with an understanding of firms' obligations within R2P. The introduction of the Internet and telecommunication technologies to countries with authoritarian governments has facilitated the imprisonment of dissidents and the surveillance of citizens while also empowering users and protestors facing human rights violations. When established information technologies are introduced to new communities, such as when Google introduced its search technology to China, or when Twitter was introduced to Iran, new patterns of use prove difficult to analyze.

This chapter proceeds as follows. First, it explores the intersection of corporate responsibility, R2P, and ICT. Second, it develops the framework for the ethical analysis of ICT generally, and uses examples of Google in China and Safaricom throughout. Third, it illustrates the utility of the framework with the case of social networks and the Arab Spring of 2009.

Corporate Responsibility to Protect through ICT

Increasingly, information and communication technology firms find themselves as a tool for freedom and human flourishing as well as a possible tool for government atrocities. Social networking site WeChat was used to organize strikes against a Taiwanese company that failed to pay into a retirement fund, while the Chinese government monitors and deletes poses on social news/politics about recent protests.

This chapter sits at the intersection of corporate responsibility, the Responsibility to Protect, and information and communication technology, as shown in Figure 7.1. Each is explained below before introducing the framework for assessing information and communication firms' corporate responsibility within R2P.

Corporate Responsibility

Corporations have responsibilities across stakeholder groups that transcend the mere obligation to be profitable. Firms exist through the mutually beneficial and sustainable relationships with stakeholders such as employees, suppliers, communicates, customers, shareholders, governments, NGOs, and even competitors. And firms have corresponding responsibilities to those stakeholders: in order for those stakeholder relationships to remain mutually beneficial and sustainable, firms consider not only the consequences to those stakeholders but also principles of fairness in making decisions.

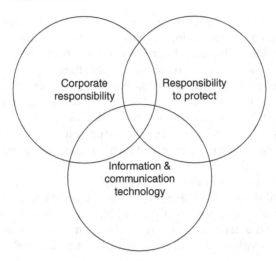

Figure 7.1 The relationship between corporate responsibility, R2P, and ICT

Firms take on these obligations based on four possible roles:

1. Firms take on responsibilities when they voluntarily enter into a relationship with a stakeholder or enter a community as part of an implicit social contract. For example, when Target opens a store in Washington, DC, it takes on responsibilities as a member of the DC community.
2. Firms may create a product or service that has the possibility for good to help the vulnerable. For example, Home Depot provides a service with the unique ability to help in a disaster, and the firm takes that responsibility seriously to pre-stock supplies ahead of a storm.
3. Firms may create a product or service that has the possibility for misuse that could cause harm. For example, mobile applications could be used to stalk victims of domestic violence through the unique design of the product.
4. Firms may be in a unique position through their knowledge and/or position within a network of stakeholders to enact change. For example, HB Fuller not only created a product – glue – that was used as a narcotic by children, but the firm was also in a unique position in a developing country to be one of the only actors in control of its own destiny. This allowed HB Fuller the role of leader and the responsibility to enact change.

Firms regularly navigate multiple stakeholder relationships and corresponding responsibilities when doing business. The challenge is in maintaining those relationships across business lines, geographic boundaries, and cultural changes.

The UN's Responsibility to Protect

The UN's Responsibility to Protect declares a state has "the responsibility to protect its populations from genocide, war crimes, ethnic cleansing and crimes against humanity." Specifically:

Each individual State has the responsibility to protect its populations from genocide, war crimes, ethnic cleansing and crimes against humanity. This responsibility entails the prevention of such crimes, including their incitement, through appropriate and necessary means. ... The international community should, as appropriate, encourage and help States to exercise this responsibility and support the United Nations in establishing an early warning capability.

Subsequent reports and analysis further emphasize the role of the international community to provide assistance to states, as well as the role of the international community to take action to prevent and halt genocide, ethnic cleansing, war crimes, and crimes against humanity.[1]

As noted by the Global Centre for the Responsibility to Protect, private actors play a pivotal role in R2P. The UN report allows for a variety of actors, including the private sector, to provide assistance in capacity building to prevent atrocities (aka Pillar II). Effective capacity building can supplement efforts by states to prevent the outbreak of atrocities and reduce the need for collective action by the international community.[2]

R2P impacts firms' general corporate responsibility in two ways. First, as members of the international community, corporations should assist in the prevention of atrocities through building capacity to protect populations even before conflicts break out. Second, firms have a responsibility during an atrocity to not only avoid assisting the perpetrator but also help the vulnerable and the victims of atrocities. These obligations link back to the sources of corporate responsibility below and in Table 7.1:

1. Firms may engage in communities in conflict where human rights abuses occur and voluntarily take on a role as a member of the local community. The decision to engage in a community in conflict carries with it a responsibility to act like a member of that community, including building capacity in populations to prevent the outbreak of atrocities and providing assistance to halt atrocities.

[1] http://responsibilitytoprotect.org/implementing%20the%20rtop.pdf; http://responsibilitytoprotect.org/index.php/about-rtop/learn-about-rtop.
[2] ICT to include telecommunication services, web and cloud services, software, consumer end use devices, telecommunication components (GNI).

Table 7.1 *Corporate responsibility and R2P*

Corporate responsibility	Within R2P	Within R2P and ICT
1. Role in the community Target in the local community	The decision to engage in a community in conflict carries with it a responsibility to act like a member of that community – including building capacity to buttress atrocities and providing assistance during an atrocity.	Safaricom, as an independently owned Kenyan company, has an obligation as a member of the Kenyan community. Safaricom benefited from the close tie to Kenya and has an obligation – which it realized – to help the vulnerable and do no harm.
2. Position to help through products and services Home Depot and hurricane relief	Firms may be in a position to assist victims of human rights violations through their products and services. Creation of product or service that has the possibility for good (help the vulnerable) in building capacity to protect populations.	Safaricom held the market for SMS bulk messaging (95 percent in Kenya), thus positioning itself as gatekeeper in the dissemination of SMS messaging in Kenya.
3. Position to harm through product and services Mobile apps and stalking	Firms may contribute to violations of human rights by aiding bad actors through products and services. Creation of a product or service that has the possibility for misuse (hurt the vulnerable) and could exacerbate atrocities.	The use of SMS text messages to initiate human rights violations in the 2007 elections illustrates the possible harm from the use of Safaricom's technology.
4. Unique position based on knowledge or physical location	Firms may be in a unique position through their knowledge and/or position within a network of stakeholders facilitating to provide assistance and build capacity for prevention of atrocities.	Safaricom is not only positioned as a gatekeeper with its technology, but its unique market power within Kenya positioned the company as a unique influence in policy negotiations with the government and mass media.

2. Firms may be in a position to help victims of human rights violations through their products and services. The creation of a product or service carries the possibility for good (help the vulnerable) in building capacity to protect populations.
3. Firms may contribute to violations of human rights by aiding bad actors through products and services. The creation of a product or service has the possibility for misuse (hurt the vulnerable) that could contribute to atrocities.
4. Firms may be in a unique position through their knowledge and/or position within a network of stakeholders to facilitate coordination of action that could provide assistance during an atrocity or to build capacity to protect populations.

Information and Communication Technology (ICT)

Both corporate stakeholder responsibility within business ethics and R2P have highlighted the importance of ICT.[3] The design of technology is value laden in that features of the design influence the possible actions and decisions of users and other actors. Understanding how a technology – including ICT – functions in its network of fellow technologies and users is critical to understanding whether the technology is ethical and the firm is being responsible (Martin 2008a).

Within R2P, the Institute for Human Rights and Business at the University of Washington School of Law notes that ICT is critical for realization of rights – civil, political, economic, social, and cultural. Firms with ICT must understand their communities' need for free expression, privacy, security, safety, and free association and assembly while using their technology (Institute for Human Rights and Business 2014). ICT companies may face issues of protecting privacy rights and freedom of expression, as well as government requests for access to user data or the removal of material.

In this way, ICT holds a special place for both R2P and corporate responsibility and business ethics. The difficulty comes in deciding the standard by which to judge or assess the ICT across global communities. The tension of abiding by home country principles versus host country rules runs through global corporate responsibility.

---

[3] While approaches to pluralism vary, key to pluralistic approaches is a move away from positioning differences as incompatible. In other words, pluralistic approaches eschew either/or solution sets. Rather than one right answer, pluralism allows for multiple right answers and a range of understandings or descriptions (Rorty 1989; Skillen 1996).

In addition, assessing technology across communities further complicates the analysis in that the technology itself may function differently in a new country. Currently, and as explored in this chapter, the introduction of ICT in authoritarian governments such as China and Iran has facilitated the imprisonment of dissidents and the surveillance of citizens while also empowering users and protestors to build support for citizens at risk. Yet, how to assess ICT is not always clear since both the technology and the surrounding stakeholder context are factors to consider.

Typically within the current ethical analysis of global innovation, the innovator is positioned as choosing between upholding one's values and becoming complicit in an immoral normative scheme in the foreign country. Solutions are framed as dichotomous based on incommensurable home country versus host country norms (Hamilton *et al.* 2009). In the case of Google in China, the organization was forced to give justifications and excuses for its complicity with the Chinese government (Dann and Haddow 2008). Firms facing R2P obligations are left with little guidance other than to exit – which might leave a population vulnerable without needed ICT.

Framework for Analyzing ICT

This chapter develops a framework for the ethical analysis of global ICT for use with R2P. Based on pluralism scholarship, the framework offered here suggests that technology should be examined by broadly considering the stakeholders of the technology, the roles and responsibilities of the actors within a particular community, and the alternatives to the innovation. The cases of ICT in authoritative regimes offer a mechanism to show the utility of such a framework. The version of pluralism utilized here requires a charitable read and open consideration of local contexts and an examination of the innovation in practice.

First, understanding ICT across cultures and borders requires understanding the roles and responsibilities of technology and stakeholders. For example, within Science and Technology Studies, Latour (2000) examines the distribution of roles and responsibility within a network of technology and stakeholders, and the important influence a technology has on the responsibility of fellow members of a social system. Latour leverages the seemingly benign examples of door closer and automobile safety devices to illustrate how roles and responsibilities are allocated to both technological and human actors to accomplish a goal. For example, a door closer's default settings (e.g. holding the door open versus closed) impacts who is viewed as responsible for closing the door (Latour 2000). At one extreme would be a door designed with a doorman assigned to the job of closing the door, relieving both the door and those who pass through from shutting the door. However, a hydraulic closer that shuts the door automatically relieves those who pass through from being responsible for ensuring that the door is closed and makes the role of doorman unnecessary. Importantly, different roles are not necessarily considered unethical only because the roles are different, allowing ICT to take on important ethical roles in R2P.

In addition to accommodating the important impact of ICT on the actions of others, the pluralistic framework moves away from dogmatism. For example, James (1907) positions pluralism as a movement against intolerance. James uses the example of an artificial clearing in the woods as being viewed by a farmer, who completed the clearing, as a personal victory. However, in coming upon the clearing, James first describes his reaction to the scene as revulsion. James saw the clearing as hideous: "The clearing which to me was a mere ugly picture on the retina, was to them a symbol redolent with moral memories and sang a very paean of duty, struggle, and success" (James 1907, 134; Rorty 1989, 38). The question for James was not whether or not he and the farmer held the same principles and values, but how seemingly incommensurable views could be redescribed. Consider how Google was judged for taking on a different role in China. Rorty notes that James's pluralistic approach to this clearing is not a reality–appearance distinction but another redescription or set of metaphors. Several descriptions of the same event are possible without asking which one is right (Rorty 1989). Redescriptions are a "tool rather than a claim to have discovered any essence" (Rorty 1989, 39).

Important for the analysis of global Internet technology, these distinct descriptions warrant an examination in and of themselves and not necessarily in reference to one right description. In other words, the farmer deserves as much consideration as James in his description of the clearing. In regards to global information technology, disruptive innovations that cross borders into new communities deserve to be considered on their own merits as novel innovations and not solely in reference to a standard of use developed in a prior community or country – for example, the US. Therefore, the criterion for success, failure, or effectiveness of an innovation is not a stable, intrinsic property of the technology but rather a contingent property studied within a stakeholder community.

Based on broader pluralism scholarship, a pluralistic approach can be broken down into key components in order to build a framework for the ethical assessment of global innovation in general and Internet technology here.

1.   *Situate ICT in Context*

Similar to James situating the clearing within the context of the farmer's world, ICT is best understood within the larger stakeholder community. Such a context helps to fully appreciate the potential role of ICT within the stakeholder community to identify and understand the participants in their environment, including stakeholders both influencing and influenced by technologies, for example google.cn and Twitter. These material and non-material actors within an innovation system co-shape each other (Johnson 2001), rely upon each other to complete tasks, and exist in a codependent relationship.

For example with Google in China, multiple governmental agencies, cybercafes, cyber police, regulated content providers, regulated access providers, NGOs, fellow citizens, users, users' families and friends, and even villagers without electricity are impacted by Google's search technology, google.cn, as in Figure 7.2.

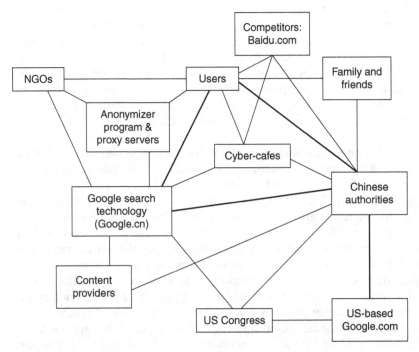

Figure 7.2 The relationship between ICT entities in China

The government was impacted by the increase in information traded among its citizens and, in reaction, increased its regulation of Internet providers and the surveillance and arrests of citizens through 30,000 Internet police and surveillance programs. This Great Firewall of China, the common name for the Chinese government's pervasive Internet surveillance and control, directly impacted all Internet activity, including google.cn (Canaves and Chao 2010).

In addition, NGOs and dissidents attempted to provide access to unfiltered information by developing tools such as proxy servers and anonymizer programs to circumvent government filters. The computer software *Fanqiang* supported a growing market for counter-surveillance software for Chinese users that was bolstered only when China blocked major sites such as Google's YouTube in March 2009 (Canaves and Chao 2010). Approximately 1 million people in China used a service provided by Global Internet Freedom (GIF) that was maintained by fifty volunteers around the world. The group was founded in 1999 by members of the Falun Gong sect living in the United States to provide unfiltered information about Falun Gong to China (Stone and Barboza 2010). In addition to proxy servers, virtual private networks (VPNs) allowed citizens to access the Internet through alternative servers that supported anonymous and unfiltered access to websites. Super-users were creative, active, and knowledgeable citizens who became an integral part of searching online in China.

2.   Analyze a Range of Roles and Responsibilities

Roles and functionalities of a technology vary based on the adopting community. Google.cn's role in China was complicated and can be described as contributing to three additional goals in China to the expected function as a search engine in less restrictive countries: (1) as a tool of censorship by Chinese authorities, (2) as a buffer between the government and the Chinese citizens, and (3) as an alternative gateway to information.

First, as has been widely reported, google.cn played an active role in government censorship by self-filtering search results. Blocking sites was not the primary method for controlling content by the Chinese; instead the Chinese authorities relied upon self-censorship by technologies such as google.cn. In this way, google.cn acts in obedient complicity (p. 459) with Chinese censorship "in a manner that results in Chinese people being unable to have access to websites to which they arguably have a right of access" (Brenkert 2009, 460).

Second, google.cn provided enhanced anonymity for users compared with alternatives. While alternative Internet technologies, such as

Microsoft and Yahoo!, have proven to be less adept at protecting the identity of their users (Martin 2008b), Google, Inc. decided to maintain all personal information associated with email and weblogs outside Chinese territory and outside the jurisdiction of Chinese authorities, thus allowing google.cn to differentiate itself from competitors and become an important part of citizens maintaining anonymity online.

Finally, google.cn supported Chinese users in accessing additional information normally censored by Chinese authorities. Google.com search technology was located outside Chinese territory, relied on a few fiber optic pipes to carry information to and from the user's computer in China, and was easily monitored and blocked through a few data checkpoints. However, google.cn resided within Chinese territory, thereby avoiding some filtering routers and allowing multiple points of connection for Chinese users. Google.cn's presence offered not just a competitive alternative to Baidu and other search technologies but also an important alternative route for users attempting to circumvent surveillance and censorship.

3.   *Compare Descriptions and Roles to Alternatives in Practice*

Finally, to enrich, enhance, and expand stakeholders is relative to alternatives in practice rather than in comparison with an objective standard of use from a previous community. Roles and responsibilities must be examined in comparison with alternative solutions rather than a single ideal based on previous patterns of use.

If the goal is more access to news and communication between citizens, google.cn and its competitors enhance the goal of providing the most information possible to Chinese citizens. If the innovation system's goal is avoiding censorship and surveillance, providing yet another route for users in China, google.cn enhances and enriches the stakeholders in Figure 7.1 by making censorship and surveillance more difficult. If the goal is to act as a buffer between Chinese authorities and Internet users in China, google.cn played an important role shielding Baidu from the censorship battle (LaFraniere 2010). "Without Google, Baidu will be very easy to manipulate," said a twenty-year-old computer science major at Tsinghua (LaFraniere 2010).

Finally, google.cn played a symbolic role in China. As noted by Hu Yong, a journalism professor at Peking University, "This is a matter of the future and whether the government's Internet policy wants to fight with the future … If this process goes on, more and more people are going to realize that their freedom of information is being infringed upon, and this could bring changes down the line" (LaFraniere 2010).

Through google.cn, Google performed a role of a fellow agitator of the Chinese authorities.

Google.cn performs its role as a buffer between the government and Chinese citizens, and as an important partner with competitors and proxy servers, to provide a complex vehicle for the dissemination of and access to censored information. Privately developed proxy servers, anonymizer programs, and Chinese users work in conjunction with Google's search technology to give Chinese citizens access to censored material and support circumventing surveillance. While google.com is able to provide broad search results, the combination of google.cn, Baidu, users, super-users, anonymizer programs, NGOs, and proxy servers provides parallel results for the Chinese citizens.

Framework for Responsible Management of ICT

	Corporate stakeholder responsibility		
	Place in context of stakeholder relationships	Identify roles and responsibilities of actors	Compare with alternatives in practice
Questions for R2P and ICT analysis	Who or what is influenced by your technology or influences the effective delivery of your service?	What are the various roles your ICT plays in the stakeholder diagram?	Are you in a unique position to effect change? Are you a hindrance to change? Is a vulnerable population better off with your presence? Are atrocities more likely or more intense with your presence?
Within R2P Safaricom in Kenya	Safaricom. NCIC, content service providers, origina-tors of bulk SMS, competition, Communication Commission of Kenya (CCK), mainstream media, Kenyan citizens.	As gatekeeper to message Kenyans with 95 percent of SMS market and 65 percent of mobile phone market. As a possible vehicle for hate speech. As a citizen of Kenya (an inde-pendent Kenyan company).	2007 elections with uncensored SMS messages to Kenyan citizens provides the alter-native to avoid.

Corporate stakeholder responsibility		
Place in context of stakeholder relationships	Identify roles and responsibilities of actors	Compare with alternatives in practice
ICT and R2P Twitter and Arab Spring	Twitter, proxy servers, multiple "front doors" (e.g. websites, texts, phones, PDAs), Iranian citizens (word of mouth), NGOs, Tor, citizens in other countries (to hide locations). Twitter in Iran is illustrative of a technological infrastructure that works to circumvent an authoritarian government and provides an example of multiple routes as an effective strategy against censorship.	As access to censored information. As a route for news to be disseminated. As a mechanism for citizens to organize.	ICT within the Arab Spring builds capacity and assists victims of atrocities by providing a news outlet giving voice to those victimized and alerting the international community as to the situation. In addition, ICT supported freedom of movement and association to empower the vulnerable.

Framework in Action: Twitter in Iran and the 2011 Arab Spring

While Internet technologies in China have drawn sharp criticism, information and communication technologies in other authoritarian countries have received praise for their ability to empower vulnerable citizens and work against atrocities by not only helping victims during an atrocity but also building capacity to protect vulnerable populations to prevent an atrocity.

Iran 2009

During protests over the Iranian national elections in 2009, foreign journalists were forced to leave Iran, and citizens became the primary providers of news and pictures (Stone and Cohen 2009). State-controlled telecommunications were shut down and then reinstated, with spotty use for weeks. Eventually, even texting became unavailable, and Twitter became the vehicle to disseminate news about the candidates and the election, as well as current and future protests (Stelter and Stone 2009).

The Iranian uprising in 2009 proved to be a precursor to the protests throughout the Middle East and northern Africa over the following two years. Similar to the start of the Iranian movement, a video of the beating to death of a twenty-eight-year-old businessman, Khaled Said, became a rallying point for protestors across Tunisia, Egypt, and Bahrain. Khaled Said had been beaten to death by Egyptian police in the lobby of a residential building. The video was eventually posted on Facebook in June 2010 with the statement "We are all Khaled Said."

Arab Spring

Six months later, Tunisian protests began what became the Arab Spring. The Tunisian government shut down the television network and closed schools and universities in January 2011 as protests began to spread throughout the capital (Worth and Kirkpatrick 2011). Using Facebook and Twitter, protestors were still able to organize demonstrations, in which many individuals were arrested and killed by the Tunisian military.

Shortly after the Tunisian uprisings, there were large protests in Egypt as well as smaller demonstrations in Bahrain, Jordan, Sudan, Yemen, and Libya, from January through March 2011 (Gettleman 2011; MacFarqhar 2011; Shadid and Bronner 2011). The original Facebook page dedicated to Khaled Said was a focal point for dissidents to communicate and organize protests in Egypt, with more than 500,000 users during the Arab Spring. Throughout these protests, social networking sites such as Twitter, YouTube, Flickr, and Facebook proved pivotal for citizens accessing censored information as well as communicating with fellow citizens.

While each country has a distinct political, economic, and demographic context for its uprising, several factors offer a common thread to tie together these demonstrations and protests and provide a link to the situation in China. First, each government sought the centralized control of information and news (Stelter and Stone 2009) by cutting long-distance phone lines, restricting access by foreigners, and owning or heavily regulating communications such as television and radio. For example, in Tunisia, the television station was shut down immediately and the owner was arrested for "grand treason" (Worth and Kirkpatrick 2011). In order to control the news, the Egyptian government owns 99 percent of all newspaper publishers and newsstands, and 72 percent of Egyptians watch the state-owned television channel (Walker and Orltung 2011). Also, regimes would slow down the Internet to make connections frustrating for citizens. After the Iranian election, the state-controlled telecom provider went down completely for part of the day, and then traffic was slow for weeks (Stelter and Stone 2009). Dictators controlled the media and offered a "parallel reality" (Walker and Orltung 2011). Similarly, Chinese authorities monitored users accessing "harmful" content that included material about democracy (for example, freedom), religious cults (such as Falun Gong), or anti-government protests (for example, Tiananmen Square) (Martin 2008b). Chinese authorities even established reporting centers to encourage citizens to report "harmful" information (McMahon 2006). In addition, China had what was called the "50-cent party," comprised of Chinese citizens who were paid 50 cents per post to flood anti-government sites with pro-government messages (Shane 2011). Controlling the information and communication technology became a precursor to atrocities such as war crimes and crimes against humanity.

Second, each government imposed strict limitations on gathering and organizing leaving populations vulnerable to human rights violations by authoritative governments. Tunisia closed universities and schools at the beginning of the protests (Worth and Kirkpatrick 2011). Dissidents were imprisoned, tortured, and killed for expressing alternative views or attending protests against the regime. Governments used pervasive tracking of individuals both online and offline. Iran and Syria used surveillance technologies by Nokia and Siemens Network in 2009 as well as CacheFlow in 2011 to monitor citizens' communications. Similarly, the Chinese government had a band of 30,000 Internet police to monitor its citizens as well as surveillance technology to ensure citizens were not breaking censorship laws.

ICT within the Arab Spring assisted victims of atrocities by providing a news outlet, giving voice to those victimized and alerting the international community as to each situation. In addition, ICT facilitated freedom of movement and association to empower the vulnerable.

1.   Situate Twitter in Context: Twitter's Stakeholders

Twitter highlights the importance of stakeholders to a technology since the technology relies heavily on many other stakeholders to act as different front doors or gateways in order to function. Unlike other Internet technologies – such as social networking sites, traditional websites, search engines, blogs, etc. – users have always been able to access Twitter feeds through multiple routes and platforms such as other websites, texts, phones, PDAs, and computers without users actually visiting Twitter's site. This tactic is normally not strategically advantageous, as Twitter cannot deliver reliable users to advertisers and hence cannot easily monetize its service (Sullivan 2009).

In Iran, Twitter's open architecture proved particularly resilient to censorship. When text messaging, Internet, and cellphone transmissions were unavailable in Iran during the political upheaval after the 2009 elections, citizens found ways to still communicate through proxy servers and software (Stone and Cohen 2009). Proxy servers are computers that are hidden or unknown to surveillance and redirect users to currently censored material. The Internet user visits the non-blocked proxy server located outside the country in order to be bounced to content normally blocked by authorities. In order to work, multiple proxy server addresses must be available to the user and not to the authorities. As noted during the summer 2009 uprisings after the national Iranian elections, in the face of an increasingly restrictive Iranian government, which was censoring millions of websites, "more than 400,000 Iranians were surfing the uncensored Web" (Markoff 2009). Shiyu Zhou, founder of the organization providing anti-censorship software and tools, said: "In China we have sent mass e-mails, but nothing like in Iran ... The Iranian people actually found out by themselves and have passed this on by word of mouth" (Smith and Cohen 2009). When the Egyptian government cut access to the Internet, page views by Egyptians on Ultra Surf, a free proxy-based privacy tool, increased ten-fold to 7.8 million page views per day from only 76,000 the day before. In other words, Internet and information technology in Iran during 2009 and the 2011 Arab Spring was possible due to the many technologies and individuals providing multiple access points to the Internet, thereby making government control much more difficult.

To increase the number of users, NGOs took an active role and developed training for citizens without access or knowledge of social networking sites. For example, Hiber was started by Jordanian Mariam Abu Adas for social media training in more remote areas during the Arab Spring. Such training was necessary for many citizens not familiar with social networking technology or how to use it safely without being monitored (Slackman 2011). Stakeholders, such as NGOs, the Global Internet Freedom Consortium, the Tor Project, or Psiphon, provided software to work around censorship and authoritarian governments, thereby allowing users to send untraceable messages and to reach censored websites (Markoff 2009; Stone and Cohen 2009).

The ability to access Twitter through multiple points proved critical with a government focussed on curtailing communication. When one communication technology was disabled by the government or became just too dangerous, an alternative was still available to utilize Twitter for communication. For example, when cell phone and Internet service was disabled, social networking technology such as Twitter or Facebook relied on "old media" technologies using a satellite to remain available (Farrell 2011). Al Jazeera, a global television station, also proved helpful in disseminating information by showing videos taken by protestors (Worth and Kirkpatrick 2011). Therefore, when Internet connections would become unreliable, previously posted videos were still available on television.

2.   *Analyze a Range of Roles and Responsibilities*

Within a controlling, authoritative context, ICTs take on decidedly different roles than in a more open environment by providing (a) access to censored news, (b) a route to disseminate news to outsiders, and (c) a mechanism for citizens to organize. These roles are critical to preventing atrocities through building capacity to protect populations even before conflicts break out as well as to help the vulnerable and victims of atrocities.

During the Iranian protests over the 2009 elections, foreign journalists were forced to leave Iran and citizens became the primary providers of news and pictures (Stone and Cohen 2009). Suddenly, Twitter became the vehicle to access news about the candidates, the election, as well as current and future protests. By allowing access to censored news, "new kinds of social media are challenging those traditional levers of state media control and allowing Iranians to find novel ways around the restrictions" (Stone and Cohen 2009). Social networking technology provided access to information not controlled by the state or other regimes. Realizing the important role of Twitter in accessing information, the US State Department began a Twitter feed in Arabic and Persian, and soon followed with feeds in Chinese, Russian, and Hindi (Landler and Knowlton 2011; Preston 2011).

In addition to providing access, social networking technologies and the community of stakeholders provided a mechanism for news to be disseminated. The forty-second video of Neda Agha-Soltan's death that began the protests in Iran was sent to a series of individuals who then posted it on Facebook. A self-immolation video in Tunisia was similarly disseminated on Facebook rather than through traditional media outlets. While in the US mainstream media was the largest user of Twitter

(Bilton 2011), the role of Twitter in the Middle East was as an alternative news source, used also by journalists to source and verify stories (Stelter 2011). As noted by James E. Katz, director of the Rutgers Center for Mobile Communication Studies, the most powerful weapon in getting around the "manipulation of the old centralized technologies" became the tiny camera inside cell phones (Preston 2011; Stelter 2011).

Finally, Facebook and Twitter were the primary tools for activists to gather, mobilize, and protest (Preston 2011). The system of social networking sites provides multiple avenues for communication, which then becomes difficult to control. Hashtags on Twitter help spread protest information (Preston 2011). Twitter users asked supporters to form an online attack on Iranian government servers, and a Facebook site gained more than 70,000 supporters for "April 6 Youth Movement" (Preston 2011). The site of the Khaled Said beating video, "We are all Khaled Said," in June 2010, remained the largest dissident Facebook page during the Arab Spring (Preston 2011), and a Facebook group called Moroccans Discuss the King had 3,000 members in five days. Women, who could not meet unaccompanied, could chat online (Slackman 2011), and social networking technologies provided new means for ordinary people to connect with human rights activists (Preston 2011).

Within a system of technology and stakeholders, each social network technology performs a role with associated responsibilities that impacts the roles and responsibilities of fellow stakeholders. Proxy servers and multiple access points gave users access to Twitter, thereby relieving Twitter from the task of ensuring its website was always accessible within tightly controlled countries. Twitter and other social network technologies gave users an outlet to disseminate news, so that journalists did not need to be the sole source of news during the protests. Social networking technologies worked jointly with a larger system of stakeholders, NGOs, citizens, cameras, satellite phones, etc. to increase access to censored information, allow wide dissemination of information, and support citizens in organizing.

3.   *Compare Descriptions and Roles to Alternatives in Practice*

Twitter and social network technologies such as Facebook made key decisions in accessing and disseminating news as well as allowing citizens to gather and organize. There were some slight modifications – for example, Facebook upgraded security for all users after Tunisian government officials used a virus to obtain local Facebook passwords (Preston 2011). However, Google and YouTube were even more willing to embrace their roles in activism during the Arab Spring. First, when the Internet was unavailable, Twitter specifically created Speak2Tweet, allowing people to leave voicemail messages that would be filed as a Twitter update. This modification made even access to the Internet unnecessary in order to disseminate news via Twitter. Later, Twitter added a local number for Speak2Tweet for Egyptians so that long-distance telephone access was not even necessary. In addition, YouTube worked with Storyful, a social media news curation service, to help people retrieve and share thousands of videos pouring in from Tahrir Square during the Egyptian uprising, thus helping citizens organize more easily (Hauser 2011).

Not all decisions supported the laudable goals of access to information and organization. Facebook shut down a popular protest page of Wael Ghonim, a Google executive who was a symbol of the revolt, when he used a pseudonym. While the requirement for real names helps Facebook ensure accountability in its users' statements and actions in a more open context, the requirement to use real names became a mechanism for surveillance in an authoritative regime. When the Egyptian government correctly identified Wael Ghonim and his role on Facebook, the executive was imprisoned for twelve days (Preston 2011). Similarly, Flickr removed pictures of Egyptian security police when the company realized that the individual who posted the pictures did not actually take the photos (Preston 2011). Requirements for identification and ownership did not support the role of these social networking sites in curtailing surveillance and disseminating news in Iran and during the Arab Spring.

Interestingly, the aftermath of the Arab Spring and Iran in 2009 suggests that the use of social networking technologies, such as Twitter and Facebook, is similarly complicated. These technologies also became actors in a system of surveillance by authoritarian governments. The Iranian government proved adept at using Internet technologies to go after activists and followed electronic trails left by activists online (Shane 2011). Iran also crowd-sourced the hunt for protestors by posting unidentified photos and soliciting input from the public in order to identify people. The very factors that brought Facebook and similar communication success have huge appeal to secret police as social network sites provide a dossier of activists. Facebook is a "great database for government now," noted Ahed al-Hindi, a Syrian activist (Shane 2011). Bloggers were imprisoned in Egypt for "insulting the military establishment based on 73 screenshots of blogs and Facebook pages" (Stack and Bronner 2011), and the Egyptian government monitored text, Skype, and email based on records found after the fall of the government (Stack and MacFarquhar 2011). Soon citizens became aware of social networking technology's dual role. In Egypt, demonstrators instructed that a twenty-six-page anti-government leaflet be passed by email and by photocopying rather than by Twitter and Facebook in order to avoid the growing surveillance of the social networking technologies (Shane 2011).

Discussion and Conclusion

The framework offered here, grounded in the pragmatic tradition of pluralism, suggests global ICT should be examined by initially considering three factors: the stakeholders of the technology, the roles and responsibilities of the actors within a particular community, and the alternatives to the innovation. To illustrate the pluralistic framework, ICT, such as Twitter in Iran and the Arab Spring, is illustrative of a technological infrastructure that works to circumvent an authoritarian government and provides an example of multiple routes as an effective strategy against censorship.

While one can mistakenly focus on Internet technology used as a tool for censorship by authoritarian governments, these technologies also play an important role in the technological infrastructure necessary for citizens to gain access to information and communicate with peers safely, thereby playing an important role in R2P. While google.cn functions as both a buffer between Chinese citizens and their government and a partner with proxy servers and competitors to provide users multiple points of access to receive and disseminate information, Twitter plays an important role as a communication vehicle between Iranian citizens and the international community. In both situations, the ICT firms worked toward the prevention of atrocities by building capacity to protect populations even before conflicts broke out. In addition, the presence of ICT helped the vulnerable and victims of atrocities and communicated the ongoing atrocities to the international community.

Given the role of proxy servers in the lives of citizens under authoritarian governments, maintaining multiple Internet gateways is critical to giving citizens alternatives paths to communicate. In respecting different environments and patterns of use, google.cn, Twitter, and other networking Internet technologies must be open to different stakeholders' systems, alternatives, and roles and responsibilities to create solutions that enrich and enhance populations. In fact, to not change the role and functionality of a disruptive ICT may ignore the very real, situated demands on stakeholders for those at risk of atrocities.

This chapter contributes to a nascent discussion around corporate responsibility and R2P. Additional questions include:

1. Who needs protecting within the idea of R2P for firms? What are the criteria for vulnerable groups needing protection? The cases offered

here are with the benefit of hindsight. And, with the case of Safaricom, a precedent was already set in 2007 highlighting the possible atrocities. However, pending atrocities are not always clear, as evidenced by the backlash against Google in China.

2. Which firms or industries might play a role within R2P? This chapter focusses on ICT, but the intersection between corporate responsibilities and the responsibility to protect needs further consideration.

3. What are the associated responsibilities of firms and managers when engaging in communities in conflict? This chapter outlines the sources of obligations for corporations generally and within the scope of R2P; however, more work should be done to specify the sources and the substance of obligations with R2P for corporations.

The Digital Dangers project is an initiative of the Institute for Human Rights and Business. It identifies six risks ICT firms face, including disconnecting or disrupting access, monitoring, evaluating, and blocking user content at the request of third parties, selling dual-use technology with possibility of misuse, complying with government orders, monitoring user content, and handing over user content and data to the state (Institute for Human Rights and Business 2014). Yet ICT firms face these issues in every country, including the United States, and without imminent risk of genocide, war crimes, ethnic cleansing, or crimes against humanity. More work is necessary to spell out the risks faced by ICT firms around R2P in particular. The Global Network Initiative is moving in that direction with practical advice for firms.

References

Bilton, Nick. 2011. "Mainstream media still drive majority of Twitter trends." *The New York Times*, February 15.

Brenkert, George. 2009. "Google, human rights, and compromise." *Journal of Business Ethics* 85 (4):453–478.

Canaves, Sky. 2010. "In China, imitation is the sincerest form of flattering Google." *The Wall Street Journal*, January 29. http://blogs.wsj.com/digits/2010/01/29/in-china-imitation-is the-sincerest-form-of-flattering-google/

Canaves, Sky and Loretta Chao. 2010. "Chinese web users use plan tech workarounds." *The Wall Street Journal*, January 15. http://online.wsj.com/article/SB10001424052748704363504575002772946324934.html?mod=article-outset-box

Dann, Gary E. and Neil Haddow. 2008. "Just doing business or doing just business: Google, Microsoft, Yahoo! and the business of censoring Chinese internet." *Journal of Business Ethics* 79, 219–234.

Farrell, Stephen. 2011. "What not to bring to Tahrir Square." *The New York Times*, February 8. http://lens.blogs.nytimes.com/2011/02/08/what-not-to-bring-to-tahrir-square/

Gettleman, Jeffrey. 2011. "Young Sudanese start protest movement." *The New York Times*, February 2.

Hamilton, J. Brook, Stephen B. Knouse, and Vanessa Hill. 2009. "Google in China: A manager-friendly heuristic model for resolving cross-cultural ethical conflicts." *Journal of Business Ethics* 86 (2):143–157.

Hauser, Christine. 2011. "New service lets voices from Egypt be heard." *The New York Times*, February 1.

Institute for Human Rights and Business and the University of Washington School of Law. 2014. "Digital dangers: Identifying and mitigating threats to human rights in the digital realm." www.ihrb.org/our-work/digital-dangers.html

James, William. 1899. "On a certain blindness in human beings." In *Talks to Teachers on Psychology: And to Students on Some of Life's Ideals*, edited by F. Burkhadt and F. Bowers. Cambridge, MA: Harvard University Press, reprint 1983.

1907. *Pragmatism, a New Name for Some Old Ways of Thinking*. Cambridge, MA: Harvard University Press, reprint 1975.

Johnson, Deborah, G. 2001. *Computer Ethics*. Upper Saddle River, NJ: Prentice Hall.

LaFraniere, Sharon. 2010. "China at odds with future in internet fight." *The New York Times*, January 16. www.nytimes.com/2010/01/17/world/asia/17china.html

Landler, Mark and Brian Knowlton. 2011. "U.S. policy to address internet freedom." *The New York Times*, February 14.

Latour, Bruno. 2000. "Where are the missing masses? The sociology of a few mundane artifacts." In *Shaping Technology/Building Society: Studies in Socio-Technical Change*, edited by W. E. Bijker and J. Law. Cambridge, MA: MIT Press, 225–258.

MacFarqhar, Neil. 2011. "Unrest spreads, some violently, in Middle East." *The New York Times*, February 17.

Markoff, John. 2009. "Iranians and others outwit net censors." *The New York Times*, April 30. www.nytimes.com/2009/05/01/technology/01filter.html?fta=y

Martin, Kirsten. 2007. "Google in China." Case BRI-005. Business Roundtable Institute for Corporate Ethics. www.darden.virginia.edu/corporate-ethics/pdf/Case_BRI-1005_Google_in_China_condensed.pdf

2008a. "Innovation, ethics, and business." Bridge Paper Series. Business Roundtable Institute for Corporate Ethics. www.darden.virginia.edu/corporate-ethics/pdf/innovation_ethics.pdf

2008b. "Internet technologies in China: Insights on the morally important influence of managers." *Journal of Business Ethics* 83 (3):489–501.

Payandeh, M. 2010. "With great power comes great responsibility – the concept of the responsibility to protect within the process of international lawmaking." *Yale Journal of International Law* 35:469. www.yjil.org/docs/pub/35-2-payandeh-great-responsibility.pdf

Preston, Jennifer. 2011. "Ethical quandary for social sites." *The New York Times*, March 27.

Rorty, Richard. 1989. *Contingency, Irony, and Solidarity*. Cambridge University Press.

Shadid, Anthony and Ethan Bronner. 2011. "Protests unsettle Jordan while most other neighbors stay calm." *The New York Times*, January 28.

Shane, Scott. 2011. "Spotlight again falls on web tools and change." *The New York Times*, January 29.

Skillen, Anthony. 1996. "William James, 'a certain blindness' and an uncertain pluralism." In *Philosophy and Pluralism*, edited by David Archard. Cambridge University Press.

Slackman, Michael. 2011. "Bullets stall youthful push for Arab Spring." *The New York Times*, March 17. www.nytimes.com/2011/03/18/world/middleeast/18youth.html?pagewanted=all

Smith, Brad and Noam Cohen. 2009. "Social networks spread defiance online." *The New York Times*, June 15. www.nytimes.com/2009/06/16/world/middleeast/16media.html

Stack, Liam and Ethan Bronner. 2011. "Egypt sentences blogger to 3 years." *The New York Times*, April 11. www.nytimes.com/2011/04/12/world/middleeast/12egypt.html?_r=0

Stack, Liam and Neil MacFarquhar. 2011. "Egyptians get view of extent of spying." *The New York Times*, March 9.

Stelter, Brian. 2011. "Twitter feed evolves into a news wire about Egypt." *The New York Times*, February 13.

Stelter, Brian and Brad Stone. 2009. "Stark images, uploaded to the world." *The New York Times*, June 17. www.nytimes.com/2009/06/18/world/middleeast/18press.html?r=2

Stone, Brad and David Barboza. 2010. "Scaling the digital wall in China." *The New York Times*, January 16. www.nytimes.com/2010/01/16/technology/internet/16evade.html?pagewanted=all

Stone, Brad and Noam Cohen. 2009. "Social networks spread defiance online." *The New York Times*, 15.

Sullivan, Bob. 2009. "Twitter 1, Censors 0: Why it's still working." *The MSNBC Red Tape Chronicles*, June 18. http://redtape.msnbc.com/2009/06/twitter-1-censorship-0-why-its-working.html

Walker, Christopher and Robert Orltung. 2011. "Lies and videotape." *The New York Times*, April 22.

Worth, Robert F. and David D. Kirkpatrick. 2011. "Seizing a moment, Al Jazeera galvanizes Arab frustration." *The New York Times*, January 27. www.nytimes.com/2011/01/28/world/middleeast/28jazeera.html

8 Corporate Responsibility to Protect Populations from Mass Atrocities

Vesselin Popovski

Introduction

The private sector has been gradually recognized as being an instrumental factor for the achievement of all three main agenda of the United Nations – peace and security, economic and social development, and human rights. Among the three, the most natural one for the private sector to contribute is the second UN agenda; in fact, the economic development cannot be even imagined without the role of private companies, being these local or multinational, small, medium, or big.

The role of the private sector for the first UN agenda – peace and security – is less clear and more debatable, but there has been a good amount of recent literature (Nelson 2000; Slim 2012) elaborating on how businesses can engage in preventing or mitigating conflicts, in post-conflict rebuilding, and, in a more limited way, in direct engagement to stop violence, reach ceasefire, and make peace.

The role of the private sector in promoting the third agenda – human rights – has gained significant recognition in the last decade, although not without serious initial critical debate (Muchlinski 2001, 31–47). The leadership and hard work of John Ruggie and others materialized in the adoption of the "Guiding Principles" and the framework for business and human rights, "Protect, Respect, and Remedy."[1]

This chapter argues that the role of the private sector is essential for both human rights and peace, and the concept Responsibility to Protect is exactly that crucial nexus that brings together and synergizes corporate responsibility for respecting human rights with corporate responsibility for maintaining peace and security.

The chapter, along with the rest of the book, introduces the notion of corporate R2P (CR2P) and offers a classification of six specific roles that the private sector can play for building R2P sensitivity and preventing

---

[1] www.business-humanrights.org/SpecialRepPortal/Home/Protect-Respect-Remedy-Framework/GuidingPrinciples. Also, www.ohchr.org/EN/Issues/Business/Pages/BusinessIndex.aspx.

mass atrocities. It starts by reflecting on the question as to whether R2P is solely a responsibility of states (state-centric approach), or whether there is scope for individuals, civil society, and the private sector to engage in R2P. Answering for the latter, the chapter lists six roles that the private sector can undertake – non-perpetrator, mitigator, assistant protector, direct protector, compensator, and re-builder – and analyzes these roles in ensuring R2P sensitivity in its activities. It discusses what can be done to motivate and incentivize companies to optimize their CR2P. The chapter then moves on to present a model code of conduct for CR2P and presents five stages of corporate involvement, before concluding with some policy recommendations.

State-centric, Individual and Corporate R2P

The concept Responsibility to Protect, universally accepted at the 2005 World Summit, originated primarily as a state-centric concept. Para. 138 of the World Summit Outcome Document refers to "each individual state" as having the R2P, but also suggests that the "international community should, as appropriate, encourage and help states to exercise this responsibility" (UN General Assembly 2005, 31). In 2009 the UN Secretary-General (SG) produced a report, "Implementing Responsibility to Protect" (UN General Assembly 2009) (hereafter "2009 SG Report"), introducing three pillars of R2P: pillar one is the responsibility of states to protect their populations; pillar two is the responsibility of the international community to assist in developing capacity of states to protect populations; and pillar three is the international community taking timely and decisive actions, when states manifestly fail to protect. It is an interesting sequence of using both states and international community when referring to who the responsibility belongs to Does the R2P belong to states? What does international community mean in this context?

I argue that pillar one and pillar three, as formulated in the 2009 SG Report, are entirely state-oriented. Even if pillar three refers to international community, it obligates the timely and decisive actions to be taken through the Security Council, effectively by its five permanent members or the most powerful states. However, pillar two – known as the "assistance pillar" – presents an opportunity for a large engagement of non-state actors and individuals. In fact, in Section III of the 2009 SG Report "International Assistance and Capacity-building" one finds numerous references to civil society and the private sector, for example encouraging "to draw on the cooperation of Member States, regional and sub-regional arrangements, civil society and the private sector" (UN General Assembly 2009, 15–22).

Paragraph 27 of the 2009 SG Report introduces what can be called "individual responsibility to protect":

Similarly, one of the keys to preventing small crimes from becoming large ones, as well as to ending such affronts to human dignity altogether, is to foster individual responsibility. Even in the worst genocide, there are ordinary people, who refuse to be complicit in the collective evil, who display the values, the independence and the will to say no to those who would plunge their societies into cauldrons of cruelty, injustice, hatred and violence. We need to do more to recognize their courage and to learn from their actions. States that have suffered such traumas, civil society and international organizations can facilitate the development of national and transnational networks of survivors, so that their stories and lessons can be more widely heard, thus helping to prevent their reoccurrence or repetition elsewhere.

Recently Ed Luck (the principal author of the 2009 Report in his capacity as SG Special Representative on R2P at the time) developed in detail the IR2P (Luck and Luck 2015). He listed seven groups of individuals related to IR2P: 1) vulnerable populations who are likely to be targeted; 2) bystanders and would-be or actual perpetrators; 3) group and community leaders; 4) national leaders; 5) leaders of influential foreign countries; 6) key officials and decision-makers in international organizations; and 7) survivors, physical and/or emotional casualties. One group clearly missing in this list are the business leaders. To exemplify, Oskar Schindler, a large industrialist in Nazi Germany, saved thousands of lives of Jews during the Nazi period, by employing them in his factories and protecting them from extradition to the concentration camps.

The move from state-centrism to individualism and corporatism can be observed not only with regard of R2P. Other concepts, such as protection of human rights or conflict prevention and peacebuilding, also initially emerged and have developed as mostly state-centric, but over the years they shifted toward inclusion of non-state actors.

R2P applies narrowly to four well-defined mass atrocities – genocide, war crimes, crimes against humanity, and ethnic cleansing. One can regard protecting populations from these crimes as part of the constitutional general responsibility of all states to protect human rights,[2] though keeping in mind the narrow scope of R2P and the very broad scope of human rights. There are many types of human rights violations – pollution and other environmental crimes, exploitation of child labor, discrimination of women, minorities, migrants, or other groups – where

---

[2] The 2005 UN Secretary-General's Report "In Larger Freedom" correctly puts R2P under the section "Freedom to Live in Dignity" (human rights) instead of "Freedom from Fear" (peace and security).

corporate responsibility would be essential and companies can play a significant role in preventing such violations, but these would not fall under the narrow scope of R2P and would not be part of the analysis here. Only human rights violations that amount to crimes against humanity – such as planned and systematic extermination, or forceful deportation of population, or destruction of cultural property, etc. – would fit into the scope of R2P.

Conflict prevention and peacebuilding are in themselves very broad activities for which the private sector can play a significant role, but as far as R2P deals only with a limited type of atrocities, its scope focusses on prevention of precisely those mass atrocities, instead of dealing generally with conflict prevention or peacebuilding. Certainly, many mass atrocities happen during wars – all war crimes by definition happen during armed conflicts – and therefore there is a natural synergy between efforts to prevent conflicts and efforts to reduce mass atrocities.

The peace and security agenda has significantly connected with the human rights agenda over the last decades, and R2P is a strong part of that connection, especially when it comes to the most serious violations. The 2014 SG report on R2P, entirely focussing on pillar two, elaborates on the role of the private sector in its Para. 26:

Private sector actors can contribute to building resilience by strengthening local economies and employing a workforce inclusive of all social groups. In some cases, private sector expertise can be mobilized through public–private partnerships to enhance the impact of national measures aimed at atrocity prevention. On the other hand, experience shows that businesses can both indirectly contribute to the commission of atrocity crimes through their operations and business practices, particularly in extractive industries, and directly enable those engaged in such acts through their products and services. Private sector actors can reduce this risk by complying with the 2011 UN Guiding Principles on Business and Human Rights, and ensuring that their commercial activities do not exacerbate social cleavages. They could also consider developing risk management tools that explicitly incorporate atrocity crime risks.

UN Security Council 2014

To develop and systematize further these opportunities and guidelines I present a taxonomy of six roles that the private sector can exercise out of R2P sensitivity to prevent, mitigate, or respond to mass atrocities.

CR2P: Taxonomy of Roles

1. Non-perpetrator
2. Mitigator.

3. Assistant protector.
4. Direct protector.
5. Compensator.
6. Rebuilder.

The first two roles are preventive, the third and fourth roles are responsive to mass atrocities, and the last two are rebuilding roles.

1.   Non-perpetrator

The role of non-perpetrator is a minimal, "do no harm" role, which requires simply that corporations do not engage in atrocities, or activities complicit to atrocities. In Nazi Germany, some industries engaged in activities associated with genocide and crimes against humanity, and these were prosecuted by the International Military Tribunal at Nuremberg and by German national courts. A landmark case or corporate responsibility for war crimes was I.G. Farben, a chemical company patenting and supplying Zyklon B, a poisonous gas used in Nazi concentration camps (Hayes 2000). At the hearings at Nuremberg the defense tried to argue that there was no hard evidence that I.G. Farben intended to supply gas to be used for human extermination. However, the judges ruled that it was sufficient for the prosecution to show that I.G. Farben supplied the gas knowing its lethal effect on people, and such knowledge in itself was a sufficient triggering mechanism for aiding and abetting liability. Individual businessmen, if not the whole corporations – Krupp, Flick, Tesch – also faced prosecution and were sentenced in complicity with war crimes, committed by the Nazis. Several banks, including Deutsche Bank, have been associated with transactions and dealing with "teeth gold" and jewels from Holocaust victims (Steinberg 1999).

Prosecuting an organization has been traditionally problematic unless it is legally characterized as criminal, like the Sicilian mafia or, in the case of Nazi Germany, the Gestapo or the SS. In the aftermath of World War II, the Allies were able to prosecute individuals for mere membership in those organizations (Kelly 2012). In recent times, the pressure has been on multinational corporations, especially those operating in politically charged or environmentally sensitive regions (Nelson 2000). For instance, in Nigeria, an investigation led by the NGO Watchdog Platform implicated the corporation Shell in fueling the armed conflict in the Niger Delta region. In a single transaction in 2010, Shell is said to have transferred $159,000 to a group known for instigating violence in the oil-rich region. This report claims that such payments indirectly contributed to the death of many civilians (Smith 2011). It should be recalled that Shell came under international scrutiny in 1994 when the Abacha regime (1993–1998) in Nigeria executed the environmental activist Ken Saro Wiwa and eight of his Ogoni compatriots for protesting Shell's environmental policies (Bennett 2001). In Indonesia, the company Freeport-McMoRan Copper and Gold Inc. (operating in Irian Jaya, West Papua) came under criticism because of serious abuses by Indonesian security forces perceived to be acting on behalf of the company. These abuses led to local rioting, civil lawsuits by the indigenous Amungme Tribal Council, and a series of campaigns against the company by leading NGOs (Bennett 2001).

During the civil war in Sudan between the Muslim Arab government and the Christian rebels in the south, the Canadian Talisman Energy and other multinational companies were criticized by NGOs for tacitly aiding through royalty payments the government in Khartoum, which engaged in grave human rights violations against civilians (Bennett 2001). Most of these companies, aware of the negative impacts of their activities, have since adopted preventive policies and are working with human rights organizations helping the local communities. Talisman, for instance, has developed a human rights monitoring program, which includes training security forces to respect human rights.

Association with a criminal organization is ipso facto prosecutable when such organization is designated as criminal. A member of Al-Qaeda or ISIS based on membership alone can be detained and prosecuted in courts in the USA and Europe. Private companies, however, have never been designated as criminal, even if jurisdictionally this is possible following from the Nuremberg charter. The acquittal of the Nazi economic minister Schacht, and the light sentence for the head of Nazi industrial production Speer, signaled a reluctance to go for a frontal attack against corporations in later trials. Krupp, I.G. Farben, and other industries, whose corporate officers underwent separate trials after Nuremberg, were never branded criminal organizations and only some of their officers were tried.

In another case, Anvil Mining Ltd., a Canadian company, was accused of complicity in atrocity crimes in the Democratic Republic of the Congo (DRC) (Spittaels and Meynen 2007). In October 2004, the Congolese Armed Forces (the FARDC) conducted torture, rapes, illegal detentions, looting and extra-judicial executions of seventy people after shelling and crushing an uprising in the town of Kilwa. Anvil Mining, located 50 km from Kilwa, provided logistical transportation to the FARDC. In November 2010 a group of Congolese citizens filed a petition in a district court in Montreal against Anvil Mining's role in the Kilwa massacre, claiming that the company's vehicles transported the Congolese soldiers and the local civilians, taken outside the town to be executed. The petition also alleged that Anvil Mining leased aircraft for the military to fly from the capital of the province to Kilwa. The legal action was taken after a repeated failure of the DRC judicial system to deliver justice – in 2006 a local military prosecutor indicted nine soldiers and three former Anvil Mining employees, including a Canadian citizen, for war crimes, but after numerous irregularities during the trial, the tribunal acquitted all defendants. The UN High Commissioner for Human Rights at the time, Louise Arbour, raised a serious concern "at the court's conclusions that the events in Kilwa were the accidental results of fighting, despite the presence at the trial of substantial eye-witness testimony and material evidence pointing the commission of serious and deliberate human rights violations" (UNHCR 2006). The Anvil Mining case is, at the time of writing, lodged in appeal at the Supreme Court of Canada. Guus Kouwenhoven, a Dutch arms trader, was accused of supplying weapons in violation of the UN embargo and in complicity with war crimes committed by Liberian troops and militias. In June 2006, The Hague District Court sentenced Kouwenhoven to eight years in prison. However, the Court of Appeal overruled the conviction and acquitted Kouwenhoven of all charges, including alleged war crimes. The prosecution brought the case to the Supreme Court, which in 2010 ordered a retrial.

In another case, Unocal (Myanmar) the plaintiffs claimed corporate liability under the Alien Tort Claims Act (ATCA) of 1789 for aiding and abetting the government's ethnic-based violence. The judges acquitted the corporation from complicity with the mass atrocities. Another case, though not R2P relevant, was the plight of the Niger Delta communities in Nigeria in 2013 for five charges of oil spills and river pollution against Shell, taking the company to a Dutch court, which acquitted Shell on four of these five, but ordered the company to compensate for the fifth count (Harvey 2013). Given the foregoing, one interesting question would be whether corporations themselves can volunteer to compensate victims, instead of waiting to be sued and ordered to do so, and this will be elaborated later when discussing the fifth role – compensator.

2. Mitigator

The private sector can contribute to preventing and mitigating mass atrocities through its networks of social investment and engagement, institutional strengthening, incorporating social and environmental codes and human rights guidelines. The role of mitigator, in contrast with the first role of non-perpetrator, can be exercised both individually and collectively. There would be an admirable accumulative and multiplying effect if companies not only develop their R2P culture but also influence other businesses through professional associations, chambers of commerce, business forums, and so on.

Ethnic or religious tensions can be mitigated in various ways, for example by employing workers in non-discriminatory ways, banning ethnic divisions in the workplace, ensuring equality of opportunities for all, providing prayer rooms for all, etc. R2P sensitivity can be developed through such positive efforts contributing to general non-discriminatory work environment and eliminating religious divisions.

Although it is rare for companies to become directly involved in peaceful settlement, and even less in military deployment (unless they provide military logistics as a core business activity), there have been examples of business engagements in mediation efforts to avoid escalation of violence and atrocities, for example in South Africa, Sri Lanka, Nepal, and elsewhere (Iff et al. 2010). One such example can be seen with Lonrho, whose founder, Tiny Rowland, given his popularity and influence in Mozambique, initiated and sustained a constant dialog between the factions in the civil war and the regional leaders in South Africa, Malawi, Zimbabwe, and Zambia, leading to the peaceful settlement in Mozambique in the 1980s (Naraghi-Anderlini et al. 2001).

Another example, documented by Desgrandchamps, shows how during the escalation of the Nigerian civil war of 1967–1970, the International Committee of the Red Cross (ICRC) lobbied large Swiss companies to send some of their senior employees to assist in mitigating the conflict and in brokering a peace agreement between the Nigerian government and the seceding Biafra Republic. Enrico Bignami, vice-president of Nestlé-Alimentana and founder of the IMEDE business school in Lausanne, engaged in tireless goodwill mediation, helping to achieve peace (Desgrandchamps 2012).

Companies can contribute to mitigation and de-escalation of conflicts through commercial or philanthropic support for humanitarian relief and through responsible management of security arrangements for their operations, thereby minimizing the risks of atrocities. The post-election violence in Kenya in 2007–2008 represents such a call, when corporations in Kenya engaged in significant peacemaking and peacebuilding efforts, documented comprehensively by the One Earth Future Report "The Role of Kenya's Private Sector in Peacebuilding: The Case of the 2013 Election Cycle," listing the following roles: sponsorship of candidates, public communication, media sensitizing, legislative advocacy, peace commitments, preventing incitement, facilitating debates, private diplomacy, active neutrality, risk management, employee management (Owuor and Wisor 2014).

Other chapters in this book reflect on these efforts in Kenya in more detail; here I would only emphasize the role of media mitigation. During the violence in 2007–2008 there was a significant ethnic incitement in the Kenyan media and the hate speech was disseminated through social media platforms; however, before the 2013 elections the private sector and the government made commendable joint efforts to ensure non-discrimination, law, and order, working closely with media and private phone service providers to eliminate hate speech, to support educational programs, to promote social cohesion, and to spread the message of "never again" as a mitigation tool against mass atrocities.

3.   *Assistant Protector*

The third role that the private sector can exercise is no longer preventive, as the first two, but emerges during atrocities. I define this role as "assistant protector," where companies offer logistics, transportation vehicles, food, water, medicine, and other supplies needed for the survival of victims of mass atrocities. Even small enterprises – bakeries, groceries, pharmacies – can be instrumental first-line respondents in critical times, rescuing people from death and starvation. An example of how a private business can be an assistant protector can be seen with the French company Nutriset, which developed a product, Plumpy'nut – a very easy-to-use paste in a plastic wrapper, supplied to severely malnourished children – and offered it to starving populations and victims of deliberate famines. Certainly, such products could help victims of both human-made and natural disasters, too.

Companies can also assist by donating services in addition to goods, such as, for example, pro bono transportation, psychological trauma relief, medical care, financial services, etc. An interesting example of the latter is the highly recognized private sector initiative Cash Learning Partnership,[3] where emergency cash transfers and vouchers across the humanitarian sector become effective tools to support populations at risk in a way that maintains dignity and choice for beneficiaries while stimulating the local economies and markets. Companies can provide humanitarian agencies with experts to assist in protecting civilians against atrocities. During the Nigerian civil war, the ICRC solicited the support of individuals, companies, and agencies to assist the large-scale humanitarian operations in Biafra. One example of a company that responded to the ICRC's plea was the Swiss Trading Company, which sent a representative, Karl Jaggi, to become the head of the ICRC delegation in

---

[3] www.cashlearning.org

Biafra in 1967 (Desgrandchamps 2012). In addition, a Swiss director of an international transport company was sent to Nigeria and entrusted with the coordination of the relief operation in the federal territory. Thus, from 1968, the key positions in the rescue operation of the ICRC were held by Swiss citizens who were recruited from political and economic circles, namely the Commissioner-General, the heads of the delegation in Nigeria and Biafra, Lindt, Schürch, and Jaggi (Desgrandchamps 2012).

During the Kosovo war in 1999, Microsoft designed a computerized registration system for the UN High Commissioner for Refugees (Bennett 2001). Other partnerships forged between corporations and international humanitarian agencies include IBM's support of ICRC's website, and Cisco Systems' support of UNDP's NetAid.org initiative, which raised more than $12 million and mobilized the involvement of 3,000 NGOs and 200 corporations to support humanitarian causes. Ericsson, a telephone company, has a partnership with the UN Office for the Coordination of Humanitarian Affairs (OCHA) and the ICRC to work on a major disaster response program, providing communication aid for humanitarian relief workers (Bennett 2001).

With the escalation of atrocities committed by Boko Haram in Nigeria in 2014, business enterprises were filling up the gap left by the state's inability to protect endangered populations. For example, businessmen in Nigeria, rallied by Nduka Obaigbena, the publisher of *Thisday* newspaper, offered $10 million to protect children through the Safe Schools Initiative established by Gordon Brown, former UK prime minister, in some of the schools in north-eastern Nigeria vulnerable to the attacks of Boko Haram (*The Economist* 2014). At a special meeting in the House of Commons on the kidnapped schoolgirls in Nigeria, charity organizations and business leaders pledged to contribute toward raising the $100 million target set by the Nigerian finance ministry for the fortification and protection of the schools against possible future attempts by Boko Haram (Brown and Brown 2014).

4.   Direct Protector

Businesses can not only assist but even provide full and direct protection in times of mass atrocities. A landmark example is Oskar Schindler, the German industrialist who saved more than 1,000 lives by employing Jews in his factories, hiding their identities, and protecting their extradition to the Nazi concentration camps. Also, no single Jew was extradited from Bulgaria to the Nazi camps during World War II, and the main factor was not the Tsar or the government (who were trying to please the Nazi occupiers) but the firm opposition of the civil society and the industrialists in Bulgaria.

During the 1994 genocide in Rwanda, Paul Rusesabagina, the manager of Hotel des Mille Collines in Kigali, used his position to save 1,268 Tutsies, who otherwise would have been killed immediately. He hid them in his hotel, rationed water from the swimming pool, and bribed the Hutu soldiers to remove the checkpoints. Although initially driven by the need to save his own Tutsi wife and their four children, he extended the protection to all Tutsies in the hotel and none of them was killed.

Other excellent examples of direct protection are companies such as Rio Tinto and Barclays, which did not abandon their offices in Zimbabwe during the violence in 2008; on the contrary, they stayed in Harare, sacrificing some profits – the primary purpose of any business – so as to help and protect their employees in difficult times. Some companies, having in mind the extremely high daily inflation, paid with food baskets instead of cash salaries, saving their employees from starvation. In Zimbabwe, companies have also formed partnerships with humanitarian agencies in times of extreme disasters so as to protect human lives: *Deutsche Post* with the UN OCHA, Siemens with the ICRC, Motorola with CARE International, for example (Binder and Witte 2007).

The role of direct protector is rare but crucial, or to use the R2P jargon – it is "narrow, but deep." Only in very narrowly defined situations will this role be activated, but these will be exactly the best tests for the corporate R2P sensitivity.

5.   Compensator

The role of compensator is interesting and different from the other roles, as it can be a result of courts' litigations and decisions, from voluntary compensations because of feelings of guilt for being implicated in mass atrocities, but also a result of bona fide willingness to help out of R2P sensitivity and to contribute generally to compensation funds for victims. The record of such responsibility, however, is not yet very promising; in fact, there remain many more lawsuits filed against multinational corporations for wrongdoings than corporations' volunteer offers of compensations. During the South African apartheid, denounced as a crime against humanity, the UN Security Council resolutions urged banks and corporations not to lend money, not to sell oil, and not to sell military technology to the apartheid government. Many companies operating in South Africa were later sued for damages as a result of their business-as-usual policies during apartheid. The lawsuits, filed with the US courts under the ATCA, which essentially allows companies trading in the USA to be sued for human rights violations anywhere in the world, were against banks – Barclays and NatWest; Citigroup and JP Morgan Chase;

Commerz and Deutsche Bank; UBS and Credit Suisse; Credit Lyonnais and Banque Indo-Suez; and also against corporations such as the Anglo American and De Beers corporations, Ford, IBM, Royal Dutch/Shell and Exxon Mobil.

The same ATCA provision formed the basis of multi-billion-dollar claims in the 1990s against Swiss banks and German and Austrian firms using forced or slave labor during the Nazi regime. In that case, the parties reached an agreement in August 1998 to settle the lawsuits in principle for $1.25 billion, and a Global Settlement for this amount was signed in January 1999. The settlement was paid by the Swiss banks and the plaintiffs agreed to release and discharge Swiss banks, the Swiss government, and other Swiss entities from any further claims relating to the Holocaust and World War II.

It would be good to see examples when companies volunteer to pay compensation to victims, instead of defending lawsuits in courts. However, we often observe the opposite – companies pay high bills to lawyers, instead of showing generosity to victims of atrocities. Winning a case in court and not paying a penny to victims will not improve the image of companies profiteering from and sponsoring regimes during which crimes against humanity were committed.

There should be ways through various schemes to incentivize companies – through tax benefits or other privileges, even if they do not feel guilty and complicit in profiting from the business atmosphere of the times when R2P crimes were committed – to engage in voluntary compensations and this would not mean in any way be an admission of guilt. Such schemes, apart from privileges in taxation and investment opportunities, can include joint public–private voluntary compensation funds.

Companies may also consider employing surviving victims of mass atrocities and their relatives, in addition to offering cash contributions. For that matter, it would be interesting to explore connections between CR2P and what has already been largely acknowledged and developed as corporate social responsibility. In fact, CR2P can be seen as part of, or as the "younger sister" of, the more general CSR, and similar mechanisms for helping the victims can be applicable.

6.   Rebuilder

Finally, the role of rebuilder is important because responsible businesses can largely support post-conflict reconstruction and reconciliation, and, accordingly, build tolerance and prevent atrocities from reoccurring. Through commercial participation in rebuilding infrastructure and investing in key sectors, companies can create conditions for resuming trade, increasing domestic and foreign investment, promoting macro-economic stabilization, rehabilitating financial institutions, and restoring legal and regulatory frameworks. Many cross-sector partnerships promote international security and explore conflict prevention, crisis management, and post-conflict reconstruction strategies that address the principal causes of conflict: corruption, poverty, and social inequality (Bennett 2002). In the Balkans, for instance, the Swiss–Swedish construction company ABB has improved and encouraged ethnic relations in the workplace by uniting Serbs, Kosovars, and Bosnians to work toward "re-building war damaged electricity infrastructure" (Bennett 2001). In South Africa, several business leaders merged two business organizations (the Urban Foundation and CBM) into the National Business Initiative, under the auspices of which the South African business leaders contributed to socio-economic reconstruction in the post-apartheid era by "developing nationwide, replicable programmes in housing delivery, education quality, local economic development and local government capacity building" (Bennett 2001). Still, it would be good to see more companies engaging in advisory services and even directly investing in post-conflict zones (Popovski *et al.* 2008).

Diaspora investors can help as first-movers, and there are many examples (Angola, Bosnia, Croatia, Liberia, Sierra Leone, South Sudan) of how they have driven the economic recovery and helped the peacebuilding efforts in countries after civil wars. ManoCap,[4] a private equity firm in West Africa, was registered by people who worked previously in humanitarian capacities in Sierra Leone for the UNDP and GOAL. ManoCap was created to generate investment opportunities (GOAL is a global NGO) by conducting in-depth market research and developing local networks. The company advertised opportunities in Sierra Leone and Liberia, where information and skills gaps exist and many businesses require pre-investment support to meet the standards required by international investors.

The six roles above are not necessarily separate circles – they can synergize creatively, forming an interactive map of CR2P. For example, most of the companies are passive non-perpetrators, but some of them go further and develop R2P-sensitivization of activities and employees, engage pro-actively in reducing ethnic intolerance, and assist government and civil society to prevent and mitigate atrocities. A company may act both as assistant and as direct protector. Also, in post-conflict situations, compensating victims and rebuilding the infrastructure can be an excellent supportive contribution for atrocities not to re-emerge in the future.

---

[4] See manocap.com.

After classifying and explaining the six corporate roles above, I would like to deliberate whether a code of conduct, or another legal instrument, can be feasible to impose obligations on the private sector to exercise CR2P.

Code of Conduct for CR2P

International law has yet to develop duties directly applicable to corporations. Historically it has placed duties on states, and more recently on individuals, but corporate responsibility has been exempt from these assignments. The conventional doctrine has asserted that only states and individuals are holders of international legal duties. Private enterprises will have duties insofar as they cooperate with actors whom international law already considers prime sources of R2P crimes – states – and insofar as their activities infringe upon the human dignity of those with whom they have special ties – individuals. A potential code of conduct can marry principles of international law concerning foreign investment, principles of corporate law more generally, *erga omnes* principles condemning genocide and crimes against humanity as crimes without territorial or temporal boundaries, and the theory and practice of human rights law.

Some may regard the code of conduct as an unnecessary idea, considering states as sufficient R2P actors, or as an impossible idea, inherently unworkable given the differences between state and corporate structures. One way to address such concerns is to put them within broader academic and policy debates about the power of multinational corporations and non-governmental organizations, the role of the state in protecting people, and the extent to which international law can and should regulate business actors. Given that most R2P crimes continue to be committed by governments, organized insurgencies, and individuals, the code of conduct can prove critical to understanding views on corporate duties and justify the need for corporate responsibility, rather than state or individual responsibility, as a means for protecting people from atrocity crimes. Inherent in this is also the tension between the imposition of R2P on businesses and the conventional view that only violations sponsored by governments or quasi-governmental actors engage international responsibility.

The code of conduct opens ways in which international actors accept duties of corporate responsibility on companies, and their recognition undercuts any conceivable doctrinal bar to such duties. The code maintains that existing international law doctrines make states and individuals responsible for mass atrocities, and provide a basis for deriving corporate duties based on four factors: the corporation's links with the government, its links with affected populations, the particular crime at issue, and the structure of the corporate entity. Reviewing the theory and provisionally applying it to some of the factual claims currently leveled at corporations, the code of conduct offers an overview of the means by which the theory of responsibility might be implemented within various arenas in which key actors prescribe, invoke, and apply international law. This includes a discussion of enforcement options, which represent one of the great challenges to international humanitarian law generally.

The code for corporate responsibility can be applied in numerous international fora, not merely courts – as excessive focus on the activities of courts diverts attention from the principal venues in which international legal argumentation is made. International humanitarian law is invoked, interpreted, and applied in diverse arenas, and some norms based on the principles of international responsibility can be incorporated by businesses themselves under economic pressure from interested shareholders and consumers, who serve as private law enforcers. Other claims can be addressed in domestic fora as legislators and government officials draft statutes, regulations, and policies.

The code should in no way suggest unilateral imposition of rules on corporations – international norms are not, and cannot be, prescribed through such a process. Wherever lawmaking occurs, the detailed elaboration of norms must directly involve all interested actors – governments, businesses, lobby groups, individuals. The code does not preclude but rather invites and assumes a role for states, corporations, and citizens in developing appropriate norms and enforcement mechanisms. The approach follows from relationships between key actors involved in the international economic activities and, in particular, foreign investments: the home state of a transnational enterprise, which itself can change as corporations become multinational.

The code is necessary also because of various demanding factors: the dramatic increase in investment by multinational companies in the developing world; the sense that the economic might of corporations has eroded the power of the state; the global telecommunications revolution, which has brought worldwide attention to the conditions of those living in less developed countries and has increased the capacity of NGOs to mobilize public opinion; the work of the WTO and the IMF in requiring states to be friendly to foreign investors. These advocacy efforts build on earlier attempts by concerned actors to focus attention on private business activity, ranging from trials of leading German industrialists for war crimes after World War II to campaigns in the 1970s and 1980s to encourage divestment from corporations doing business in South Africa. They are based on the growing acceptance that business enterprises should be held accountable for R2P crimes taking place within their sphere of operations. Corporations, for their part, can respond in numerous ways, from denying any duties in the area of R2P to accepting voluntary codes that constrain their behavior.

One problem is whether there could be an objective standard by which to appraise claims that various business activities are responsible or irresponsible from the perspective of R2P. To what extent can corporations be responsible for atrocities when investing in a country where genocide occurs? How can businesses know that the government is planning to commit atrocities? What if corporations with the tacit consent of the government exploit workers from ethnic or religious minorities, paying low wages or providing bad working conditions (as in the case of Shell and the Niger Delta communities in Nigeria).

The code can assess the recent progress in adopting anti-discriminatory principles (such as Sullivan, McBride), the ban on provocative religious or political emblems at the workplace, other examples of how anti-discriminatory recruitment of people belonging to minorities can de-escalate tensions, and serve as a preventive tool against ethnic and religious violence and mass atrocities. The code can also look at decisions challenging private business activity in areas in which they occur, for example the Security Council Resolution 1306 (2000) condemning illegal trade in diamonds and fueling the civil war in Sierra Leone, and urging private diamond trading associations to establish a regime labeling diamonds of legitimate origin. The South African Truth and Reconciliation Commission devoted Chapter 2 of its final report (1998) to the involvement of the business sector in the practices of apartheid. Human Rights Watch established a special unit on corporations and human rights and issued two reports in 1999, one accusing Enron Corporation of corporate complicity in human rights violations by the Indian government, and another accusing Shell, Mobil, and other international oil companies operating in Nigeria of cooperating with the government in suppressing political opposition. Citizens of Burma and Indonesia sued Unocal and Freeport-McMoRan and accused those companies of violating human rights. These cases can build enthusiasm for applying a similar model for R2P crimes.

Finally, a code of conduct can demonstrate a model of corporate engagement in R2P including the following five stages:

1. *Gather knowledge and give early warning.* Identify and share intelligence on vulnerabilities and potential dangers of ethnic or religious violence and signal concerns, for example on emerging discriminatory practices.
2. *Prioritize risks.* Risks, identified in the knowledge-gathering process, are assessed and prioritized, so as to plan preventive or responding actions.

3. *Map activities*. Following identification, early warning, and prioritization, companies map activities to mitigate tensions and contribute to the protection of populations.
4. *Coordinate*. After risk analysis and reflecting on inputs of stakeholders, companies collaborate with other actors in direct or indirect efforts to protect endangered groups.
5. *Remedy victims*. Companies offer contributions to compensation funds and other schemes, rebuilding the lives of those who suffered, and reconciling the society.

There might never be an equality of arms in lawsuits between powerful corporations and sufferers, so voluntary bona fide commitments to alleviate the victims of atrocities can be drafted in a code of conduct for CR2P that can also establish some process of arbitration that private enterprises may have with governments, international organizations, non-governmental organizations, and individuals. Without an agreed and adopted code, there might continue to be both excessive claims made against private actors and counterclaims by corporate actors against their accountability. Decision-makers considering these claims – whether legislatures or international organizations contemplating regulation, courts facing suits, or officials deciding whether to intervene in a dispute involving business and R2P – will respond in an ad hoc manner, driven by domestic priorities or by legal frameworks that are likely to differ significantly across the world. The resultant atmosphere of uncertainty will be detrimental to both R2P and the economy. Therefore, establishing a code of conduct with regard to CR2P could be a timely and useful exercise.

Conclusion

This chapter identifies an existing gap and develops the concept of CR2P as a different but related responsibility to state-centric R2P and to individual R2P. It argues that similarly to the way the role of the private sector has been recognized in the peace and security agenda, and in the human rights agenda, it is high time to recognize CR2P as a natural nexus between the other two agendas. CR2P can also be well linked with CSR – already a well-established field of both knowledge and practice.

The chapter introduces six roles that the private sector can exercise – non-perpetrator, mitigator, assistant protector, direct protector, compensator and rebuilder – and analyzes those roles from the point of view of necessity, feasibility, and impact. It presents some best practices already emerging, but also expresses concerns with gaps, for example the failure to recognize and compensate victims of atrocities.

The chapter also argues that establishing a code of conduct with regard to CR2P is a timely and useful exercise. Such a code can list the following stages of corporate involvement: knowledge gathering, early warning, risk prioritization, activity mapping, coordination, and remedy for victims.

References

Bennett, Juliette. 2001. "Business in zones of conflict: The role of the multi-nationals in promoting regional stability." Prepared for the UN Global Compact Policy Dialogues, January. www.unglobalcompact.org/issues/con-flict_prevention/meetings_and_workshops/Reg_stability.html

2002. "Multinational corporations, social responsibility and conflict." *Journal of International Affairs* 55 (2).

Binder, Andrea and Jan Martin Witte. 2007. "Business engagement in humani-tarian relief: Key trends and policy implications." Humanitarian Policy Group background paper, Overseas Development Institute, London.

Brown, Gordon and Sarah Brown. 2014. "Safe schools meeting held at House of Commons." The Office of Gordon and Sarah Brown, July 3. http://gordonand-sarahbrown.com/2014/07/safe-schools-meeting-held-at-house-of-commons/

Bruderlein, Claude. 2000. "The role of non-state actors in building human secu-rity: The case of armed groups in intra-state wars." Centre for Humanitarian Dialogue. http://statebuildingmonitor.files.wordpress.com/2012/01/the-role-of-non-state-actors-in-building-human-security.pdf

Bryer, David and Edmund Cairns. 2010. "For better? For worse? Humanitarian aid in conflict." *Development in Practice* 7 (4):363–374.

Democratic Control of Armed Forces (DCAF) and Geneva Call. 2014. "Armed non-state actors: Current trends and future challenges." DCAF Horizon 2015. Working Paper, 1–23.

Desgrandchamps, Marie-Luce. 2012. "Organizing the unpredictable: The Nigeria-Biafra war and its impact on the ICRC." *International Review of the Red Cross* 94 (888):1409–1432.

Duffield, Mark. 2010. "NGO relief in war zones: Towards an analysis of the new aid paradigm." *Third World Quarterly* 183:527–542.

The Economist. 2014. "Boko Haram's impact on Nigeria: Education in crisis." May 9. www.economist.com/blogs/baobab/2014/05/boko-harams-impact-nigeria?page=1&spc=scode&spv=xm&ah=9d7f7ab945510a56fa6d37c30b6f1709

Fagin-Jones, Stephanie and Elizabeth Midlarsky. 2007. "Courageous altru-ism: Personal and situational correlates of rescue during the Holocaust." *Journal of Positive Psychology* (2):136–147.

Fishkin, Rebecca L. 2011. *Heroes of the Holocaust.* Mankato, MN: Compass Point Books. http://books.google.co.za/books?hl=en&lr=&id=L5nwr9B9F0kC&oi=fnd&pg=PT3&ots=mHAG0mzMGo&sig=iOt1ei_t0c1Wzf1hzpx082Vbmko#v=onepage&q&f=false

Glaser, Daryl. 2007. "South Africa and the limit of civil society." *Journal of Southern African Studies* 231:5–25.

Habib, Adam and Rupert Taylor. 1999. "South Africa: Anti-Apartheid NGOs in transition." *Voluntas: International Journal of Voluntary and Nonprofit Organizations* 10 (1):73–82.

Harvey, Fiona. 2013. "Shell acquitted of Nigeria pollution charges." *The Guardian*, January 30. www.theguardian.com/environment/2013/jan/30/shell-acquitted-nigeria-pollution-charges

Hayden, Robert M. 1996. "Schindler's fate: Genocide, ethnic cleansing, and population transfers." *Slavic Review* 55 (4):727–748.

Hayes, Peter. 2000. *Industry and Ideology: I.G. Farben in the Nazi Era.* Cambridge University Press.

Haywood, Robert and Jeffrey French. 2009. *Potential roles for non-state actors and non-territorial sovereign organizations in reducing armed violence.* Research Report. Broomfield, CO: One Earth Future Foundation. http://1earthfuture.org/sites/1earthfuture.org/files/documents/publications/file_55.pdf

Hazlett, Chad J. 2008. "Resistance to genocidal governments: Should private actors break laws to protect civilians from mass atrocity?" *Human Rights Brief* 15 (3):24–28. www.wcl.american.edu/hrbrief/15/3hazlett.pdf

Human Rights Without Frontiers. 2013. "Role of civil society in preventing genocide and mass atrocities, a case study: Liberia." Symposium on Cultural Diplomacy and Human Rights: Collaboration of Civil Society in Preventing Genocide and Mass Atrocities. Berlin, May 30. www.hrwf.net/images/advocacy/2013/2013genocideprevention.pdf

Iff, Andrea, Damiano Sguaitamatti, Rina M. Alluri, and Daniela Kohler. 2010. "Money makers as peace makers." Working Paper Series, No. 2, SwissPeace.

International Coalition for the Responsibility to Protect. 2012. "Voices from civil society: Global efforts to prevent mass atrocities." http://responsibilitytoprotect.org/Voices2012_final(1).pdf

International Committee of the Red Cross. 2008. "Enhancing protection for civilians in armed conflict and other situations of violence." www.icrc.org/eng/assets/files/other/icrc_002_0956.pdf

2011. "Improving the protection of civilians in situations of armed conflict." Fellows' Working Paper. www.hks.harvard.edu/cchrp/research/working_papers/ImprovingProtectionOfCiviliansInArmedConflict.pdf

Kaldor, Mary. 2001. "A decade of humanitarian intervention: The role of global civil society." In *Global Civil Society*, edited by Helmut Anheier, Marlies Glasius, and Mary Kaldor. Oxford University Press. www.gcsknowledgebase.org/wp-content/uploads/2001chapter51.pdf

Kelly, Michael J. 2010. "The status of corporations in the travaux preparatoires of the Genocide Convention: The search for personhood." *Case Western Reserve Journal of International Law* 4(1).

Kelly, Michael J. 2012. "Prosecuting corporations for genocide under international law." *Harvard Law & Policy Review* 356 (6):339–368.

Linn, Ruth. 2003. "Genocide and the politics of remembering: The nameless, the celebrated, and the would-be Holocaust heroes." *Journal of Genocide Research* 5 (4):565–586.

Luck, Edward C. and Dana Zaret Luck. 2015. "The individual Responsibility to Protect." In *Reconstructing Atrocity Prevention*, edited by Sheri Rosenberg, Tiberiu Galis, and Alex Zucker. Cambridge University Press.

Muchlinski, Peter. 2001. "Human rights and multinationals: Is there a problem?" *International Affairs* 77 (I):31–47.

Naraghi-Anderlini, Sanam, Ed Garcia, and Kumar Rupesinghe. 2001. "Nonconventional diplomacy." In *Journeys Through Conflict: Narratives and Lessons*, edited by Hayward R. Alker, Ted Robert Gurr, and Kumar Rupesinghe. Lanham, MD: Rowman and Littlefield, 208–209.

Nelson, Jane. 2000. "The business of peace: The private sector as a partner in conflict prevention and resolution." International Alert Council on Economic Priorities, The Prince of Wales's Business Leaders Forum, July 21, 2014. www.internationalalert.org/sites/default/files/publications/The%20Business%20of%20Peace.pdf

Oliner, Samuel P. and Pearl M. Oliner. 1992. *Altruistic Personality: Rescuers of Jews in Nazi Europe*. New York: Touchstone Press. http://books.google.co.za/books?hl=en&lr=&id=7Ze0ohBVFY0C&oi=fnd&pg=PR9&dq=saving+Jews+from+genocide+by+Oskar&ots=wo-9dMxhIZ&sig=vBxvg0t_bfxre-6P7CZZMpKaoU8#v=onepage&q&f=false

Owuor, Victor Odundo and Scott Wisor. 2014. *The role of Kenya's private sector in peacebuilding: The case of the 2013 election cycle*. Research Report. Broomfield, CO: One Earth Future Foundation. http://oneearthfuture.org/sites/oneearthfuture.org/files//documents/publications/kenyaprivatesector-policybrief_1.pdf

Oxfam Australia. 2009. "NGOs and the prevention of mass atrocity crimes: A practical workshop for NGOs to develop and share strategies to implement the Responsibility to Protect in the Asia Pacific Region." Workshop Outcome Document, November 23–24. http://responsibility-toprotect.org/Oxfam%20R2P%20workshop%20outcome%20doc%20March%202010-2.pdf

Popovski Vesselin, Obijiofor Aginam, and Nicholas Turner. 2008. "Foreign direct investments in post-conflict zones." Policy Brief, United Nations University.

Schneckener, Ulrich and Claudia Hofmann. 2011. *NGOs and non-state armed actors: Improving compliance with international norms*. United States Institute of Peace Report.

Shlensky, Jane. 2003. "Considering other choices: Chiune Sugihara's rescue of Polish Jews." Paper prepared for and delivered to Japan Studies Association Conference "Reconsidering Hiroshima/Nagasaki," Hiroshima Peace Museum, Hiroshima, Japan, June 24–27. http://faculty.ccp.edu/faculty/DFreedman/HCS/Shlensky.pdf

Slim, Hugo. 2012. "Business actors in armed conflict." In *International Review of the Red Cross* 94, 887. www.icrc.org/eng/resources/international-review/review-887-business-violence-conflct/index.jsp

Smith, David. 2011. "Shell accused of fuelling violence in Nigeria by paying rival militant gangs." *The Guardian*, October 3. www.theguardian.com/world/2011/oct/03/shell-accused-of-fuelling-nigeria-conflict

Spearin, Christopher. 2008. "Private, armed, and humanitarian? States, NGOs, international private security companies and shifting humanitarianism." *Security Dialogue* 39 (4):363–382.

Spittaels, Steven and Nick Meynen. 2007. *Mapping interests in conflict areas: Katanga*. International Peace Information Service Report. www.ipis-research.be/maps/Katanga/20070813_Mapping_Katanga_ENG.pdf

Steinberg, Jonathan. 1999. *The Deutsche Bank and its Gold Transactions During the Second World War*. Munich: C.H. Beck.

Streitfeld-Hall, Jaclyn D. 2014. *Responsibility to Protect: Can we prevent mass atrocities without making the same mistakes?* CIVICUS State of Civil Society Report. www.civicus.org/index.php/en/expert-perspectives/2015-the-responsibility-to-protect-can-we-prevent-mass-atrocities-without-making-the-same-mistakes

Truth and Reconciliation Commission of South Africa. 1998. *Truth and Reconciliation Commission of South Africa Report*. Cape Town: Truth and Reconciliation Commission.

United Nations General Assembly. 2005. "2005 World Summit Outcome." Document A/Res/60/1, October 24. www.un.org/womenwatch/ods/A-RES-60-1-E.pdf

2009. *Implementing the Responsibility to Protect: Report of the Secretary-General,* A/63/677 (January 12). www.unrol.org/files/SG_reportA_63_677_en.pdf

United Nations Office of the High Commissioner for Refugees (UNHCR). 2006. Global Report 70349. www.unhcr.org/501f7d2e2.html

United Nations Security Council. 2000. *Security Council Resolution 1306 on the Situation in Sierra Leone*, S/RES/1306 (July 5). www.refworld.org/docid/3b00f27918.htm

2014. *Fulfilling Our Collective Responsibility: International Assistance and the Responsibility to Protect: Report of the Secretary-General,* A/68/947 (July 11). http://responsibilitytoprotect.org/N1446379.pdf

Wiesnew, Stephen Matthew. 2012. "Humanitarian frames and humanitarian soft power in Darfur." *Interagency Journal* 3 (2):66–70. http://thesimonscenter.org/wp-content/uploads/2012/05/IAJ-3-2-SpecialEditionSpring2012.pdf

World Federalist Movement Institute for Global Policy. 2014. "Summary of the Responsibility to Protect: Report of the International Commission on Intervention and State Sovereignty (ICISS)." Accessed June 12. www.responsibilitytoprotect.org/files/r2psummary.pdf

Wundheiler, Luitgard N. 1986. "Oskar Schindler's moral development during the Holocaust." *Humboldt Journal of Social Relations* 13 (1/2):333–356.

Alex J. Bellamy

The Responsibility to Protect can be understood as a "global effort" to prevent and end genocide and mass atrocities. In their contribution to this volume, Victor MacDiarmid and Tina J. Park provide a thorough account of the norm's emergence since it was first articulated in 2001. Yet, until quite recently, international and scholarly debate focussed almost exclusively on the role of states and the international institutions they comprise (Bellamy 2009).[1] This is unsurprising in some respects given that states remain the principal actors in world politics, have specific legal obligations for the protection of populations from genocide and mass atrocities, wield immense material power capable of both imperiling and saving whole populations, exercise exclusive sovereign authority within their own territories, and are the source of a unique international authority to enforce collective decisions vested in the UN Security Council. What is more, as some of the contributors to this volume have observed, the 2005 World Summit vested the responsibility to protect specifically in the UN's Member States.

Almost from the outset, however, it was recognized that states could not achieve the goals of R2P alone. Non-state armed groups, civil society organizations, and the private sector would all have a role to play if the goal of preventing and ending atrocities was to be achieved. This point, about the important role of non-state actors, was recognized by the UN Secretary-General in his 2009 report on *Implementing the Responsibility to Protect*. But while research has burgeoned on non-state armed groups as perpetrators of mass atrocities and sometimes as facilitators of protection, and a global movement of civil society organizations has emerged to support the goals of R2P, the role of the private sector in atrocity prevention remains relatively obscure.[2] That is why the preceding chapters are so timely and important.

[1] By genocide and mass atrocities, I mean genocide, war crimes, ethnic cleansing, and crimes against humanity. See "Responsibility to Protect" (Bellamy 2009).
[2] That said, there is a related literature on corporate responsibility and genocide. For a useful overview of this literature see "Business in Genocide" (Stel 2014).

In this reflective chapter, I examine three questions that have recurred in the previous chapters: why include the private sector in our consideration of atrocity prevention? What roles does the private sector play? And what can be done to enhance the sector's contribution to atrocity prevention? In short, I argue, first, that the private sector is an important but often missing part of the prevention puzzle; second that, whether consciously or not, it fulfills a number of important roles that need to recognized and understood if the private sector is to be better harnessed for atrocity prevention; and third, that there are a number of modest ways of incorporating the sector more fully into atrocities prevention.

Why Look at the Private Sector?

We need to begin with a clarification and an objection.

As some of the other contributors have observed, it is quite difficult to talk about a "private sector" in part because the sector is so large and heterogeneous and in part because of some lack of conceptual clarity. The "private sector" refers to that part of the economy that is not controlled by the state, and comprises individuals and companies that operate to make profit. As such, it is distinct from both the state and state-controlled businesses and from "civil society" or, more accurately, the "not-for-profit sector." As a sector, it comprises everything from a single-person small business to a major multinational corporation whose annual turnover dwarfs the GDP of most of the UN's Member States. The picture is further complicated by the sector's functional breadth, spanning almost every area of human endeavor. One of the principal tasks for those who continue the work begun in this volume will be to demarcate and disaggregate different types of private actors so that we may get a more complete understanding of their roles and potentialities.

The "objection" is the suggestion that the private sector is a peripheral consideration at best because of the apparently tangential connection between atrocity crimes and the business sector (a point mentioned and convincingly disputed by Fort and Westermann-Behaylo) and because the 2005 World Summit referred only to the responsibilities that states have to protect their populations from genocide and mass atrocities, assist others, and take timely and decisive action when all else is judged likely to fail. Because of this it might be objected that not only is the private sector no substitute for the state, it has neither the moral obligation nor the global mandate to act to promote R2P since the concept speaks only of the responsibilities of states and the "international community."

The question of whether R2P confers responsibilities on specific actors, i.e. states and particular institutions, or whether it is limited by its failure to do so has been hotly debated (Pattison 2010; Erskine 2013; Ralph 2013; Roff 2013). As agreed by Member States in 2005, R2P involves three layers of responsibility, relating to different sets of actors. The first is a specific obligation that rests on sovereign states to protect their own populations. The second is a general and diffused responsibility awarded to the "international community" to assist states to protect their own populations and to utilize diplomatic, peaceful, and other peaceful means to that end. The third is a set of special responsibilities bestowed upon the UN Security Council – this is a responsibility that states have to protect populations in other countries from genocide and mass atrocities. It is a responsibility specifically bestowed by the UN's Member States upon the Security Council but one which, by virtue of the UN Charter's demand that states comply with the Council's decisions, ultimately rests on all states.[3]

One question raised in the preceding chapters is whether the conferral of responsibilities onto the "international community" might imply the imposition of duties on actors other than states and whether this might include the private sector. This is an unpromising line of argument, in part because states typically understand the term "international community" to refer to some grouping of states, and in the context of the World State was clearly intended to refer to UN Member States as a whole. It is also an unpromising line of argument, because it cannot be advanced without untangling the intricate webs of state responsibility agreed in 2005.

It is most straightforward to demonstrate the point that the use of the phrase "international community" was meant to refer to states by examining the question of "timely and decisive response" to genocide and mass atrocities. The World Summit recognized the Security Council's special responsibility with respect to the protection of populations from atrocity crimes. Certainly political and normative in content, rather than legal (Luck 2010, 349, 363), these responsibilities nevertheless make it more difficult for the Council to do nothing in the face of atrocity crimes (Chesterman 2011, 279). This much has become evident in the Council's practice since early 2011.

In para. 139 of the World Summit Outcome Document, Member States acknowledged an international responsibility to "use appropriate diplomatic, humanitarian and other peaceful means, in accordance with

---

[3] With the degree of responsibility for enforcing the UN Security Council's decisions related to their capacity to do so. On this, see *Humanitarian Intervention* (Pattison 2010).

Chapters VI and VIII of the Charter of the United Nations to help protect populations from genocide, war crimes, ethnic cleansing and crimes against humanity." Para. 139 does not leave this international responsibility "disembodied" in the sense that it fails to identify a specific bearer of responsibility (Pattison 2010). On the one hand, it stipulates that the responsibility should be exercised "through the United Nations." On the other, Chapters VI and VIII of the Charter identify specific roles for different UN organs, primarily (but not exclusively) the Security Council.

The most obvious responsibility bestowed on the Council by para. 139 relates to the second element of R2P's third pillar: "We are prepared to take collective action, in a timely and decisive manner, through the Security Council, in accordance with the Charter, including Chapter VII, on a case-by-case basis and in cooperation with relevant regional organizations as appropriate, should peaceful means be inadequate and national authorities manifestly fail to protect their populations from genocide, war crimes, ethnic cleansing and crimes against humanity" (para. 139). In terms of the locus of responsibility, this sentence opens with "we," indicating that the responsibility lays with each individual Member State rather than with an "international community" that might include non-state actors. What is more, this shared responsibility is delegated specifically to the Council, which is expressly identified as the appropriate agent. The Council can therefore be thought of as bearing special responsibilities relating to R2P. It is also, of course, the only agent in world politics that holds the international legal authority to authorize the use of military force and other means of coercion outside a context of self-defense.

Thus, it seems fairly clear that, as agreed in 2005, R2P is a largely state-based concept inasmuch as the responsibilities it confers are laid specifically upon states and state-based institutions. It would be difficult, therefore, to defend the inclusion of the private sector in debates about implementing R2P on the grounds that responsibilities were conferred upon them as members of the "international community." An alternative route is to recognize that, on the one hand, although it was states that made a commitment to R2P, states alone would be incapable of achieving R2P's goals, and, on the other hand, irrespective of whether or not it is consciously recognized, private sector actors are already involved in facilitating and preventing genocide and mass atrocities. Preventing and ending atrocities will require determined action by non-state actors, too. As Fort and Westermann-Behaylo point out, not only do businesses play a role in building a more peaceful world, they have an important stake in doing so.

210   Alex J. Bellamy

No sooner had the ink dried on the 2005 World Summit agreement than it became clear that some non-armed groups, such as the FDLR and the M23 in the Democratic Republic of the Congo, Boko Haram in Nigeria, al-Shabaab in Somalia, the Lord's Resistance Army across southern Sudan, Uganda and the DRC, and more recently Islamic State in the Middle East, posed at least as great a threat to civilian populations as do badly behaved states. It was clearly not enough that states accepted obligations under R2P – it was imperative that those obligations extended to non-state actors, too. In some theaters, such as the Middle East, this concern extended to the private companies subcontracted to use force for a variety of purposes.[4] This was a point recognized and reinforced in successive reports on R2P by the UN Secretary-General.

But there are other grounds for thinking that states alone are incapable of achieving the goals set forth by R2P. Two decades of scholarship on the protracted civil wars that emerged after the Cold War demonstrated how the violent competition for resources, often valuable natural resources, had literally hollowed out states and replaced (to the extent that they had ever existed) state structures with hybrid forms of authority based on networks of patrimony, economic exchange, and violence.[5] As the struggles to build peace in places such as the Democratic Republic of the Congo, Central African Republic (CAR) and South Sudan attest, the re-establishment and re-imposition of state authority are not sustainable in the long term without deeper transformations within civil (meaning outside the state) society. What is more, although there have been some notable successes in the use of state-based diplomacy for atrocity prevention, most obviously in the case of Kenya in 2008–2009, there is growing recognition that the most effective sources of escalation prevention and resilience to triggers come from within vulnerable societies themselves (McLoughlin 2014). From this perspective, prevention is best served by identifying and augmenting the resources that societies already have with which to resist genocide and mass atrocities.

Of course, this is but one facet of a broader set of phenomena connected with globalization. It is increasingly the case that the options before governments and their capacity to act and shape outcomes autonomously are conditioned and limited by the forces of globalization. All states, including powerful ones, are constrained by the movement of capital, resources, people, and ideas across borders to the extent that very few have a full range of policy options from which to select or the capacity for entirely autonomous action. For a significant number of

---

[4] On which, see *Corporate Warrior* (Singer 2008).
[5] For example, see *International Peacebuilding* (MacGinty 2011).

states – including most of those experiencing chronic risk of genocide and mass atrocities – this means that those with the trappings of formal authority often do not enjoy (if they ever did) what Stephen Krasner labeled "domestic sovereignty" – the practical capacity to exert effective control over the territory of the control (Krasner 1999). What is more, even when states do enjoy formal "control," global forces make it more difficult for them to translate control into desired outcomes. While sovereignty continues to play a powerful constitutional role in international society (Cohen 2012), the capacity of sovereigns to autonomously determine their own fate, and that of their people, has been diminished by globalization.

Size matters, too. The private sector generates and marshals financial resources that exceed those of most states. For example, were it a state, Walmart's GDP would be in the world's top twenty-five, greater than South Africa's and significantly greater than the GDP of countries such as Pakistan and Thailand. Indeed, the cumulative annual turnover of the USA's seven largest corporations is roughly equivalent to the annual GDP of the African Union as a whole. The private sector is therefore a vast and potentially significant player in most societies and therefore an important piece of the puzzle of preventing genocide and mass atrocities.

For all these reasons, and more, it is safe to conclude that although R2P was born as an agreement between states, it is an ambition that cannot be achieved by states alone. Not only do the threats and challenges extend well beyond the world of states, states are themselves enmeshed in networks and structures that are beyond the control of any one of them. Thus, the ability of states to protect their own populations and those of other countries is intimately connected to the role played by non-state actors of one form or another. To date, when it has focussed on the non-state sector, scholarship on atrocity prevention has tended to focus on non-state armed groups as sources of threat (as with Boko Haram in Nigeria) or sometimes protection (as with the Kurdish *peshmerga* in Kobane) and the roles played by civil society in inciting and instigating violence or preventing it and resolving disputes. Relatively little attention has been paid to the role of the private sector.

This problem is compounded by the fact that where attention has been paid to the private sector, this has generally been to focus on the contribution it makes to the economic drivers of civil war that so often create the conditions for genocide and mass atrocities.[6] While it

---

[6] A large literature emerged in the late 1990s, showing how predatory economic practices laid the groundwork for civil war. For a classic statement of the "conflict trap" theory, see *The Bottom Billion* (Collier 2008, 117–137).

is certainly important to recognize – and counter – these effects, it is equally important to understand that this is only part of the equation; the private sector can also play a role in preventing genocide and mass atrocities. Beyond the many specific examples detailed in this volume, there is a major structural reason for thinking that the private sector has a role to play. As Fort and Westermann-Behaylo point out, evidence suggests powerful links between economics and the risk of genocide and mass atrocities: rich and middle-income economies confront generally lower risks than poor economies; the equitable distribution of wealth across ethnic groups produces less risk than the unequal distribution of wealth; economic shocks and rapid downturns can lead to the "scape-goating" of minority groups and trigger crises that eventually give rise to genocide and mass atrocities. The trends work in both directions: economic decline and shocks can precipitate conflict, leading to atrocities, but the reverse is also true in that growing income can help reduce atrocity risks. It is not a coincidence that the economic rise of East Asia was accompanied by a dramatic decline in the incidence of mass atrocities there (Bellamy 2014).

That is why the insights offered in the preceding chapters are so important, because they speak about a missing part of the prevention puzzle. They are so timely because international society's failure to respond effectively to the crisis in Syria reveals both the limits of what states can achieve by themselves – especially when their perceived interests are not aligned with the goals of human protection – and the urgent need to mobilize all available resources to the goals of R2P. This is the essence of the UN Secretary-General's call for the implementation of R2P to be "narrow but deep": an approach that is single-mindedly focussed on the prevention of genocide and mass atrocities, but one that draws upon all the resources available to us. By excluding the private sector from consideration, or limiting that consideration to the sector's negative aspects, students of atrocity prevention have inadvertently limited understanding of the factors contributing to prevention and have foreclosed the potential mobilization of huge reservoirs of resources. Although it is too early to draw definitive judgments about what types of preventive action work and in what circumstances (and developing a more systematic approach to evidence gathering and lessons learning is crucial), Edward and Dana Luck have usefully identified five factors that appear to serve the interests of protection well: early and sustained engagement, coordinated and collaborative efforts by actors at different levels, leverage over key players and a willingness to use it, civil society's preparedness to provide a moderating voice, and the specific targeting of individuals in key positions (Luck and Luck 2015). Each of these factors involves, potentially, actors beyond the state and implies roles for the private sector.

In summary, fulfilling R2P is not a task that states can accomplish by themselves. Non-state actors matter, too, including the private sector, which has been largely overlooked by scholarship on atrocity prevention. There are at least five reasons why it is appropriate and necessary to consider the role played by the private sector in atrocities prevention.

First, because R2P is universal and enduring: that is, it applies everywhere, all the time. As the UN Secretary-General has argued, there is never a situation in which R2P does not apply for that would imply that there are contexts in which there is no duty to protect populations from mass atrocities (UN Security Council 2012, para. 13). The responsibilities of protection always exist; what differs is the best way of exercising them in any given context. With that in mind, where private sector actors accept their part or not, they do have a moral responsibility to do what they can. It is always, therefore, legitimate to ask whether they are contributing to the prevention of mass atrocities or to their commission.

Second, because the private sector is effectual: whether for good or bad, consciously or not, the private sector influences the course of events in countries at risk of genocide and mass atrocities. The private sector is not aloof from the forces that drive and inhibit genocide and mass atrocities, and nor should it be treated as such. Leaving it out of analysis risks omitting potentially important drivers of violence or sources of resilience. Excluding it from the politics of prevention needlessly limits the levers that might be pulled to assist the cause of prevention.

Third, the forces of globalization are eroding the distinctions between public and private, national and international, spaces: on the one hand, advanced liberal states are turning increasingly to public–private partnerships and subcontracting to the private sector as ways of delivering services more effectively, including services associated with security. On the other hand, many post-colonial states are effectively hybrid political orders that combine formal state institutions with a variety of less formal, non-state practices and institutions.[7]

Fourth, the disruption of distinctions between the public and private are and should be heightened when atrocities are perpetrated, especially when this occurs in contexts of civil war or state fragility. In such situations, the state might be dysfunctional, its authority spatially limited, while private actors might assume more responsibility for basic functions such as governance and security.

---

[7] For a good exposition of this concept in the context of eastern DRC, see *Violent Capitalism* (Raeymaekers 2014).

Fifth, the private sector and mass atrocities are co-related. On the one hand, the private sector has a powerful stake in the prevention of genocide and mass atrocities. The profit motive is the defining characteristic of the private sector and there is abundant research demonstrating that armed conflict and mass atrocities disrupt economies, retard growth, and therefore inhibit the accumulation of wealth by private business. On the other hand, economies – which are largely shaped by the private sector – shape atrocity risks inasmuch as struggling economies that inhibit opportunities can help give rise to risk while flourishing private sectors can place significant downward pressure on risk.

Private Sector Roles in Atrocity Prevention

To understand the positive roles that the private sector actors could play in helping to prevent genocide and mass atrocities, it is important to understand the roles that they play already. The question, after all, is not one of whether or not such actors should be involved since, whether consciously or not, private sector actors are involved in the processes that lead to, or prevent, genocide and mass atrocities. The preceding chapters in this volume have performed a useful and much-needed task by providing insights into the many roles fulfilled by private sector actors and different ways of categorizing them. To better understand the relationship between these roles and practices of atrocity prevention, it might be useful to conceptualize the different roles along a spectrum of action ranging from "perpetrator" at one end to "protector" at the other, and to think about the function of these roles at different stages of the prevention cycle. Of course, when considering the different roles that private sector actors can play it is important to remember the wide variation in their type, scale, and capacity to influence.

In his chapter, Popovski usefully identified six potential roles fulfilled by private sector actors. Other chapters, especially that by Fort and Westermann-Behaylo, either used slightly different language to describe similar roles, or else identified different roles that fall within the spectrum of possibilities suggested by Popovski. This spectrum is summarized in Table 9.1.

At one end of the spectrum, private sector actors can be the direct perpetrators of genocide or mass atrocities. That is, they are sometimes directly and knowingly involved in the commission of atrocity crimes. Although there are no modern examples of private sector actors constituting the primary perpetrators of mass atrocities, there are historical examples of private companies being directly responsible for what

Table 9.1 *Private sector actors*

Type	Role
Active perpetrators	• Company employees as direct perpetrators of violence (including private security companies) • Companies part of systems of extermination
Direct assistants to perpetrators	• Provision of direct assistance (e.g. transportation) to perpetrators • Patterns of cooperation with perpetrators
Indirect assistants to perpetrators	• Financial support to perpetrators through trade, royalty payments, etc. • Provision of material support through sale of key goods and services, etc.
Bystanders	• Remain passive in the face of genocide and mass atrocities
Indirect supporters of prevention	• Promotion of gentle commerce • Reinforce common humanity • Non-discriminatory human resource practices • Norm builders • Investment decisions that break down horizontal inequalities • Support for GDP growth • Business diplomacy
Direct supporters of prevention	• Material support to prevention • Promote values of peace/create and police norms of behavior • Promote conflict resolution • Coordinate comprehensive efforts
Rescuers	• Provide safe havens • Facilitate escape • Provide information/early warning

today would be described as an atrocity crime (Kelly, M. 2012, 340). For example, in 1623, the Dutch East India Company tortured and beheaded twenty people it suspected of plotting against its spice trade in Amboyna. Indonesia. There are, however, recent cases in which private security personnel have been responsible for the commission of crimes that, in some circumstances, could be described as war crimes or crimes against humanity. These include the well-documented abuses by personnel working for Blackwater in Iraq (Kelly, E. 2012). More recent history has provided examples of private companies engaged within systems of mass extermination. Perhaps the most obvious example is the dozens of German companies that operated civilian workers' camps to exploit the labor of Jews and other imprisoned groups prior to their extermination in the Holocaust. As the story of one of those involved in this practice, Oskar Schindler, shows, private sector actors were fully aware of the system of extermination of which they were a direct part.

More commonly, however, private sector actors have aided the perpetration of genocide and mass atrocities through the provision of direct or indirect assistance. Direct assistance involves the provision of services or other resources to actors known to be perpetrators of genocide or mass atrocities. Popovski provides the example of Anvil Mining, which transported members of the Congolese Armed Forces (FARDC) to Kilwa, where it had a mine, to suppress a rebellion through extra-judicial executions. There are numerous examples of the provision of indirect assistance by private sector actors. By indirect assistance, I mean the provision of goods or services that provide material assistance to the perpetrators of mass atrocities, but where this is not provided with the intent of supporting such violence. Popovski, for example, describes how Talisman Energy and other multinational companies aided the Sudanese government's campaigns in Darfur and elsewhere through the transfer of royalty payments. Other examples include the foreign companies that supplied Rwanda with the machetes used to perpetrate the 1994 genocide, and the companies that helped Saddam Hussein amass a massive stockpile of chemical weapons, which he then employed against Kurdish civilians (Kelly, M. 2012, 320).

Most common of all, though, is the next role – that of bystanders.[8] This is a morally and legally ambiguous role that in general demands greater understanding and explanation, and is a function that the concept of the "individual R2P" can shed useful light upon (Luck and Luck 2015). Popovski describes this role as "non-perpetrators," requiring a "do no harm role." For Popovski, private sector actors that do not facilitate atrocities fall into this category. Although "non-perpetrator" is a useful legal phrase, it perhaps obscures the fact that the passivity in the face of genocide and mass atrocities to which it alludes actually helps facilitate these crimes. It is this additional consideration that is captured by the label "bystander," for bystanders are individuals or groups that are witnesses to events leading to genocide and mass atrocities but that choose to do nothing in response. Bystanders can be usefully further delineated into internal bystanders – those within the perpetrating society – and external bystanders – those with knowledge but who sit outside the perpetrating society itself. "Bystanders" are not neutral in situations of mass atrocity – their decision not to obstruct perpetrators or help

---

[8] See *Roots of Evil* (Staub 1992).

victims facilitates the commission of these crimes. Indeed, for atrocities to occur at anything beyond a modest and selective level, it is necessary that the vast majority of private actors "stand by" and do nothing.

Beyond "bystanders" we move into the positive roles that private sector actors can play in supporting prevention. As indirect supporters of prevention, private sector actors stop short of taking conscious steps to prevent atrocities or shield victims, but through their everyday actions and policies represent a challenge to the forces of escalation and a source of resilience and prevention. They fulfill these roles in a number of ways. For example, as Fort and Westermann-Behaylo point out in this volume, they can facilitate positive and mutually beneficial interactions between groups through gentle commerce. Or, as Jonas Claes points out, companies might resist ethnic, religious, or gender discrimination by pursuing an inclusive and non-discriminatory approach to recruitment and promotion for entirely self-interested reasons (because hiring and promoting on merit produces the most efficient outcomes). For similar reasons, they might foster the constructive management of difference within their organizations. In these ways, acting out of a sense of self-interest and in the name of economic efficiency, companies help challenge the politicization of difference that can lead to atrocities and reinforce a sense of shared humanity. By doing so, they help reduce general and horizontal inequalities through their investment and employment decisions, making it more difficult for political agitators to stimulate conflict by aggravating economic grievances. When they behave this way, private sector actors help to reinforce the norms and cultures that challenge atavistic ideologies and practices of hate speech and incitement. As Fort and Westermann-Behaylo show, they can also use their own diplomatic capacities to promote human rights and resolve tensions indirectly through resolving business "problems" – such as when tech companies work around government restrictions, allow their employees time for volunteer work, and help societies navigate through pressure points.

It is also necessary to recognize the important role that the private sector plays in helping societies rebuild after conflict, and the strong connection this has to the prevention of future crimes. Economic reconstruction plays a pivotal role in helping states and societies recover from war, and the forging of a vibrant private sector is central to that, though it is important to ensure that the "marketization" of economies does not lead to their capture by the very elites that led the country into war.[9]

---

[9] On which, see *At War's End* (Paris 2004).

Beyond that, private sector actors can be active supporters of prevention – and the preceding chapters have shed light on the many ways they might do this. As Popovski shows, they can provide logistical support to help prevention efforts and can offer pro bono services to support the various needs of those charged with atrocities prevention. In her chapter, Kirsten Martin shows how the information technology sector can employ its expertise in a variety of ways to support atrocity prevention, from enabling early warning through crowd sourcing and data analysis to monitoring and blocking hate speech and incitement.

As Patrick Obath and Victor Owuor show in this volume, one recent example of a comprehensive and joined up approach to active atrocity prevention is that of the Kenya Private Sector Alliance (KEPSA), an industry association comprised of some 200 organizations that took active steps to prevent violence during the country's 2013 election.[10] In the year immediately preceding the election, KEPSA implemented a campaign aimed at promoting peaceful elections and a peaceful transition of power, which included private meetings with key political actors, the promotion of peace in the wider community through initiatives such as a theme song for peace and a network of peace ambassadors, and a series of public events designed to reinforce the message. Individual members utilized their capabilities to support the endeavor. For example, mobile phone provider Safaricom issued guidelines on how to block hate messages and took steps to prevent the spreading of messages inciting violence through the mobile phone network.

Having been insufficiently organized to adopt an active role in prevention in 2007–2008, KEPSA played an important role in the successful effort to prevent violence during Kenya's 2013 election. As Obath and Owuor show, its experience carries with it some important lessons, not least relating to the capacity for private sector groupings to foster positive norms and encourage actors to adopt certain types of behavior. Not only did KEPSA actively promote peace within the wider Kenyan society, but it also created powerful norms that prescribed certain types of behavior within the business sector as appropriate or inappropriate. In particular, it promoted a politics of non-confrontation, and created a powerful social incentive for companies to move from "bystander" positions to "active supporters of prevention." These effects were amplified, Obath and Owuor show, by the group's cooperation with other types of actor in the non-government sector, including faith-based and community groups.

---

[10] Also see "Responsibility to Protect" (Alleblas 2015).

This brings us to the final role, that of rescuer. Alain Lempereur and Rebecca Herrington describe this role well in their contribution to this volume. As rescuers, private sector actors do whatever they can to protect civilians from harm, including providing safe haven, facilitating escape, containing perpetrators, providing early warning, or maintaining a steady flow of information to the outside world. Often improvising in the face of great adversity, these actors helped save thousands of lives through their direct – indeed, heroic – actions.

Integrating the private sector more fully into the practice of atrocity prevention essentially requires action to encourage companies to move down the scale toward more direct and active support for prevention. That is, it means action designed to (1) encourage those that have supported perpetrators to move toward becoming passive bystanders, (2) encourage bystanders to support prevention, and (3) encourage those that provide indirect assistance to consider taking more direct roles where appropriate. With these points in mind, the following section examines ways of developing understanding and practice with respect to the role of private sector actors in preventing genocide and mass atrocities.

Harnessing the Private Sector for Atrocity Prevention

How might private sector actors be better harnessed for atrocity prevention? This section leaves to one side the question of deterring companies from perpetrating or supporting (whether actively or indirectly) genocide and mass atrocities, as these are largely issues of monitoring and reporting, ensuring criminal accountability, expanding accountability to include complicity, and examining different types of deterrence to secure compliance with basic global norms and laws. These issues have been expertly canvassed elsewhere in this volume, especially by Popovski, and are the subject of a fairly extensive legal literature.[11] Instead, my focus in this section is on ways of harnessing the private sector to support atrocity prevention, and in particular on the ways in which the private sector can help support and promote national resilience to atrocity crimes. By "resilience" I mean the capacity of a society to withstand crises that could give rise to genocide and mass atrocities. Although international actors often have an important role to play in preventing these crimes, the key determinants of whether a crisis will spiral into atrocities lay deep within societies themselves. As such, this section briefly explores

---

[11] For example, see "Categories of Corporate Complicity" (Clapham and Jerbi 2001), "Setting the Framework" (Kaleck and Saage-Maass 2008), and "Prosecuting Corporations" (Kelly, M. 2012).

how private sector actors contribute to prevention before examining what needs to be done to persuade these actors to play a more important role and how they might be integrated into atrocity prevention efforts going forward.

From the analysis in the preceding chapters, it appears that private sector actors can make one or more of four critical contributions to social resilience. I categorize these as:

- norm diffusion;
- non-cooperation;
- service provision;
- active prevention.

These terms should be self-explanatory from the preceding discussion. Norm diffusion refers to the capacity of private sector actors to diffuse norms relating to inclusiveness, non-discrimination, equality of treatment, the rule of law, and rejection of violence through their everyday practices. As Lempereur and Herrington point out, this is achieved most effectively when companies are integrated into the surrounding community. Thus, private sector actors help instantiate global norms and reinforce a sense that incitement, hate speech, discrimination, and violence are socially unacceptable. Indeed, by enforcing policies of non-discrimination internally, companies can mount a direct challenge to hate speech and incitement, and promote more inclusive models of behavior as viable alternatives. Evidence from social psychology tells us that social pressures such as these that define the limits of appropriate behavior exert a powerful influence on human behavior (Zimbardo 2008). The idea of non-cooperation draws upon theories of non-violent change and is a development of the concept of "bystander." Companies that do not play an active role in prevention can nevertheless be a positive influence by simply refusing to cooperate with those engaged in inciting or perpetrating genocide and mass atrocities. Evidence shows that the commission of these crimes on a mass scale is possible only in conditions of acquiescence by a significant portion of the community. If the section of that community most responsible for generating wealth refused to cooperate, it would be very difficult for perpetrators to persist.

The final two categories, service provision and active prevention, relate to the variety of positive roles played by private sector actors, described earlier and in preceding chapters. The preceding chapters provide us with a long list of positive functions performed by private sector actors, which bears repeating here simply for the purpose of reinforcing the message about the need to better harness them. These roles include:

- promoting peace, non-violence, and non-discrimination;
- using their financial influence to deter leaders from atrocities;
- providing material support to the not-for-profit sector;
- providing logistical and infrastructure support for atrocity prevention efforts;
- organizing and supporting public demonstrations of opposition to discrimination and violence;
- supporting the rule of law and ensuring that employees comply with their legal obligations;
- gathering, analyzing, and disseminating information about emerging risks and ongoing atrocity crimes;
- supporting international organizations in conducting protection needs assessments;
- using whatever resources they have (personnel, monetary, transportation, etc.) to help the vulnerable to find safe haven or to flee;
- using their resources to persuade/encourage perpetrators to alter course;
- communicating information to the outside world, including through internal channels within a country;
- using functional positions to address specific prevention issues – for example, communications companies can block hate speech and incitement and disseminate information about atrocities and early warning;
- assisting in the learning of lessons from past cases.

While these activities are certainly no substitute for state responsibility, they can certainly make all the difference to the lives of thousands of civilians when atrocities strike. Just as importantly, however, as the example of KEPSA in Kenya attests, they can make a powerful contribution to more comprehensive strategies of prevention. It is precisely the development of comprehensive, nationally based but internationally supported strategies such as this that should lie at the heart of future efforts to prevent genocide and mass atrocities.

But as well as understanding how private sector actors behave in contexts of mass atrocities, we need to know why they behave in the ways they do, if those engaged in atrocity prevention are to do better at harnessing these actors. In the first section, I argued that because civil war and instability are generally bad for the economy, private sector actors have a direct interest in their prevention. Unfortunately, in practice, interests are rarely aggregated in such a rational fashion. Thus, confronted with their own narrow and short-term interest, private sector actors face strong incentives to accommodate regimes or other powerful actors that perpetrate mass atrocities. Although sometimes private sector actors might share the perpetrators' goals, their actions are usually explained as being driven by the profit motive and calculations about how best to achieve and enhance profits in unstable situations. In contexts of escalating violence, companies face difficult choices about how to maintain their competitive advantage, protect their investments, and, a particular problem in resource-driven civil conflicts, secure their access to natural resources (Van der Wilt 2006, 255). Often, in such circumstances, some level of complicity (whether active or passive) appears warranted in order to protect the company's financial interests.

While the profit motive is undoubtedly significant, concern for profits alone cannot explain the wide variation of responses to atrocity crimes exhibited by private sector actors which, as noted earlier, spans the range from willing perpetrator to active rescuer. Clearly other factors, such as the company's global position, the identities and interests of its leadership, and the moral commitments of its personnel play a significant role, too (Tripathi 2010, 133). In particular, the type of business culture fostered within organizations can play a significant role in decisions about whether to support, ignore, or prevent atrocity crimes. Those that value goal attainment above all else might be more susceptible to complicity than those that subscribe to strong moral principles, as managers are driven and rewarded to do whatever they can to maintain profit margin despite conditions of violent conflict or mass atrocities (Van Baar and Huisman 2012).

As such, it is important to understand that although the "profit motive" is a powerful determinant of private sector behavior, the way it is understood and pursued is not immutable. Instead, it is open to contestation and reconstitution within organizations. This means that there is scope for influencing behavior by incorporating atrocity prevention considerations into global dialogue, and expectations, about corporate social responsibility. But this also needs to be a "bottom-up" exercise led by local business leaders who set their own expectations about the tangible roles that private sector actors can play in preventing genocide and mass atrocities. Once again, KEPSA provides an excellent example. Through this "bottom-up" approach, global conversations about the role of the private could be broadened in scope to include non-western actors, and especially the emerging Asian multinationals and panoply of local businesses in various parts of the world that can influence affairs within their own community.

But beyond this sort of global norm building, based on the models already established by the UN's efforts in corporate social responsibility, how can the private sector be better incorporated into global strategic thinking about atrocities prevention? What can the UN, in particular, do to better engage with, and harness the potential of, private sector actors? The answer is connected to a broader issue confronting atrocity prevention: the need for the field as a whole to move beyond an approach characterized by broad and generic discussions about risks and "prevention tools" and ad hoc responses to imminent crises toward more of a finely grained understanding of specific problems and carefully tailored strategies for addressing them.

The first step is to ensure that private sector actors are consulted over, and incorporated into, assessments of risk and resilience in given countries. This would help open opportunities for engagement and relationship building and, through the very process of inviting participation, would create positive social inducements for private sector actors to become involved in atrocity prevention. The first stage of any serious attempt to prevent atrocities is the development of a detailed understanding of country situations. Country assessments are necessary to identify local sources of risk, and as the UN Secretary-General noted in his 2010 report on "Early Warning and Assessment," need to provide a "moving picture," not a one-off snapshot (UN General Assembly 2010). Being a moving picture, assessments need not always emphasize the prediction of genocide and mass atrocities. Their principal purpose is to build situational awareness, and to identify specific sources of risk and potential sites of escalation. In some conditions, however, such as prior to an election or at the onset of civil strife, assessments might examine the likely trajectory of events as a guide to policy and contingency planning (see below). As noted earlier, private sector actors are embedded within their communities and are often well placed to provide information about the situations they confront. Allowing this information to flow into the assessments of organizations such as the UN would not only improve the quality of the overall analysis but would also begin to engage private sector actors in thinking about relevant risks.

An important corollary to risk assessment is the need to identify local sources of resilience that international policies and programs might impact upon or support. To date, early warning assessments have tended to focus only on the sources of risk (McLoughlin 1999); they have not identified the local actors, institutions and processes that might help to mitigate these risks. As a result, analysts have been hard pressed to explain why some countries that exhibit underlying risk succumb to mass violence while others that exhibit an equal, or sometimes greater, level of risk appear to avoid mass killing, leading the UN Secretary-General to call for further research on this topic (UN General Assembly 2009). Situational assessments provide only part of the picture if they focus only on risk and not on the local sources of resilience. Evidence deduced from observations in some of those countries suggests that a diverse range of factors might foster national resilience to genocide and mass atrocities. These factors include:

- the fragmentation of political authority (which makes it difficult to build a coalition in support of atrocities);
- cultures that promote equality between ethnic groups and high levels of economic integration between those groups;
- strong and relatively independent judiciaries;
- vibrant civil and private sectors that can exert a brake on tendencies toward extremism and violence;
- opposition groups that have dedicated themselves to non-violence (which makes it difficult for governments to justify widespread open violence, as in the case of Zimbabwe);
- legitimate political leadership that listens to non-state sources and is willing to sacrifice narrow self-interest in order to avoid violent conflict.

International efforts in support of prevention are likely to be both more efficient (delivering more added value for equal or less investment) and effective (better able to prevent genocide and mass atrocities) if they are directed wherever possible to supporting local sources of resilience.

The focus on local resilience implies a different ethos to that of more traditional conceptions of structural prevention. The latter has tended to assume that outsiders know which deep structures give rise to violent conflict and which do not in any given society, and to foster interventions that support the former. By contrast, a focus on resilience starts with an understanding of the local institutions, dynamics, groups, individuals, and other factors that provide bulwarks against genocide and mass atrocities, and asks what can be done to support these already existing sources of strength in a way that does not impose particular prevention templates on individual situations. Clearly, as the preceding discussion has demonstrated, private sector actors can be important sources of resilience. This needs to be identified and supported.

Associated with this, harm mitigation is an important part of atrocity prevention and it is imperative that organizations such as the UN avoid exacerbating risks through the unintended consequences of their actions. This requires a form of "due diligence" of the type already employed by some organizations operating in conflict situations, and called for by some of the other contributors to this volume. Known as "conflict sensitivity," some government programs that deliver aid in conflict settings (e.g. the US Agency for International Development (USAID) and the U.K. Department for International Development (DFID)) employ frameworks to assess the impact of their aid on the social environment.

It is important that such work is done on a systematic basis and that it includes sensitivity to atrocity risks. Being on the "shop floor" of national economies, private sector actors are well placed to advise on harm mitigation, especially relating to the unintended impact of international policies on horizontal inequalities. At the same time, major employers could themselves be encouraged to consider their role in mitigating unintended harm caused by recruitment and investment strategies. For example, some economic strategies that prioritize growth could inadvertently increase horizontal inequalities, proving counter-productive in the long run.

Beyond developing analysis of risk and resilience to guide its assessments, the UN could examine ways of receiving information about risks and potential triggers from private sector actors. Indeed, patterns of trade and business confidence sometimes provide the first visible indications of deeper fears within a community. Although it came as a surprise to some UN officials and state delegations in New York that the 2007 elections in Kenya gave rise to communal violence and atrocities, it was not unexpected among experts and private sector actors inside the country (Sharma 2012). Although we have some understanding of the triggers of genocide and mass atrocities, there is no substitute for the sort of heavily contextualized analysis that can be offered from within communities. As several of the preceding chapters have demonstrated, private sector actors have sometimes warned of atrocities and ongoing information about patterns of violence. Given that such finely grained information is often difficult to come by, establishing networks for the exchange of information and analysis between private sector actors in vulnerable countries and those charged with providing early warning advice in the UN would help strengthen the latter's capacity (as well as reinforcing connections with potential sources of resilience).

The value of these networks, which have to be established in advance, comes into sharp relief in crises involving the potential commission of genocide and mass atrocities. As the case of Kenya in 2013 (in contrast to Kenya in 2008–2009) shows, there is immense value in the development and implementation of national strategies to prevent violence, and private sector actors have a critical role to play. The underlying purpose of advance early warning assessment is to identify those countries or regions that require this sort of pre-planning and the potential triggers to violence. One key priority for the UN ought to be to explore options for facilitating and supporting these strategies in the countries that need them. Sometimes, as in Kenya, potential triggers are so well signaled in advance that national actors can take the lead. In other circumstances, however, it may be that the UN itself will have to take the initiative in bringing together national partners for prevention. Whatever approach is taken, it is clear from the preceding analysis that private sector actors should be part of the process. While it may not be possible to replicate KEPSA in every case, that is certainly a model of collective private sector action that could guide future strategies.

In the midst of mass atrocities, the nature of both the work and the relationships involved changes once again. However, the inclusion of private sector actors in networks focussed on preventing makes it more likely that these actors will take steps to do what they can to protect vulnerable people. Understanding that this will be inevitably small in scale, nevertheless it is imperative that international actors such as the UN do what they can to (1) utilize opportunities where they exist (for example, by taking up opportunities to use logistical support and services provided by private sector actors) and (2) support local endeavors by private sector actors (for example, by receiving, analyzing, and passing on information, assisting in "rescue," and promoting safe havens). Ideally, in such situations, the UN or other relevant organizations would develop a comprehensive response strategy. Although great strides have been made in the past few decades to include non-governmental organizations in these processes, little consideration is given to private sector actors, including those – such as chambers of commerce – that might represent significant parts of the population. By forging key relationships with private sector actors in advance, UN officials and others can build them into their networks of response. Through this, it may be possible to develop more comprehensive responses to genocide and mass atrocities that make better use of human and material resources already in situ.

The atrocity prevention field also needs to become more systematic in its approach to learning lessons and to develop repositories of knowledge about the types of actions that produce good effects in different sorts of situations and the full range of preventive actions undertaken by different actors. Efforts to prevent electoral violence in Kenya in 2013 involved the government, international organizations and foreign governments, civil society, private sector groups such as KEPSA, and prominent individuals. Understanding, precisely, who did what and to what effect is important for enabling better prepared and targeted strategies for prevention in the future.

But these initiatives ought to be mindful of the barriers of participation confronted by private sector actors, such as those identified by Jill Shankleman in her chapter on the attitudes of extractive industries. As Shankleman points out, however negligible the risk, private sector actors are likely to resist adopting "responsibilities" for protection that might encumber them with legal duties and expose them to litigation. They are also, she shows, typically reluctant to become embroiled in political affairs or concerns related to the potential use of military force. What is more, although genocide and mass atrocities are "high cost" events, they are also "low probability," making it difficult for private sector actors to sustain a business case for investment.

Conclusion

In his 2009 report on *Implementing the Responsibility to Protect*, UN Secretary-General Ban Ki-moon called for a "narrow but deep" approach to atrocity prevention and response that marshaled all the resources at the international community's disposal (UN General Assembly 2009). Until relatively recently, however, the theory and practice of atrocity prevention have tended to overlook the roles played by a significant section of society – the private sector. Reflecting on the preceding chapters in this volume, this chapter has set out the case for including private sector actors in prevention practice (primarily on the grounds that, whether recognized or not, these actors are effectual), reviewed the various roles played by private sector actors, and suggested some modest steps that might be taken to better incorporate them into the planning and practice of atrocity prevention. In so doing, it suggested there was a broad synergy between the goal of integrating the private sector into atrocity prevention and translating that agenda into actualized practice on a more systematic basis. What is required, it suggested, is a more fine-grained and "bottom-up" approach to prevention that takes local sources of risk and resilience as its starting points and builds from there. There is much that stronger partnership between organizations such as the UN and private sector actors can do to facilitate that sort of approach to making atrocity prevention a "lived reality."

References

Alleblas, Tessa. 2015. "The Responsibility to Protect and the private sector: Making the business case for private sector involvement in mass atrocity prevention." Working Paper 5, presented at The Hague Institute for Global Justice, January 14–15.

Bellamy, Alex J. 2009. *The Responsibility to Protect: The Global Effort to End Mass Atrocities*. Cambridge: Polity.

"The other Asian miracle: The decline of mass atrocities in East Asia." *Global Change, Peace, and Security* 26:1.

Chesterman, Alex J. 2009. "Leading from behind: The Responsibility to Protect, the Obama Doctrine, and humanitarian intervention after Libya." *Ethics and International Affairs* 25:279.

Clapham, Andrew and Scott Jerbi. 2001. "Categories of corporate complicity in human rights abuses." *Hastings International and Comparative Law Review* 24:339.

Cohen, Jean L. 2012. *Globalization and Sovereignty: Rethinking Legality, Legitimacy and Constitutionalism*. Cambridge University Press.

Collier, Paul. 2008. *The Bottom Billion: Why the Poorest Countries are Failing and What Can Be Done About It?* New York: Oxford University Press, 117–137.

Erskine, Toni. 2013. "Moral agency and R2P." In *Oxford Handbook on the Responsibility to Protect*, edited by Alex J. Bellamy and Tim Dunne. Oxford University Press.

Kaleck, Wolfgang and Miriam Saage-Maass. 2008. "Setting the framework: Corporate accountability for human rights violations amounting to international crimes: The status quo and its challenges." *Journal of International Criminal Justice* 8 (3):699–724.

Kelly, Emily. 2012. "Holding Blackwater accountable: Private security companies and the protections of use immunity." *Boston College International and Comparative Law Review* 35:3.

Kelly, Michael J. 2012. "Prosecuting corporations for genocide under international law." *Harvard Law and Policy Review* 6:340.

Krasner, Stephen. 1999. *Sovereignty: Organized Hypocrisy*. Princeton University Press.

Luck, Edward C. 2010. "The Responsibility to Protect: Growing pains or early promise?" *Ethics and International Affairs* 24 (4):349, 363.

Luck, Edward C. and Dana Z. Luck. 2015. "The individual Responsibility to Protect." In *Reconstituting Atrocity Prevention*, edited by Sheri Rosenberg and Alex Zucker. Cambridge University Press.

MacGinty, Roger. 2011. *International Peacebuilding and Local Resistance: Hybrid Forms of Peace*. London: Palgrave.

McLoughlin, Stephen. 2014. *The Structural Prevention of Mass Atrocities: Understanding Risk and Resilience*. London: Routledge.

Paris, Roland. 2004. *At War's End: Building Peace After Conflict*. Cambridge University Press.

Pattison, James. 2010. *Humanitarian Intervention and the Responsibility to Protect: Who Should Intervene?* Oxford University Press.

Raeymaekers, Timothy. 2014. *Violent Capitalism and Hybrid Identity in Eastern Congo: Power to the Margins*. Cambridge University Press.

Ralph, Jason. 2013. "The international criminal court." In *Oxford Handbook on the Responsibility to Protect*, edited by Alex J. Bellamy and Tim Dunne. Oxford University Press.

Roff, Heather. 2013. *Global Justice, Kant and the Responsibility to Protect: A Provisional Duty*. London: Routledge.

Sharma, Serena K. 2012. "The 2007–08 post election crisis in Kenya: A success story for the Responsibility to Protect?" In *Responsibility to Protect: From Principle to Practice*, edited by Julia Hoffmann and Andre Nollkaemper. Amsterdam: Pallas Publications.

Singer, Peter W. 2008 (revised). *Corporate Warrior: The Rise of the Privatized Military Industry*. Ithaca, NY: Cornell University Press.

Staub, Ervin. 1992. *The Roots of Evil: The Origins of Genocide and Other Group Violence*. Cambridge University Press.

Stel, Nora. 2014. "Business in genocide – understanding the how and why of corporate complicity in genocides." Working Paper 2014/28, prepared for Maastricht School of Management Conference, September 4, Maastricht, The Netherlands.

Tripathi, Salil. 2010. "Business in armed conflict zones: How to avoid complicity and comply with international standards." *Politorbis* 50 (3):133.

United Nations General Assembly. 2005. "2005 World Summit Outcome." Document A/Res/60/1, October 24. www.un.org/womenwatch/ods/A-RES-60-1-E.pdf

2009. *Implementing the Responsibility to Protect: Report of the Secretary-General*, A/63/677 (January 12). www.unrol.org/files/SG_reportA_63_677_en.pdf

2010. *Early Warning, Assessment and the Responsibility to Protect: Report of the Secretary-General*, A/64/864 (July 14). www.responsibilitytoprotect.org/N1045020(1).pdf

United Nations Security Council. 2012. *Responsibility to Protect: Timely and Decisive Response. Report of the Secretary-General*, A/66/874-S/2012/578 (July 25).

Van Baar, Annika and Wim Huisman. 2012. "The oven-builders of the Holocaust: A case study of corporate complicity in international crimes." *British Journal of Criminology* 52 (6):1033–1050.

Van der Wilt, Herman G. 2006. "Genocide, complicity in genocide and international v. domestic jurisdiction: Reflections on the Van Anraad case." *Journal of International Criminal Justice* 4 (2):255.

Zimbardo, Phillip. 2008. *The Lucifer Effect: Understanding How Good People Turn Evil*. New York: Random House.

10   The Way Forward: Discovering the Shared Interests between Business and R2P

John Forrer and Conor Seyle

Introduction

International actors interested in preventing and mitigating mass atrocities achieved a notable breakthrough with the formal adoption in 2005 of R2P principles by the United Nations General Assembly. A decade later, the recent experiences in the Ukraine, Iraq, Syria, and Burma underscore the profound challenges that remain to realize that vision for global peace and security. The gap between the aspirations for R2P and its efficacy to date suggests that more work is needed in both designing and implementing R2P policies and practice aimed at atrocity prevention. One dimension of that work is a more complete and sophisticated understanding of the role of business in R2P. The contributors to this book make a convincing case, one of the necessity for all public and private actors to include businesses of all types in the discourse and practice of R2P. The challenge moving forward in crafting roles for business that are more concrete and operational is the discovery of where business and R2P interests align, and identifying those actions that achieve the realization of these mutual interests.

Drawing from the findings and insights presented in this volume, we highlight some guidance and actions relevant and applicable for involving business in R2P, and describe a practical framework for engaging private sector actors and other institutions in a collaborative process of discovery to support R2P. This is not an easy or obvious task. Incorporating private sector actors into R2P dialog and practice faces a number of challenges. Traditionally, nations are presumed to have responsibility for addressing issues of peace and security within their own borders and internationally. Many public and private sector actors would not see business engagement with R2P as being appropriate or even legitimate. In addition, there is a presumed gulf between the interests of private sector actors focussed on the day-to-day demands of their business and the state and international actors focussed on their specific legal or institutional mandates. In this view, businesses focus on profits and must attend to issues associated

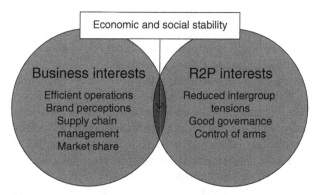

Figure 10.1 Overlap between business and R2P interests as frequently perceived

with competitiveness, risk, regulation, and reputation. They will act in the interests of their shareholders and stakeholders to maximize shareholder value. And these endeavors have little to do with preventing, or responding to, mass atrocities. Figure 10.1 sets out our assessment of where mainstream literature and most people now understand the overlap between shared business and R2P interests.

The Relationship between Business and R2P

The arguments laying out why businesses are not interested in supporting R2P are familiar; they are in many ways the same arguments lodged to explain why private sector actors should be unmotivated more broadly to support peace. In the case of peace overall, these arguments have been largely discredited. As we discussed in the Overview chapter, and as referenced by many other authors in the book, a literature has emerged over the past fifteen years documenting the role that businesses can play in promoting peace. These findings have informed and inspired the exploration of the role of business and R2P.

The business and peace literature forecasts a vast common ground of shared interests for business and R2P. It suggests that economic and social stability offers a rich claim for discovering new and constructive roles for business and R2P. A key in moving forward is to recognize that shared interests exist not just in stability in the abstract but in how that stability is achieved. For example, advancing environmental sustainability, supporting equitable societies, respect for human rights and rule of law, accountable governance and transparency, support for anti-corruption, among others, contribute to making communities more peaceful, more stable, and undermine justifications for race-, ethnic-, religion-, or gender-based animosities and conflict. And these conditions in turn lessen the likelihood of mass atrocities.

These same efforts help maintain or bring about more favorable business climates. It is much easier to sell services or goods when communities are peaceful, there is limited structural violence, markets are not disrupted, and people are not being uprooted by violent conflict. Supply chains do not operate efficiently if there is conflict that disrupts markets and commerce. Planting and harvesting are neglected and goods cannot be produced or transported without great risks of losses when violence and fighting persist in the area. Of course, wars and conflict fuel their own kind of commerce and in specific sectors, but nearly all businesses prefer a "peace economy" over a "war economy." Businesses have a vested interest in minimizing conflict and promoting stability in the areas where they are engaged. The means by which this is achieved articulate the shared interests of business and R2P.

As these shared interests are discovered and applied, it is useful to recognize that businesses may not always endorse or support specific R2P policies and recommendations put forward by international actors or third-party advocates. In practice, business leaders are confronted with a large number of issues and challenges, with limited time and resources at their disposal. R2P options and trade-offs need to be assessed in the context of the strategic goals of a business. Businesses should be allowed the discretion to address R2P in the ways of their own choosing – sometimes they will align with recommended policies and practices and other times they will not. Moreover, the competitive nature of markets means that even businesses that are strongly motivated to support R2P may not be in a position to dedicate all the resources and efforts requested. The unwillingness of business to support or take an R2P action does not necessarily indicate the absence of interest in or commitment to R2P. Businesses have to develop their own approach given the organizational and market constraints they face. The guidance and actions identified by the authors in this book provide insights into the prospects and possibilities for the role of business and R2P. However, discovering shared business and R2P interests should reflect the specific conditions at that time and in that community that make sense for businesses and other parties.

Despite the popular perception that the shared business and R2P interests are small and limited, this book demonstrates that in fact there are limitless confluences between the issues that reside within the domains of peace and atrocity prevention and those in business. Figure 10.2 presents

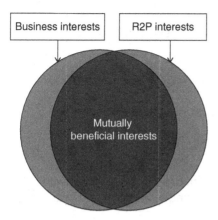

Figure 10.2 Actual relationship between business and R2P interests

what we believe to be the real situation with regard to business and R2P interests.

A Framework for Discovering Shared Business and R2P Interests

Given the rich but largely unrecognized common cause between the interests of business and those interested in R2P, we propose a framework for how to engage the private sector and government entities and other third parties in support for R2P. Figure 10.3 sets out this framework graphically in three stages. This framework is based on our experiences as researchers and practitioners working in getting businesses involved in peace, and in particular our perception that partnerships engaging businesses in support of R2P should start with an acknowledgment and understanding of the interests of the different actors involved, and work from this starting point to move toward longer-term engagement.

This framework is presented as a linear model that develops from the earliest stages of discovery, through limited and specific activities conducted out of mutual self-interest, into larger forms of systemic engagement, and changes in institutional policy and practice. The real world is never so neat, and in practice this approach should be adapted to the specifics of each individual location or community. If the political conditions allow for direct and sustained engagement without specific proposed activities, for example, then this opportunity should be seized. A rigid linear approach that tries to follow the above steps without adaptation will probably miss important opportunities. With that important caveat,

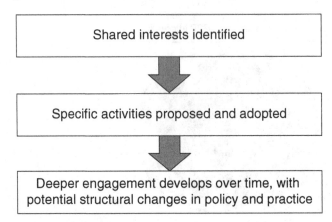

Figure 10.3 Framework for discovering shared business and R2P engagement

the framework described above provides one approach for engaging private sector actors in atrocity prevention that accepts as a starting point the fact that for many institutions in both the private and public sectors there are few perceived shared goals. We believe that when this framework is employed to develop a process of discovery, and peace and business actors work together to engage with atrocity prevention, the people and institutions involved will come to see the direct overlap between their interests.

Shared Interests Identified

We argue that institutions interested in developing partnerships in support of R2P should begin by working across sectors to identify shared interests in the context of the local conditions affecting peace and stability: particularly in the context of an imminent or ongoing atrocity; neither businesses nor R2P-focussed I(N)GOs will have the time or inclination to engage in general discussion or abstract engagement with theoretical ideas. Instead, calls for cross-sector coordination should be couched in terms of the specific and limited interests of each institution. In the case of specific threats of atrocity, this could mean specific appeals to businesses to meet to discuss the threat of violence and its potential impact on business operations. Similarly, businesses reaching out to NGOs or IGOs interested in R2P should lead with the specific idea of contributing to atrocity prevention. Examples from this book may be valuable in contributing to this kind of cross-sector identification of shared interests.

For example, Fort and Westermann-Behaylo in Chapter 2 offer examples of how companies can shape their general and day-to-day operations in ways sensitive to stability and peace. In the initial identification of shared interests, all parties should search for concrete, actionable proposals that address R2P issues but also advance their specific individual and institutional goals. Linking the shared goals with specific outcomes that benefit individual parties makes for a more sustainable and meaningful collaboration. As suggested by several authors in this volume, including Obath and Owuor in Chapter 5 and Shankleman in Chapter 6, working through umbrella associations and organized groups of firms can be particularly useful for accomplishing this.

Specific Activities Proposed and Adopted

In support of the operationalization of discovered shared interests, the next stage in the framework is the identification of specific activities that can be undertaken by businesses to support R2P. Cases presented in this volume include a fairly large range of such activities that may be considered as starting points, ranging from Lempereur and Herrington's suggestions in Chapter 3 that firms develop individual capacity to support R2P prevention, to Obath and Owuor's list of activities carried out by KEPSA, including direct diplomacy and peaceful messaging. In Chapter 7, Kirsten Martin suggests that "firms may be in a position to help victims of human rights violations through their products and services. The creation of a product or service carries the possibility for good (help the vulnerable) in building capacity to protect populations," and in Chapter 8 Vesselin Popovski supports this through his words. "Companies can contribute to mitigation and de-escalation of conflicts through commercial or philanthropic support for humanitarian relief and through responsible management of security arrangements for their operations, thereby minimizing the risks of atrocities."

The recommendations in this volume provide a starting point from both theory and history, laying out what kinds of activities businesses can take up in support of R2P. There is no cookie-cutter solution, however, and none of these activities should be taken as a panacea or used uncritically. Those institutions interested in bringing together firms and institutions interested in atrocity prevention should take care that any specific solution proposed must fit with the capacities and the interests of both the firms and the R2P-supporting institutions being brought to the table, and also be calibrated to the specific conflict dynamics in the country of operations. The examples in this book can serve as a starting point for what kinds of work can be done, but should be fit to the specific needs and abilities of groups being engaged with.

Deeper Engagement and Structural Change Develops Over Time

If initial engagement between different institutions is successful in identifying contextually specific shared interests and some specific activities that can advance them, it sets a strong foundation for a continued process of engagement that can support more structural and long-lasting efforts incorporating business into R2P. These efforts include lasting change in the policy and practice of business or political actors, not just one-off actions or reactive engagement. In order to accomplish such changes, if there is interest in them, then institutions should look to develop structures for cross-sector engagement that bring in communities, peacebuilders, local governmental institutions, and other groups of stakeholders. As with the specific activities discussed above, contributors to this volume also have some models for how systematic institutional change can be achieved. In Chapter 5, Obath and Owuor provide one model for this kind of structured and sustained engagement. As stated there, "key political actors have private sector interests … The actors are therefore able to communicate with other businesspeople about these common interests, sharing a language of needs and interests that helps the actors see the economic importance of political stability." Local politicians, with an interest in stability both for their careers and for, in this instance, economic gain, can serve as an efficient engagement channel for private actors. Kirsten Martin also speaks on engagement, stating that "firms may be in a unique position through their knowledge and/or position within a network of stakeholders facilitating to provide assistance and build capacity for prevention of atrocities."

This larger engagement may be codified into formal changes in policy and practice at the firm or international organization level. In addition to articulating specific aspects of the framework for identifying mutual interests, the authors in this book have offered larger guidelines on what the idea of private sector engagement in R2P can mean for policy and practice around R2P. Reflecting the diversity of perspectives on what R2P and atrocity prevention can look like, the authors have offered a variety of perspectives on what the larger guidelines for institutional practice might be. Jonas Claes in Chapter 4 laid out an "early warning/early prevention" guideline that the private sector can follow to construct its own policy on ensuring that atrocities and disasters are stopped before they happen. Another in-depth guideline presented by our authors can be seen in Chapter 3 by Alain Lempereur and Rebecca Herrington. Their "3P" framework shows one approach that private actors may use to assess conflict and gives tools for engaging with how businesses should assist, how to correctly identify the problem, and the process of what they can do to assist. Looking more at state actors, MacDiarmid and Park in Chapter 1 argue that businesses should be considered an extension of the existing system, not a replacement: "The focus of our attention should not be on replacing the capacities and roles already played by the international organizations like the UN or regional bodies, or a state's primary responsibilities, but about how best to fill the gap found in our existing mechanisms for protection capacity."

This kind of larger structural change may be the most effective way of formalizing and operationalizing the role of the private sector in R2P – but it's also likely to be the type of change that will face the most resistance from both firms and other institutions. Because of this, structural change is certainly an important element of approaches to engaging business in R2P, but it may not be useful for programs attempting to accomplish this engagement to present R2P as the sole goal of engagement. Other forms of activity and engagement that accomplish more limited goals can be effective outcomes in directly addressing specific R2P situations and building blocks supporting the argument that there is a need for structural change.

Conclusion

The authors in this volume realize the perceived differences between peace interests and business interests are sizable, and for at least the near term, such perceptions will persist. Any setting of an agenda for actions that anticipate business support of R2P should start with an appreciation of these pre-conceptions. At the same time, the contributors to this book have delivered "proof-of-concept" demonstrations that there are substantial shared business and R2P interests and mutually beneficial approaches. They provide an invaluable inventory of possibilities and potentials for roles businesses can play in R2P. Their findings are not the last word on the subject but the first discoveries: a "head start" in helping us understand where shared business and R2P interests may reside and what actions could be taken to make them manifest. In this volume and in this concluding chapter we have attempted to avoid two potential pitfalls that can easily come out of a discourse at this stage: either an uncritical argument that the way forward is obvious and easy, or a pessimism that says that operationalizing these ideas is doomed to failure.

In our analysis, the state of play as captured by the contributors to this volume is that there are both solid analytical reasons and compelling examples that demonstrate the potential for private sector engagement in R2P. These are set against the reality that for many firms and international institutions, the current perception is that the interests of these institutions are so far apart as to make concrete engagement difficult.

Based on the claims made by the contributors here, and our own experiences working to engage firms in peacebuilding and good governance, we describe with examples a method for involving R2P actors and firms in a process of discovery. It starts with a focus on shared business and R2P interests, and progresses to identifying specific activities that each entity can take – unilaterally and collaboratively – to support these same interests, and ultimately develop long-term and structural changes that address R2P issues

The suggestions on the role of business in R2P offered here are practical approaches, quite emphatically not as moral principles that we argue should determine either business or state behavior. We are not seeking to impose or ask certain actions of the private sector, but instead to explain and propose what it can reasonably do, under the proper circumstances. Similarly, our proposed actions are offered to state and other non-state actors in the spirit of pragmatic advice: engaging with business in the interest of accomplishing shared goals rather than a normative claim about which institutions warrant inclusion in these discussions. Finally, we make no claims as to larger theoretical issues about institutional legitimacy or the appropriate structure of global institutions, but instead offer these principles as our analysis of how states and businesses can work together to support atrocity prevention and cessation.

In this chapter, we have attempted to lay out one way for negotiating the rocky path leading from this starting point to a more systemic engagement between R2P actors and the private sector. The contributors to this volume have provided a set of actions that businesses and interested institutions may consider. Not every approach is appropriate for every situation, and the specific activities and engagement strategies considered will need to be selected and tuned for the unique conditions of any specific R2P violation. This list is not comprehensive, and we invite other authors to add to the suggestions in this book.

Our hope is that the various approaches that our authors have provided will act as the spark for private enterprise to progress its relationship with peacebuilders around the world. In addition, we hope to have given adequate analysis of such to ensure that private enterprise can effectively operate with peacebuilders. As the current relationship between business and peace resides nearer to the bleak unengaging extractive industry side of the business spectrum, we believe that there is promise for a much brighter and productive relationship between the private sector and peace. Such a relationship may demonstrate the error in a limited understanding of institutional self-interest, and underscore the close associations between what's good for peace and what's good for business.

Index

Abacha, Sani, 190
ABB, 197
Adas, Mariam Abu, 177
Afghanistan, 141
Africa Union, 124
African Commission on Human and
    Peoples' Rights, 36
African Union, 26, 45, 47, 124, 211
Al Jazeera, 178
Al Shabaab, 210
Albright, Madeleine, 106
Algeria, 12
Alien Tort Claims Act (ATCA), 191,
    195, 196
Allende, Salvador, 17, 18
Al-Qaeda, 190
Aluminium Corporation of China
    (Chinalco), 144
American International Group, Inc., 117
Amnesty International, 107, 147
Amung, 190
Anglo American, 196
Angola, 197
Annan, Kofi, 11–12, 13, 21, 22, 23, 38, 98,
    104, 125, 127
Anvil Mining, 190–91, 216
apartheid, 18, 195, 197, 200
Apple, 53
Arab Spring, 163, 174–75, 176, 177,
    179–80, 181
    and social media, 175–76
Árbenz, Jacobo, 1
Arbour, Louise, 191
Auschwitz concentration camp, 72, 88
Australia, 12, 144, 145
Austria, 196
authoritarian regimes, 163, 168, 174, 176,
    177, 180, 181
Axworthym Lloyd, 37
Azerbaijan, 147

Bahrain, 175
Baidu, Inc., 172–73
Balkans, 10, 197
Baltic and International Maritime Council
    (BIMCO), 108
Bangladesh, 109, 110
Bankier, Abraham, 71
Banque Indo-Suez, 196
Barclays, 195
Barclays Bank, 117, 195
BBC, 93, 117
Bharti Airtel Limited, 117
BHP Billiton, 144
Biafra, 192, 193, 194
Bignami, Enrico, 192
Bizimungu, Augustin, 88
Blackwater Company, 215
Blair, Tony, 40–41
Boko Haram, 194, 210, 211
Bosnia, 37, 38, 140, 197
Bosnia-Herzegovina, 24
Boutros-Ghali, Boutros, 21
Brazil, 43, 145
Britain. *See* United Kingdom
British Petroleum, 156
Brown, Gordon, 194
Buddhism, 56
Bulgaria, 194
Burma, 147, 200, 230
Bush, George W., 40
business and peace field, 2, 3, 4, 52, 58,
    103, 185, 231, 238
business diplomacy, 62–65
Business for Peace Foundation, 2, 62

CacheFlow, 176
Cambodia, 140
Cameroon, 147
Canada, 12, 36, 37, 38, 101, 144, 190, 191
capitalism, 20, 55, 73

CARE International, 195
Cash Learning Partnership, 193
Caux Round Table (CRT), 74
Cental Intelligence Agency, 18
Central African Republic, 46, 109, 138,
    141, 149, 150, 210
Central Organisation of Trade Unions
    (COTU), 127–28
Centre for the Responsibility to Protect,
    36, 165
Chad, 141, 203
Chile, 17, 18
China, 55, 63, 144, 148, 149, 154, 163,
    168, 169–73, 174, 176, 177, 178,
    181, 182
Christianity, 55, 117, 131, 190
    Catholicism, 54, 55, 71, 87
    Protestantism, 54, 55
Chua, Amy, 55
Cisco Systems, 194
Citigroup, 117, 195
climate change, 98
CNBC, 117
Coca-Cola Company, 117
Code of Conduct, 186, 198–201, 202
Cohen, Roberta, 40
Cohen, William, 106
Cold War, 10, 17, 20, 21, 37, 210
Collins, Randal, 54
colonialism, 18, 56, 60
Columbia, 57
Commerz, 196
conflict diamonds, 13, 15
conflict minerals, 148
Congolese Revolutionary Army, 210
Convention on the Prevention and
    Punishment of the Crime of
    Genocide, 101
corporate foreign policy, 53–54
corporate philanthropy, 65, 156
corporate social responsibility (CSR), 3–4,
    45, 64, 74, 91, 99, 105, 138, 139,
    146–47, 153, 155, 157, 163–65,
    166, 167, 181, 182, 185, 188, 189,
    196, 198, 199, 201, 206, 222
Côte d'Ivoire, 37, 104, 141
Credit Lyonnais, 196
Credit Suisse, 196
crimes against humanity, 3, 9, 10, 13,
    24, 35, 37, 41, 42, 82, 99, 138,
    140, 156, 157, 165, 176, 182, 187,
    188, 189, 195, 196, 198, 206,
    209, 215
Croatia, 197
cross-sector collaboration, 197

Cyprus, 54, 55, 57
Czechoslovakia, 72, 78, 89

Darfur, 216
De Beers Corporations, 196
democracy, 4, 55, 89, 118, 176
Democratic Republic of the Congo, 138,
    141, 144, 148, 150, 190, 191,
    210, 216
Deng, Francis, 40
Deshpande, Rohit, 80, 81
Deutsche Bank, 189, 196
Deutsche Post, 195
Diageo, 117
Dodd--Frank Wall Street Reform and
    Consumer Protection Act 2010,
    148, 149
Dutch East India Company, 215
duty to rescue, 83, 85

Early Warning and Assessment, 223
ebola, 155, 156
Egypt, 21, 63, 175, 176, 177, 180
El Salvador, 57
Eldoret, Kenya, 121, 126
Electoral Commission of Kenya (ECK),
    120, 121
Emalia Factory, 71–73, 86
Embu, 120
Enforcing Responsibility to Protect: the
    Role of Parliamentarians, 36
Enron Corporation, 200
Environmental and Social Impact
    Assessment (ESIA), 151
Environmental Impact Assessment
    (EIA), 151
Equatorial Guinea, 150
Ericsson, 194
ethnic cleansing, 3, 9, 10, 13, 24, 35, 40,
    41, 42, 99, 138, 140, 157, 165, 182,
    187, 206, 209
European Union, 36, 89, 148, 149
Evans, Gareth, 12
extractive industries, 4, 6, 99, 138–58, 188,
    226, 239
Extractive Industries Transparency
    Initiative (EITI), 98, 142, 150
ExxonMobil, 144, 153, 196, 200

Facebook, 175, 178, 179, 180
Falun Gong, 171, 176
Fanqiang, 171
Federation of Kenya Employers, 119, 127
Firestone, 147
Flickr, 175, 180

Ford Motor Company, 196
Foundation of Labor, 74
France, 55, 76, 87, 193
Freeport-McMoRan Copper and Gold
    Inc., 190, 200
Friedman, Milton, 64
Friedrich Krupp AG, 189, 190
Fry, Douglas, 56, 60
Fulfilling our Collective Responsibility:
    International Assistance and the
    Responsibility to Protect, 36
Fund for Peace Index of Fragile
    States, 140

Gabon, 150
Gaza, 37
General Electric, 117
General Motors, 51, 52, 117
Geneva Convention of 1949, 4
genocide, 3, 5, 9–11, 13, 24, 35, 36,
    40–42, 47, 52, 53, 69, 70, 75–77,
    79, 82, 84, 89, 92, 99, 104,
    107, 138, 140, 165, 182,
    187, 189, 195, 198, 200,
    206–16, 219–27
Genocide Convention 1948, 112
Genocide Prevention Task Force, 106,
    109, 110
gentle commerce, 52, 57, 58, 60–62, 63,
    64, 65, 66, 215, 217
Germany, 18, 27, 63, 71, 72, 73, 74, 89,
    187, 189, 194, 196, 199, 215
    National Socialism, 27, 71, 72, 74,
    78, 82, 85, 87, 89, 187, 189, 190,
    194, 196
Gestapo, 189
Ghana, 124
Global Internet Freedom Consortium,
    177
Global Network Initiative, 182
Global South, 40, 41, 43
Global Witness, 1, 147, 149
globalization, 15, 21, 22, 23, 210,
    211, 213
GOAL Global, 197
Google, 63, 117, 163, 168, 169, 170–72,
    173, 179, 180, 182
Google China, 170–73, 181
Great Rift Valley, Kenya, 122, 126
Gross-Rosen concentration camp, 72
Guatemala, 1, 56
Guinea Bissau, 141

H.J. Heinz Company, 63
H.B. Fuller Company, 164

Habyarimana, Juvenal, 75
Hague Center for Global Justice, 2
Haiti, 37, 141
Harare, Zimbabwe, 195
Hess, David, 65
Hiber, 177
High-level Panel on Threats, Challenges,
    and Change, 13
    A More Secure World Our Shared
    Responsibility, 40
Hinduism, 55, 131
Hitler, Adolf, 59
Holland, 69
Hollywood, 70, 71
Holocaust, 69, 71–73, 82, 189,
    196, 216
Home Depot, 164
Horn of Africa, 108
Hotel des Mille Collines, 70, 75–79, 86,
    87, 89, 92, 195
Hotel Rwanda, 70, 75
Huawei Technologies Company, 117
Human Rights Watch, 107, 200
Hussein, Saddam, 40, 216
Hutu, 75, 76, 77, 86, 87, 195

I. G. Farben, 189, 190
imperialism, 17, 41
India, 55, 82, 110, 149, 200
Individual Responsibility to Protect
    (IR2P), 16, 32, 186–87, 198,
    201, 216
Indonesia, 190, 200, 215
information and communication
    technology (ICT), 4, 6, 14, 17, 30,
    63, 107, 162–82, 218
Institute for Economics and Peace, 2
Inter Religious Council of Kenya
    (IRCK), 131
intergovernmental organizations (IGO),
    98, 234
Interhamwe, 75, 76, 87, 89
Internally Displaced Persons (IDP),
    40, 128
International Alert, 142
International Business Machines
    Corporation, 194, 196
International Chamber of Commerce,
    19, 108
International Commission on Intervention
    and State Sovereignty (ICISS), 12,
    13, 39, 40, 101
    report, 12–13, 39–40, 42, 102, 109
International Committee of the Red Cross
    (ICRC), 192, 193–94, 195

International Council on Mining and
    Metals (ICMM), 142, 146, 153
International Finance Corporation (IFC),
    151, 152, 158
Social and Environmental Performance
    Standards, 151, 152
International Monetary Fund, 199
International Organization of
    Employers, 19, 26
Internet, 61, 62, 162, 163, 169, 170, 171,
    172, 174, 176, 177, 178, 179,
    180, 181
Inter-Parliamentary Union Assembly, 36
Iran, 163, 168, 174–75, 176, 177, 178,
    179, 180, 181
    and social media, 174–75, 177
Iraq, 37, 40–41, 46, 58, 104, 109, 141,
    215, 230
Ireland, 54, 55, 56, 57
Islam, 55, 117, 131, 190
Islamic State in Iraq and the Levant
    (ISIL), 37, 190, 210
Islamic State of Iraq and Syria. *See* Islamic
    State in Iraq and the Levant (ISIL)
ITT Corporation, 17, 18

Jagad, Mallika, 80
Jaggi, Karl, 193, 194
Jordan, 175, 177
JP Morgan Chase, 195
Judaism, 69, 71–73, 74, 78, 85, 86, 88,
    187, 194, 216

Kalenjin, 120
Kang, Karambir Singh, 79–80, 94
Kashmir, 110
Keeley, Lawrence, 59
Keneally, Thomas, 71
Kenya, 3, 4, 6, 26, 30, 37, 46, 104, 116–
    34, 166, 173, 192, 193, 210, 218,
    221, 225, 226
Kenya Africa National Union
    (KANU), 118
Kenya African Democratic Union
    (KADU), 118
Kenya Association of Manufacturers, 119
Kenya Flower Council, 119
Kenya National Chamber of Commerce
    and Industry, 119
Kenya Private Sector Alliance (KEPSA),
    119–20, 123–34, 218, 221, 222,
    226, 235
Kenya Revenue Authority (KRA), 125
Kenyatta, Mzee Jomo, 118
Kenyatta, Uhuru, 118

Khartoum, Sudan, 190
Kibaki, Mwai, 118, 120–21, 124, 125, 126,
    127, 128
Kigali, Rwanda, 70, 75, 77, 195
Kikuyu, 118, 120
Kilwa, Democratic Republic of the Congo,
    190–91, 216
Kimberley Process Certification Scheme,
    13, 15, 142, 144, 149, 150, 151
Ki-moon, Ban, 26, 35, 42, 43, 46, 227
Kirby, Michael, 37
Kisumu, Kenya, 121, 123
Kobanî, Syria, 211
Kosovo, 11, 38, 194, 197
Kouwenhoven, Guus, 191
Kraków, Poland, 71, 72
Kraków-Płaszów concentration camp, 72
Kuffor, John, 124
Kupchan, Charles, 52
Kurds, 211, 216
Kyrgyzstan, 37, 109

Lafarge, 117
Lashkar-E-Taiba, 79
l'Etude des Methodes de Direction de
    l'Entreprise (IMEDE), 192
LG Electronics Inc., 117
Liberia, 37, 147, 152, 155, 156, 191, 197
Libya, 43, 104, 138, 141, 142, 147,
    155, 175
Lonrho, 192
Lord's Resistance Army, 210
Luhya, 120
Luo, 120

Magna Carta, 61
Malaysia, 110, 144, 145
Mali, 147
ManoCap, 197
Marx, Karl, 73
McDonald's, 55
Media Owners Association (MOA),
    119, 131
Meru, 120
Micro and Small Enterprises
    Federation, 127
Microsoft, 117, 172, 194
Middle East, 31, 55, 145, 175, 179, 210
military-industrial complex, 64
Mkenya Daima, 116–17, 130–33, 134
Moi, Daniel Arap, 118
Mombasa, Kenya, 123
Mooney, Erin, 40
Morris, Ian, 52
Motorola, 195

Mozambique, 192
Mubarak, Hosni, 63
Multilateral Investment Guarantee Agency
    (MIGA), 139
Mumbai, India, 5, 70
Murphy, Craig, 18
Musyoka, Kalonzo, 120, 124
Myanmar, 144, 191

"narrow but deep," 9, 35, 46, 195,
    212, 227
Nairobi, Kenya, 118, 121–24, 125
National Accord and Reconciliation
    Agreement, 127–28
National Business Initiative, 197
National Cohesion and Integration
    Commission, 130
National Petroleum Corporation (CNPC),
    144, 148
National Rainbow Coalition (NARC),
    118, 119
nationalization, 17
NatWest, 195
Nazi. *See* Germany, National Socialism
neo-classical economic theory, 1
neo-mercantilism, 51, 52
Nepal, 192
Nestlé, 192
Netherlands, 69, 73, 74, 191
Nicaragua, 56
Niger Delta, Nigeria, 189, 191, 200
Nigeria, 1, 141, 189, 190, 191, 192, 193,
    194, 200, 210, 211
Nokia, 176
norm entrepreneurs, 13, 35
Norms on the Responsibilities of
    Transnational Corporations and
    Other Business Enterprises with
    Regard to Human Rights, 23
North Korea, 37
Norway, 26, 145
Ntaryamira Cyprien, 75
Nutriset, 193

Obaigbena, Nduka, 194
Obama, Barack, 104
Odinga, Raila, 120, 121, 123, 124, 125,
    126, 127
Ogoni, 190
Old Mutual Group, 117
One Earth Future Foundation, 2
    The Role of Kenya's Private Sector in
        Peacebuilding
        The Case of the 2013 Election
            Cycle, 192

Orange Democratic Movement (ODM),
    120, 121, 126, 133
Orange Democratic Movement
    (ODM)-Kenya, 120
Organisation for Economic Cooperation
    and Development (OECD), 149
    Guidelines for Multinational
        Enterprises, 138, 149
Organization of the Petroleum Exporting
    Countries, 17

Pakistan, 110, 141, 211
Palestine, 56
Party of National Unity (PNU), 120
Peace Research Institute Oslo (PRIO), 2
Petrie Report, 43
Petrie, Charles, 43
Petronas, 144, 145, 147, 153
Philips Electronics Company, 73–75,
    85, 86, 93
Philips, Frederick (Frits), 69, 73–75, 78,
    86, 87, 88, 94
Pinker, Steven, 57, 59–61, 63
Poland, 71, 89
protection of civilians (POC), 38, 154
Psiphon, 177
public-private partnerships, 11, 15, 46,
    103, 108, 188, 213

Red Cross, 93, 147
Refugee Policy Group, 40
Responsibility while Protecting, 43
Responsible Sovereignty: International
    Cooperation for a Changed
    World, 35
Rights Up Front Initiative, 43–44
Rio Tinto Group, 144, 195
Rowland, Tiny, 192
Royal Dutch Shell, 1, 144, 153, 154,
    189–90, 191, 196, 200
Ruggie, John, 23, 45, 185
rule of law, 39, 61, 220, 221, 231
Rusesabagina, Paul, 70, 75–79, 85, 86, 87,
    88, 89, 94, 195
Rwanda, 5, 10, 11, 23, 24, 37, 38, 54, 70,
    75–76, 77, 82, 86, 87, 88, 89, 122,
    140, 195, 216

SABENA Company, 70, 75–76, 92
Safaricom, 163, 166, 173, 182, 218
Safe Schools Initiative, 194
Sahnoun, Mohamed, 12
Said, Khaled, 175, 179
Samsung Electronics Limited, 117
Saudi Arabia, 145

Saudi Aramco, 145
Sauvant, Karl, 17, 21, 26
Saxegaard, Per, 62
Schindler, Oskar, 69, 71–73, 74, 76, 77,
    78, 80, 85, 86, 87, 88, 89, 93, 94,
    187, 194, 216
Schindler's List, 71
Schutzstaffel (SS), 86, 189
Security and Exchange Commission
    (SEC), 148
Serbia, 38, 197
Siemens, 117, 176, 195
Sierra Leone, 197, 200
Skype, 180
Social and Environmental Management
    and Monitoring Plan
    (SEMMP), 152
    Emergency Response Plan, 152, 153
social media, 64, 94, 177, 178, 180, 193
Somalia, 37, 38, 141, 210
South Africa, 26, 28, 56, 192, 195, 197,
    199, 211
South African Truth and Reconciliation
    Commission, 200
South Sudan, 24, 138, 141, 144, 147, 149,
    154, 197, 210
Srebrenica, Bosnia and Herzegovina, 23
Sri Lanka, 24, 43, 57, 109, 192
Stanbic Bank, 117
Standard Chartered Bank, 117
standard operating procedures (SOP), 89,
    90, 93, 94, 95
Stec, Stefan, 76
Sudan, 46, 141, 149, 175, 190,
    210, 216
Sullivan Principles, 28
Sweden, 197
Swiss Trading Company, 193
SwissPeace, 2
Switzerland, 192, 194, 196, 197
Syria, 24, 37, 46, 104, 109, 141, 176,
    212, 230

Taiwan, 163
Taj Mahal Hotel, 70, 79–81, 82, 86, 87,
    88, 89, 91, 92, 93
Talisman Energy, 190, 216
Target, 164, 166
Tata Group, 80, 85, 91
Thailand, 211
This Day Newspaper, 194
Timberland, 65
Tor Project, 177
Total S.A., 117, 147, 153, 154, 161
Tunisia, 175, 176, 178, 179

Tutsi, 75, 77, 195
Twitter, 63, 163, 170, 174–81

Uber, 62
UBS, 196
Uganda, 122, 210
Ukraine, 58, 230
Unilever, 80
United Fruit Company, 1
United Kingdom, iv, 18, 97, 110, 117, 128,
    141, 145, 150, 194, 224
United Nations, 5, 9–12, 14, 16–23, 25,
    26, 29–31, 37–47, 75–77, 82, 86,
    89, 93, 98, 101, 102, 118, 140,
    154, 165, 185, 206, 207, 209,
    222–27, 237
    Agenda for Peace, 21
    Centre on Transnational
        Corporations, 21
    Charter, 11, 13, 14, 19, 38, 41, 42, 43,
        208, 209
    Charter of Economic Rights and Duties
        of States, 18
    Code of Conduct on Transnational
        Corporations, 14, 17
    Commission on Human Rights, 23
    Corporate Responsibility to Protect
        Human Rights, 45
    Declaration and a Programme
        of Action on the Establishment
        of a New International Economic
        Order, 17
    Development Programme, 194, 197
    Economic and Social Council, 18,
        19, 21, 25
    Environmental Program, 118
    Framework for Business and Human
        Rights, 153
    General Assembly, 4, 11, 12, 17, 21,
        25, 36, 41, 42, 43, 44, 46, 47, 102,
        108, 230
    Global Compact, 2, 22, 98, 99, 105,
        146, 153
    Guiding Principles on Business and
        Human Rights, 23–27, 40, 45, 138,
        142, 151, 153–54, 185, 188
    High Commissioner for Human
        Rights, 191
    High Commissioner for Refugees, 31, 194
    Human Rights Council, 23, 25, 26, 36,
        43, 44, 45
    Human Settlements Program, 118
    Implementing the Responsibility to
        Protect, 10, 13, 15, 26, 42, 102,
        186, 206, 227

International Trusteeship System, 19
Joint Office on Genocide Prevention and Responsibility to Protect, 30
New International Economic Order (NIEO), 17
Office for the Coordination of Humanitarian Affairs (OCHA), 194, 195
Office of Special Adviser on the Responsibility, 42
Office of the Prevention of Genocide, 47
Office of the UN High Commissioner for Human Rights, 45
Office on Genocide Prevention and the Responsibility to Protect, 108
Peacebuilding Commission, 44
Presidential Statement on the Protection of Civilians in Armed Conflicts, 38
Responsibility to Protect Report 2014, 23, 28
Secretary-General, 4, 9, 10, 11, 12, 13, 14, 15, 16, 18, 21, 23, 25, 28, 35, 36, 40, 42, 43, 44, 45, 46, 47, 102, 103, 108, 127, 132, 149, 151, 187, 206, 210, 212, 213, 223
Security Council, 11, 12, 13, 21, 36, 38, 40, 41, 42, 43, 44, 102, 103, 104, 108, 186, 195, 206, 208, 209
Special Representative for Business and Human Rights, 23
Universal Declaration of Human Rights, 154
UNSC resolutions
  UNSC Resolution 1265, 38
  UNSC Resolution 1296, 38
  UNSC Resolution 1306, 200
  UNSC Resolution 1674, 42
  UNSC Resolution 1706, 42
We the Peoples, 22, 23
United States, vii, 1, 2, 16, 18, 20, 23, 32, 40, 53, 63, 71, 74, 97, 102, 104, 106, 110, 121, 133, 139, 141, 143, 145, 146, 148, 149, 150, 169, 171, 178, 181, 182, 190, 195, 211

Senate Select Committee on Intelligence Activities, 18
United States Department of State, 178
United States Institute of Peace, 2, 98, 139
Unocal Corporation, 191, 200
upstream prevention, 105–11
Urban Foundation, 197

Vision 2030 Secretariat, 130
Voluntary Principles on Security and Human Rights (VPSHR), 142, 150–51
Vught concentration camp, 74, 78

Walmart, 211
war crimes, 3, 9, 10, 13, 24, 35, 41, 42, 52, 53, 99, 138, 140, 165, 176, 182, 187, 188, 189, 191, 199, 206, 209, 215
War on Terror, 40–41
Watchdog Platform, 189
WeChat, 163
Weiss, Thomas, 40
Wiwa, Ken Saro, 190
Woodrow Wilson International Center for Scholars, 139
World Bank, 139, 142, 151
World Economic Forum, 1999, 22
World Summit, 9, 13, 22, 24, 31, 35, 36, 37, 41, 42, 46, 99, 101, 186, 206, 207, 208, 210
  Outcome Document, 13, 14, 15, 35, 37, 41–42, 99, 102, 186, 208–9
World Trade Organization, 199
World War II, 5, 56, 69, 71, 82, 189, 194, 196, 199

Yahoo!, 172
Yazidi, 104
Yemen, 37, 141, 175
YouTube, 171, 175, 179, 180
Yugoslavia, 54, 58

Zambia, 192
Zimbabwe, 141, 149, 192, 195, 224
Zyklon B, 189

Printed in the United States
By Bookmasters